The Harder They Fall

"The strength of these always honest and affecting anecdotes is, in fact, their variety of paths to recovery; the diversity should help this excellent volume appeal to a wide audience."

—PUBLISHERS WEEKLY

"Addiction to alcohol and other drugs is a complex medical problem. However, one of our major obstacles to effective treatment and recovery is stigma. *The Harder They Fall* provides us with stories of courage, passion, commitment, and triumph. Each depicts their own struggle with a debilitating disease and their ultimate decision to choose life over death. These stories are very inspirational and will serve to provide help and hope to those who may still be suffering, as well as put a face on recovery. It is an excellent read for all of us who have been affected by addiction."

—STACIA MURPHY, President, National Council
on Alcoholism and Drug Dependence, Inc.

"Read this book! Here are the *real* winners in life. The best and the brightest with devastating illnesses, living clean, sober, confident, happy lives. If you want to know about alcoholism and addiction and how to get 'weller than well,' read this book!"

—CAPTAIN RONALD E. SMITH, Chairman of the Department of
Psychiatry, National Naval Medical Center, and for twelve
years the Psychiatric Consultant to Congress

"These compelling and intimate narratives provide an illuminating look at celebrity . . . the addiction, the loss, and the recovery process."

—HAROLD OWENS, Director, Addiction
Recovery Services, MusiCares Foundation

"Here are the stories of twenty-one celebrities who had everything until their abusive chemicals showed them that, at the bottom, they had nothing at all. These pioneers in the modern drug abuse epidemic eventually each found their way into recovery, even redemption. They tell of the joy of finding a way of being that is more precious than fame and fortune."

—ROBERT L. DUPONT, M.D., White House Drug Czar
for President Richard Nixon
and President Gerald Ford (1973–1977)
and author of *The Selfish Brain*

The Harder They Fall

Celebrities Tell Their Real-Life Stories

of Addiction and Recovery

Gary Stromberg

Jane Merrill

HAZELDEN®

Hazelden
Center City, Minnesota 55012-0176

1-800-328-0094
1-651-213-4590 (Fax)
www.hazelden.org

ISBN-13: 978-1-59285-156-0

Library of Congress Cataloging-in-Publication Data
Stromberg, Gary, 1942-
    The harder they fall : celebrities tell their real-life stories of addiction and
    recovery / Gary Stromberg, Jane Merrill.
        p. cm.
    ISBN 1-59285-156-8
        1. Celebrities--Drug use. I. Merrill, Jane. II. Title

    HV5824.C42S87 2005
    616.86'092'2--dc22   2004060938

Any viewpoints and opinions expressed in this book belong to the authors and
interviewees, and are not necessarily endorsed by Hazelden.

09 08 07 06 05 6 5 4 3 2

Jacket design by Theresa Gedig
Interior design by David Spohn
Typesetting by Tursso Companies

To David and Emily, and in memory of Fred E.

—GARY STROMBERG

To my four stars—Emma, Burton, Julie, and Rosalind

—JANE MERRILL

Contents

Foreword
by Lewis Lapham

ABOUT THE SELF-DESTRUCTIVE IMPULSES NATIVE to the Age of Aquarius nobody was better informed than the late Terry Southern. As a writer, he favored the darker shades of comedy (the screenplay for *Dr. Strangelove*, the preposterously pornographic novel *Candy*); as a pilgrim on the many roads to expanded consciousness, he experimented with every form of substance abuse rooted in an ancient religion or known to modern science. His satirical pieces occasionally appeared in *Harper's Magazine*, and late at night in one or another of the uptown bars that catered to the New York literary trade, I sometimes came upon the author himself, contemplating what was left of the ice in a glass of gin, remarking on the number of his talented acquaintances—actors, authors, film directors, action painters, stand-up comics, lead guitarists—who had gone missing in the forests of addiction. He attributed the casualty rate to the heavy prices paid for the promise of transcendence, and in a season marked by a sharp upturn in the bad news incoming from the American dream of military grandeur in Vietnam, I remember him saying to the assembled company at a table in Elaine's, "There is no power on earth that can loosen a man's grip on his own throat."

I don't know whether the lyric was his own, or whether he borrowed it from a California Zen master or a Bob Dylan song, but by 1969 the point was not one that provoked an argument. The social revolutions of what was proving to be a not-so-joyous decade had rallied to the cry of freedom, in all its tenses and declensions—freedom for and freedom from, freedom then and now. The word appeared on everybody's tie-dyed shirt or sign, went well with protest movements and psychedelic dope, marched south for civil rights, drifted west with the surfboards and the sun. And yet, as had been noticed by both F. Scott Fitzgerald and Ernest Hemingway during a previous age of American exploration in the wilderness of the self, freedom had its faults, seldom turned out to match the commercial advertising copy, went more or less directly south.

As an editor often exposed in the early 1970s to writers newly arrived on the heights of commercial celebrity or literary reputation, I noticed that their fear of failure was surpassed by their fear of success. So also but more obviously, similar states of anxiety descended upon the movie stars and the musicians. Becoming suddenly famous, they were granted license to say and do as they pleased, to ask and have and send the bill to Zurich. Being American, they had been born in the assurance of their certain virtue and perfect innocence. The money and the television cameras taught them otherwise. At liberty to discover in themselves traits of character of which they had no prior knowledge—also criminal tendencies, monstrous wishes, perverse desires, a comprehensive repertoire of antisocial behaviors—some of the most observant members of the troupe turned away in horror from what they saw in Medusa's mirror. Terrified by the freedom to play any role or tune that might come fantastically to mind, they looked for ways to turn to stone—acquired inhibitions, developed a capacity for the self-inflicted wound, applied for early admission to the nearest cage. A drug or alcohol addiction served the purposes of the prison cell, which, by the fashionable standards of the day, established one's credentials as an enemy of the system or the state but offered the further advantage of remaining silent while seeming cool.

The twenty-one traveler's tales collected in this book at hand prove the exceptions to Southern's heavy rule of thumb. Each individual speaks to his or her own experience of wrestling with what they mistook for a muse of fire or an angel of deliverance. They testify not only to their own particular courage and strength of will but also to the truth of Sigmund Freud's general theory of *Civilization and Its Discontents*, predicated on the recognition of never-ending war between the instinct toward life and the instinct toward death, Eros and Thanatos, contending for "the evolution of civilization" and "for the life of the human species . . . this battle of the giants that our nursemaids try to appease with their lullaby about Heaven."

Acknowledgments

Our gratitude goes first to the individuals who welcomed us into their lives and gave us their stories.

We also thank those who led us to them: Claire "ToneeQua" Baker, Tony Barger, Bob Barney, Sarah Brown, Doc Danner, Nicolette Donen, Joel Dorn, Steve Farhood, Paul Fishkin, Rift Fournier, Shep Gordon, Trudy Green, Peter Himberger, John Kaye, Amy Kurland, Jennifer Lee, Toby Mamis, Michelle Marx, Tony Morehead, Thom Mount, Dean Peterson, Sooze Plunkett-Green, Walt Quinn, Arnie "Tokyo" Rosenthal, Joe Safety, Bill Stankey, and Ethlie Ann Vare.

There were others who helped us refine our conception of the project: Janie Chang, Tom Connor, Jacques de Spoelberch, Chris Filstrup, Laurie Filstrup, Emma Filstrup, Diane Glynn, Alan Katz, Stacey Kivel-Green, Jordan D. Luttrell, Leslie Pallas, Donnie Wahlberg, and Wayne Zimmerman.

And finally those who made this book a reality: our learned literary agent, Drew Nederpelt; the extraordinary editorial team at Hazelden—Becky Post, Kate Kjorlien, and especially Karen Chernyaev, our wise and gentle editor; and Kim Weiss, head of public relations at HCI.

Locally, our heartfelt thanks go to the reference department of the Westport Public Library and our fellow grunters at the Westport, Connecticut, YMCA.

The authors and Hazelden gratefully acknowledge the following:
"We've Only Just Begun," words and music by Roger Nichols and Paul Williams, copyright ©1970 Irving Music, Inc., copyright renewed, all rights reserved, used by permission. "Freefall" by Laurie Anderson, ©1994 Difficult Music, from the album *Bright Red*, reprinted with the permission of the author. "NyQuil" from *Ultramarine* by Raymond Carver, copyright ©1986 by Raymond Carver, used by permission of Random House, Inc. "Gris Gris Gumbo Ya Ya," by John Creaux, ©1998 Warner-Tamerlane Publishing

Corp. (BMI) and Skull Music (BMI), all rights on behalf of Skull Music (BMI) administered by Warner-Tamerlane Publishing Corp. (BMI), all rights reserved, used by permission, Warner Bros. Publications U.S. Inc., Miami, FL 33014. Excerpts from *Pryor Convictions: And Other Life Sentences* and *Richard Pryor: Here and Now* used by permission of Richard Pryor and Jennifer Lee. Harvey Shapiro, "It Seems to Me" from *How Charlie Shavers Died and Other Poems*, ©2001 by Harvey Shapiro and reprinted by permission of Wesleyan University Press. "The Rhinoceros" by Richard Morris in *Assyrians*, published by The Smith in Brooklyn, New York, ©1968, reprinted 1991, p. 68, reprinted with permission. "Man's Feet Are a Sensational Device," from *The Poems of Marianne Moore* by Marianne Moore, edited by Grace Schulman, copyright ©2003 by Marianne Craig Moore, executor of the estate of Marianne Moore, used by permission of Viking Penguin, a division of Penguin Group (USA) Inc. "Welcome to My Nightmare," copyright 1975 Sony/ATV Songs LLC, Ezra Music and publisher(s) unknown, all rights on behalf of Sony/ATV Songs LLC and Ezra Music administered by Sony/ATV Music Publishing 8 Music Square West, Nashville, TN 37203, all rights reserved, used by permission. "Whiskey and Lace," copyright 1977 Sony/ATV Songs LLC, Ezra Music and publisher(s) unknown, all rights on behalf of Sony/ATV Songs LLC and Ezra Music administered by Sony/ATV Music Publishing 8 Music Square West, Nashville, TN 37203, all rights reserved, used by permission. "Poems for the Young and Tough" from *The Flash of Lightning Behind the Mountain: New Poems* by Charles Bukowski, edited by John Martin, copyright ©2004 by Linda Lee Bukowski, reprinted by permission of HarperCollins Publishers Inc. "Final Curve" from *The Collected Poems of Langston Hughes* by Langston Hughes, copyright ©1994 by The Estate of Langston Hughes, used by permission of Alfred A. Knopf, a division of Random House, Inc. "My Battle with Life" from *Northside Poetry* by Tone One, copyright ©1999 by Anthony Matos, published by Writer's Club Press, used by permission of Tone One. "The Dead Dads," "Empty Stage," and "Nothingsville, MN" from *The Beforelife: Poems* by Franz Wright, copyright ©2000 by Franz Wright, used by permission of Alfred A. Knopf, a division of Random House, Inc. "Baptism" from *Walking to Martha's Vineyard* by Franz Wright, copyright ©2003 by Franz

Wright, used by permission of Alfred A. Knopf, a division of Random House, Inc. "Heartattack and Vine," written by Tom Waits, ©1980 Six Palms Music Corp., all rights reserved, reprinted with permission. "The End," words and music by The Doors, copyright ©1967 Doors Music Co., copyright renewed, all rights reserved, used by permission. "Let a Man Come In and Do the Popcorn," by James Brown, ©1970 (renewed) Dynatone Publishing Company (BMI), all rights on behalf of Dynatone Publishing Company (BMI) administered by Unichappell Music Inc. (BMI), all rights reserved, used by permission, Warner Bros. Publications U.S. Inc., Miami, FL 33014.

Introduction by Stephen Davis
Redemption Songs

THIS IS A BOOK OF MIRACLES: not supernatural miracles, but superhuman ones. The people talking in this volume speak only for themselves, but they represent some of the bravest and most determined folks anyone is likely to encounter.

Some of them are back from the dead. Some are not.

I wish Elvis were in this book. If someone had only gotten to him, weaned him from the entire pharmacopoeia, he'd be the greatest gospel singer in the world today.

I wish Jimi Hendrix had a recovery narrative. Can you imagine?

If only Bob Marley had a redemption song.

If someone had intervened on Jim Morrison, he might have developed into the champion American poet and filmmaker he always wanted to be.

But Jim was on a suicide mission. Mission accomplished.

What about Lenny Bruce, brilliant social critic and gadfly, who OD'd in Los Angeles in 1966, where the cops hated him for telling the truth and gave their crime-scene photos of his tied-off corpse to the gutter press. We really could have used Lenny Bruce later on in that decade.

Same with John Belushi, that "fucking idiot" (his own brother's words). Same with Janis Joplin and Brian Jones, both dead at twenty-seven of dope and pills. Same with John Bonham, protean drummer of Led Zeppelin, who drank himself to death. Same with Gram Parsons, who mixed country music with rock and then killed himself with a shot of smack.

Same with Kurt Cobain, the *auteur* of Nirvana, who might have used heroin as an analgesic to ease his chronic irritable bowel syndrome, and then ended it all in a martyrdom operation.

Tennessee Williams. Judy Garland. Jack Kerouac. Marilyn Monroe. F. Scott Fitzgerald. Hank Williams. Bon Scott from AC/DC. Dee Dee Ramone. Shannon Hoon. Whatever your age, whatever your generation—name your poison.

The talent we have lost to drink, drugs, and plain human despair is unbelievable.

But in their defense, most of these angelic burnouts had nowhere to run. They died, in most cases, isolated by fame and too hopelessly addicted to help themselves.

"No one could save them," Jim Morrison sang, "save the blind tiger."

It's hard to imagine anyone intervening on Elvis. When he died in 1977, addicted to pills, Betty Ford was the First Lady with a prescription drug problem, not a famous treatment institute. There were no well-known and widely publicized treatment centers other than the few discreet clinics that deployed systemic methods of deprogramming addicted people, usually wealthy or famous, and teaching them how to live in their own skins. Alcoholics Anonymous was there, of course, but until the eighties, this Twelve Step method was stigmatized as a program for old lushes, not for movie stars and young musicians in their prime. Prisons, mental hospitals, and indiscriminate electroshock therapy were the end of the road for the rest of us—"hopeless" alcoholics and junkies.

Anyway, interfering with someone else's life in the existential sixties and disco seventies was totally uncool, really unforgivable. People were supposed to do their own thing, even if it was killing them. Internal freedom was an integral part of the ethos of the sixties, an era when expanded consciousness was synonymous with social change and artistic endeavor.

Most of the people whose stories of quiet heroism are told in this book came of age and into their fame during the sixties. These were the years when the massive post-war generation launched themselves into a maelstrom of spiritual crises, political unrest, new religious visions, sexual adventurism, and, most important, a rare opportunity for change and reform. For millions, the sixties ideals of reclaiming and embracing the senses were inspired by a generation's embrace of marijuana, previously confined to the worlds of bohemia and jazz. The decade's communitarian ideals—protest and reform, emotional intensity, the transience of nature, expansion of consciousness—often depended on marijuana and LSD for a shortcut to nirvana.

Rolling and smoking a joint was a legit anti-establishment statement.

Popping a tab of Purple Haze or Orange Sunshine was a blow against the empire.

"But I would not feel so all alone," Bob Dylan sang to us in one of his imperative bulletins of coolness. *"Everybody must get stoned."*

Nobody, but nobody, tried to contradict Bob Dylan, the god of the sixties.

The crucial role that illegal drugs played in sixties movements like civil rights, the anti–Vietnam War movement, and the sexual revolution has yet, in my opinion, to be acknowledged and fully understood. Western culture at that time was driven by the preferred drugs of its artistic icons. Alcohol inspired the abstract expressionist painters. Heroin virtually owned jazz. LSD can't be separated from the Merry Pranksters and the Grateful Dead. Andy Warhol's superstars lived and worked on amphetamines. The reggae stars regarded ganja as a sacrament and meditation, not as a means to get high. Then the drugs got harder as the old ideals faded into the disco seventies. Cocaine fueled the 4/4 beat on the dance floor. Heroin came into youth culture with the punk bands and never left. In more recent times, the rave scene depends on Ecstasy and other so-called designer drugs for its energy and trance states.

Society and its politicians responded with the unending War on Drugs and "just say no." The joke was on us. It still is.

There are some common threads that weave through these often stirring narratives of recovery: initial success fueled by various stimulants, the inevitable crash and burn, and then somehow, often at the last possible moment, against all odds, and often having been dragged kicking and screaming into a rehabilitation program, finding redemption in the quiet, steely, disciplined, deeply personal processes of healing the self, making peace with inner demons, and finding a renewed way to live.

The experience I bring to writing this introduction devolves from my work with Aerosmith, the legendary American rock band. Twenty years ago, the five musicians in this hardest-partying group began a process that eventually resulted in long-term sobriety for them all. They would be telling you their story themselves, except they already have, both in their collective autobiography, *Walk This Way*, and in countless interviews since

1990. Today they prefer to serve by example rather than continue to trumpet their successful, long-term sobriety.

For readers unfamiliar with how improbable this outcome is, let me give you the back story.

Aerosmith began their run for the rainbow in the early seventies, part of the new blood that replaced the mass die-out of the sixties rock stars: Jones, Hendrix, Joplin, Morrison.

Inspired by the Rolling Stones, the Yardbirds, and Led Zeppelin, the young musicians followed Arthur Rimbaud's artistic imperative—the systematic disordering of the senses—by actually outdoing their rock idols' Dionysian consumption of drink, dope, powders, and pills. Asked how they were able to sustain their creative energy over the course of the decade, one of the guitar players told me that as they became wealthy, they were able to afford higher-quality drugs. Everyone, especially the girls, said that Aerosmith was the stonedest, craziest, highest-risk band of them all.

Then, of course, the horror began. Junkie behavior is always the same, whatever the addiction. By the end of the seventies, the once charismatic leaders of the band were ridiculed in the press as "The Toxic Twins." They fought each other like blind tigers. As the drugs took their toll, key members of the band dropped out, and it looked like Aerosmith was headed for the scrap heap of rock history.

Then someone did something. Someone actually helped.

His name was Tim Collins. He was a young, Boston-based talent manager with a taste for cocaine and an Irish American gift of gab. It took him a year to get the five original members of Aerosmith back together. Then he realized that there was no way this band could achieve the hardest act in show business—"The Comeback"—if the musicians were closet dope fiends. After giving up his own considerable addictions, Collins began to consult with mental health professionals in order to research new ways of saving lives jeopardized by addiction and self-destructive behavior, like those in Aerosmith. It took five years of psychic jujitsu to get everyone in the band clean and sober.

By the mid-eighties, the shameful stigma was off addictive behavior in America after both Betty Ford and Kitty Dukakis were treated for abusing pills. And by the last of the eighties, Aerosmith was back on the radio with "Dude (Looks Like a Lady)." Even the Reverend Little Richard was praising them to the skies as the epitome of good old American filth.

Tim Collins's underreported achievement remains one of the most successful interventions in the brief history of rehab. As of this writing, Aerosmith has been sober for almost two decades and remains one of the biggest acts of the rock movement. They've sold millions of records and concert tickets, and they've done it stone cold sober.

My chance to see this in action came a few years ago, when I was invited to accompany Aerosmith on a world tour. Rock journalists don't usually learn much on a big tour because, in most cases, the band's energy goes into the performances and the parties afterward. But I learned something crucial on this tour.

I had been on the road in the seventies with Led Zeppelin and other bands of the day, so I knew how weird it all could get. I wondered how Aerosmith could summon their fierce, nubile muses every night without the artificial expansion of consciousness for which this band had once been notorious.

As we began to fly around the world, I started going to Alcoholics Anonymous meetings with members of the band. Tokyo. Frankfurt. Milan. London. At night, I marveled at the poignancy of their sober but still wild performances. The band's old drug mystique had been replaced by an iron determination to survive at the top of their profession. They attacked their performances with a cool ferocity I'd never seen in a band before, night after night.

When they had the relapse urge, they went to meetings. In our conversations, they explained what they had learned: An addict's relationship with the drug is the most important relationship in his or her life. Everything else slips away. Enter the callous, antisocial behavior, followed by borderline personality disorder. Nothing matters, though. Addiction is the ultimate bad relationship. The drug is reliable, constant, and never abandons the user.

Aerosmith taught me that the user has to abandon the drug.

This idea is what this book is all about: the quiet, individual acts of personal willpower that have succeeded in maintaining long-term sobriety by some of the most interesting people in America. True, they are all celebrities or the celebrated, but within this subgroup, we have the testimony of a congressman, a boxer, a poet, a jockey, a rodeo cowboy, a baseball player, as well as writers, comedians, musicians, and actors. These stories may come from prominent people, but they definitely relate to the daily life struggles of us all. Watching them interweave with the times is unique in my experience as a reader.

Above all is the sheer immediacy of these accounts. Saw-toothed, stripped down, exposed, and gratefully alive, these people and their stories combine into one of the oldest forms of literature: the quest saga. These people have dedicated themselves to seeking new worlds—and to new ways of living in them. I hope these interviews will inspire you as they have moved and encouraged me.

Introduction by Gary Stromberg

THEY STARTED ARRIVING AT MY Malibu Canyon home not long after sunrise that bright spring morning. The early birds were there to have first crack at the "good stuff." It was listed as an estate sale, but what it was essentially was a last ditch effort at raising some cash to finance my exit. Since the bank had already foreclosed on my house, there seemed little sense in trying to keep its contents. Items big and small, valuable and not so valuable, were on display throughout the three Spanish colonial–type buildings that comprised my self-styled hacienda. A plush new pool table, a thousand or so record albums, items from a well-outfitted kitchen, gold records commemorating my association with hit music and film projects, paintings of varying value including my prized original by Jonathan Winters, all kinds of velvet- and leather-covered furniture right out of the hippie culture I grew up in—everything I had acquired in my years of aggressive consumption was on display and for sale. I even got a friend to remove the original stained-glass windows from many of the rooms and replace them with clear panes. I thought these might bring a pretty penny, but the bank, which sent a representative to observe this fire sale, had other ideas. Unless I replaced the stained glass immediately, they were going to lock me out of the house, nullifying the thirty days they gave me to vacate.

Two years earlier, I had purchased this beautiful villa on two-plus acres of prime coastal foothill land at the suggestion of my business manager. I was riding high at the time, having finished producing my second major-studio feature movie. Who had any inkling that twelve years of nonstop drug use was about to take me down?

When things were going good, I had a sense of being invincible. The Midas touch. I had helped build a hugely successful public relations firm, Gibson & Stromberg, representing a virtual who's who of contemporary music talent in the sixties and seventies. Touring the world with the Rolling Stones and Pink Floyd. Helping launch the careers of Elton John, the gnome-like Marc Bolan of T-Rex, Cat Stevens, The Doors, Earth, Wind & Fire, Steely Dan, James Taylor, Steppenwolf, Three Dog Night, Jethro Tull. The list went on.

Life was a ball, an exhilarating wild ride. In 1974, I was asked to do the publicity for the music festival that was to precede the Muhammad Ali–George Foreman "Rumble in the Jungle," which was the subject of the Academy Award–winning documentary *When We Were Kings*. Two hundred and fifty American and African musicians assembled in Kinshasa, Zaire, for an unbelievable musical event. Being a huge fight fan, I immediately headed for the Ali training camp and eventually was introduced to Drew "Bundini" Brown, Ali's inimitable corner man. One thing led to another, and the next thing I knew, Bundini and I were riding with our guide into neighboring Swaziland, a postage stamp–sized country where we heard that the German pharmaceutical giant, Merck, had a factory producing pharmaceutical cocaine. Talk about kids in a candy store!

Even when my drug use escalated to the point where I lost touch with my business and watched it disintegrate, I still didn't recognize that I had a problem. Another career was what I thought would fix it.

Because of the success of my public relations firm, I was given a chance at producing a movie. Universal Studios decided that a concept for a film I had come up with called *Car Wash* was worth a shot. Two years of hard work, ever-increasing drug use, and more than my share of good fortune found me riding high once again. The movie was a pretty big hit, and I was believing all the bullshit.

Before long I was producing my second movie, a little confection entitled *The Fish That Saved Pittsburgh*, a loony comedy about basketball and astrology, with a strong dose of R & B music, that was conceived and written in one rollicking night of gluttonous coke snorting. It was during the filming of *Fish* that things really began to take a turn for the worse. By now I was using with complete abandon, ingesting dangerous amounts of cocaine and heroin. I was on location in Pittsburgh, ostensibly in charge of the production of the movie, but things were out of control. Costs for the filming were skyrocketing, and no one was running the show. The studio bosses, needless to say, were losing patience, and several phone calls to me expressing their concern did little good. Finally they took matters into their own hands and sent a pair of representatives to our location and physically removed me from command. The next thing I remember was waking up in some fancy hotel room and looking around, trying to figure out what was going on. Merritt Island, Florida, is where they forced me to detox and come to my senses before I was allowed back on the film set.

The movie was a financial disaster, as was my career. Word began to spread that my drug use was out of control and that my work was erratic, at best. I was quickly becoming unemployable, and it wasn't long till the roof fell in.

In the summer of 1980, after losing my house, my woman, and my career to the excesses of wild living and drug abuse, I took the suggestion of one of my last remaining friends, Shep Gordon, and moved to Kihei, Hawaii, on the sun-baked island of Maui. Shep, Alice Cooper's manager and a real maven in the music business, had a sprawling beachfront home there and thought getting away from Los Angeles would do me some good. Nothing like carefree island life to get one's shit together.

My game plan was simple. Try to stop using drugs, excluding the ubiquitous Maui Wowie pot everyone over there smokes, and the five, six, or ten daily beers you need to keep hydrated under the powerful tropical sun.

On Maui I had nothing to do but be with me, and that didn't seem like such a great gig. True, the islands are spectacular and the living was easy and grand, but alone at night, I had plenty of time to contemplate the mess I had created. I also had some physical healing to do. Years of abuse had left me worn down, and I took this opportunity to repair some of the damage. Having kicked my heroin addiction for the third or fourth time and knowing that coke use in Hawaii was absurd—why would anyone want to be jacked up in such a laid-back place—I started on a mission of wellness. I attacked it like most things in my life, with blind resolve to accomplish something. Hawaii is a mecca of health, so this was a relatively easy task. I took up running in 1980, a discipline I have continued to this day, and saw benefits right away. I also joined a "seniors" six-man Hawaiian outrigger canoe team, made up of six guys over the age of thirty-five. We trained at sunrise each morning, and on weekends we paddled in long-distance races on the open ocean. I started eating with some consciousness, even took to occasional fasts and began to embrace vegetarianism. Restoring my body was easy, but my mind and soul would require greater effort.

A year later I was back in Los Angeles trying to pick up the pieces. Virtually broke, I moved back into the house I was raised in. A forty-year-old failed big shot living with his parents. Feelings of utter defeat were creeping back. I was trying to stay clean, but life without hope was impossible. Once again drugs got the better of me, and I began chipping again. I remember one night my great friend Joel Dorn, a brilliant, underappreciated record producer, was visiting from New York. It was my mother's birthday, and she suggested I bring him over for dinner. The rest of the story is what Joel remembers. Apparently I was high when he arrived, and midway through dinner I nodded out . . . right into a full plate of Mom's brisket and mashed potatoes. Joel pulled me up by my hair and made some excuse about how "tired" I was, but the hurt and shock showed all over my parents' faces. Joel never lets me forget that night.

Not long after this, a miracle occurred in my life. I was browsing the newspaper on a quiet Sunday morning when I happened across an article about a new Twelve Step program that had recently begun in my area. Without knowing why, I picked up the phone and made a call. That very same day I was attending my first meeting, and soon after, I began my journey into sobriety.

> Strength came where weakness was not known to be,
> at least not felt; and restoration came
> Like an intruder knocking at the door
> of unacknowledged weariness.
>
> —William Wordsworth, "The Prelude"

That was a little over twenty-two years ago, and it's been quite a trip. Looking back over the years and my history of substance abuse, here is what I can say is true for me: It started out as great fun. For someone shy like me, drugs made me bigger and bolder. Eventually drugs and alcohol got the best of me. The fun became depravity. I was without purpose, wrestling with my demons, and lost. The facade fell. I crashed and burned, but the will to survive took over. I was given the greatest gift I've ever received: sobriety. And with it came a new life.

Jane notes that pain, growth, and spiritual evolution don't belong only to those with an addiction. In my view, it is all a means to an end. Through grace, people shuck off the bark of all kinds of sickness and despair. We believe that you don't have to have gone through addiction to identify with the days of doubt and nights of sorrow, the enlightenments and transformations of the recovering addict. What we can see as particularly characteristic of many in recovery is their candor about their struggles and their humor about themselves.

Jane and I became running companions long ago, and runners talk. She encouraged me to tell 1001 stories, morning after morning, while she responded on the uphill. For instance, she found delightful the camaraderie I took for granted from the shakers and movers in the entertainment world. The land of carefree living seemed exotic to her. She would shake her head at the wretched misery that some of the *jeunesse dorée* fell into. She wanted to record these incidences of human spirit, and as we ran, this became the genesis of our book.

In the following chapters you are going to meet some remarkable people. I hope their stories will touch your heart, and if you have issues with substance abuse, perhaps they will inspire you to seek help.

Fame is a bee.
It has a song—
It has a sting—
Ah, too, it has a wing.

—Emily Dickinson, No. 1788

Paul Williams
(singer, songwriter)

PAUL WILLIAMS AND I MET in the hotel restaurant at the DoubleTree
Hotel in Westwood, California, on a bright, robust Sunday afternoon,
two hours before we were to attend a memorial service for our
mutual friend Buddy Arnold. Buddy called himself "the world's oldest Jewish junkie." He had more than twenty-two years of sobriety
and cofounded, along with his wife, Carole Fields, the Musicians'
Assistance Program (MAP), which has helped more than 1,500
addicted musicians find their way to rehab.

Paul showed up in a natty outfit consisting of a tailored black suit,
black dress shirt, and snazzy black-and-lavender patterned tie. I was
feeling underdressed in my customary jeans, black polo shirt, and dark
blue blazer. We checked each other out and decided that each was
dressed appropriately, although Paul removed his tie before entering
the memorial service.

After an initial exchange of hugs and small talk, we got down to
business. I soon was marveling at Paul's uncanny ability to quickly
reach that intimate place where sharing becomes extraordinarily
personal. As he started telling me his story, his face took on an assured
look of one who has traveled this road before. Paul loves talking about
sobriety and how it changed his life. Because we have this in common and have been friends for more than thirty years, there is a
tremendous ease in our exchanges. Paul speaks with authority and

impressive insight these days, having explored at depth his own road to recovery. He still has the wonder and excitement of a newcomer, though.

A couple of times during the telling of his story, we were locked eye-to-eye, our heads only a foot or so apart. I noticed he began to tear up, which caused the same response in me, and we instinctively locked hands, as if to assure each other that each of us understands.

As has happened many times over the years, we ended our conversation with words of how much we love each other, and how we appreciate having each other in our lives. I'm one lucky dude to have a friend like Paul.

I was raised in a household where alcohol was a reward for a good day's work. My consciousness was that alcohol was a payoff. Dad came home to a drink, his wife, and his kids. As I look back on it, it was really in that order. He walked in the house, got the drink, and he probably had one in the bar on the way home. My father spoke about the fact that he never missed a day's work because of drink, so he must have had some misgivings—the old "methinks he doth protest too much."

Alcohol was a reward for being a grown-up. He went to work, he did the job, and came home and drank. I picture my father with his friends around him, and how they talked about the same things again and again and again. And argued about the same things again and again too. They lived their lives in a revolving door of mini-dramas.

My dad would come home and say, "There are three things we're not going to talk about tonight, guys: politics, religion, or the goddamn job. Because when we talk about them, we fight." So that would be the decision. And then they would have a couple of drinks and the conversation always led to three things: politics, religion, and the goddamn job. And he and his friends fought. And then he got angry, and then he'd cry, and all the emotions came out. My dad was a pretty emotional man when he drank. He would get me up in the middle of the night and sit me on his lap to sing for him. And he would cry when I sang: "Listen to my son, listen to *my son*."

My mother says that I was four or five when she was in a department store and all of a sudden I was gone. She turned around and couldn't find me. She found me on a counter with a fistful of money, singing. Music was a part of me. It was in my DNA to make music, evidently. So this was from infancy to thirteen. But after my dad died, it felt like all that went away. I was thirteen when my father was killed in an alcohol-related car wreck, a single-car accident. His death stopped the music in me. My mother was suddenly a widow in her forties with no money. My dad left not a penny of insurance. He left not a dollar in the savings account. So my mother went out to work, and I was told essentially she could afford one child, and that was my little brother.

I was then manipulated out of the household by an aunt and uncle. They more or less stole me, and I was shipped off to live with them in Long Beach, California. In a way, I lost both parents.

The important element of my childhood that I look back on now is that my dad was in construction and we moved all the time. By the time I was in the ninth grade, I'd been to nine different schools. I was always the new kid in school. I was always the littlest kid in school. The kid with the slow body clock. I looked as though I was five grades behind everybody else. The way I deal with the world—reduced to a defensive craft—was born then. You know, I'll walk on stage and do a short joke. Reduce yourself to a cultural stereotype if it makes the world safer! And that's an element of my own life that I deal with today. I mean that I walk on stage and make jokes about people grabbing me in Ireland and saying, "Where'd you hide the gold, you little bastard?" It's the same thing in a way as me being in the third grade and being the new kid who looks like he belongs in kindergarten making a joke about myself.

Because we recognize these elements of our personality doesn't mean we can discard them. Or necessarily that we need to. That's something I'm coming to understand—that my joking about looking like a leprechaun in Ireland gives pleasure to some people. They relax when I'm on stage and then we can enjoy the music and each other's company.

I was raised in a household whose location was constantly changing. And yet there were certain kinds of people that traveled with us. We were kind of gypsies . . . construction brats . . . construction gypsies. And the way we lived changed from location to location. If we went to Denver for a year, there were great places to live and we'd have a nice house. Go to Lucasville, Ohio, and there's nothing but a trailer to rent. There were four people in a twenty-four-foot trailer when my dad was killed. My dad died two days short of his sixtieth birthday. So when I turned sixty, and every day since, has had special significance. From the time I've been sober, I've always said that every day is a gift. It's all a gift. But this has double meaning for me now—the fact I'm living days my father never lived.

So, at thirteen, my father dead, I was shipped off to live with an aunt and uncle who were black belt alcoholics. She would wait up and taunt him into a physical confrontation. I remember lying in bed and hearing the knife drawer slam open and sounds of the hysteria. They had a lot of money and he would spend it. He was a second husband after the first died, and there was great drunkenness in the house. My aunt was my dad's half-sister. But I never fit in that house. And all of a sudden I'm a new kid in the ninth grade, in high school, but with the slow body clock and not fitting in at all.

Even when my dad was alive, I'd have a glass of beer at picnics or at the table, which was not a big deal. I remember drinking with other kids and the ritual of "let's get drunk and throw up and be somebody." It made me feel like one of the boys. I hit puberty after I left high school, where I was still a little boy. My physical maturity came extremely late. What happened was I was very small—I used to be short! When I was nine, my mom and dad were worried about me being small, so we went to the doctor and they did an experiment. I was given male hormones—what you have in your system when you hit puberty. What this did was it gave me an erection and my voice lowered and the whole deal. It also stops your bones from growing. So the reason that I am five-two instead of six-foot like my brother is they gave me male hormones. If they had left me alone, I would have been whatever I was going to be. So it kind of screwed up my whole physiology, and I matured a lot slower.

I'm now in my sixties and there's still a thirty-three-year-old lurking within me. I was thirty-four at fifteen, and I'm thirty-four today. But during those high school years, in a way, I became very good at coping with that. I avoided the showers. I avoided gym. I got through.

Losing my father and the dislocation from family ended my singing for a while. During my teenage years, I was a James Dean wannabe. I wanted to be an actor. I was actually able, with that tunnel vision of "won't take no for an answer," to make a living at it for a lot of years. Eventually to the point where I was broke and not making a living. I got so bored I started writing songs—that classic case of when God slams one door shut, another one opens.

In a lot of ways, I behaved like an alcoholic long before I began drinking like one. I think there were elements of alcoholism in the way I acted. The fact that I was nineteen or twenty with no prospects, and absolutely convinced that I was going to make it as an actor. Came out here, lived on somebody's couch, let them pay the bills, kept track of it so I could pay them back. And always managed to get a job. They'd maybe be a year apart, but I was the only one who kept getting a job. Shot a commercial for Parsons' Ammonia, did a movie called *The Loved One* with Jonathan Winters— worked three months on that. Slept on a couch. Paid the guy I'd been living with the back money I owed him. Got another movie two years later. My faith was immense. I believed I was born to be on the silver screen, completely ignoring the fact that I simply didn't fit into any casting mold. The second movie I was cast in was *The Chase* with Marlon Brando and Robert Redford. I made enough money to bring my mom to the coast to take care of her. At least that was the plan. By the time *The Chase* was released, I had about four or five lines in it. I was practically an extra in the film. Hardly a star-maker.

It wound up that I did bring my mother out to California, ostensibly to take care of her, and then I wound up living on her couch. Living with her going to work and paying the bills. And me a twenty-seven-year-old all of a sudden sitting up all night with a guitar, doodling, writing songs for my own amusement. And out of that writing songs for my own amusement I thought, "You know what? Maybe I can do this." I went to Lee Leseef who had White Whale Records and played him all my songs, and he signed me to a contract as a writer and an artist. And six weeks after I had signed the contract, Lee called me into his office and let me go. He said, tearing up the piece of paper, "I don't think you have a future in music. Your stuff is . . . I don't know what to do with it." So I went home going, "Wow, he's wrong! . . . I hope he's wrong!"

In the meantime, I had written some songs with Biff Rose. He was a brilliant young writer, and when he was given a publishing deal at A & M Records, I rode his coattails in the door. They liked his songs, including some that I'd written. I went over and said, "Where's my part of this? I get an advance too." And Chuck Kaye, the publisher at A & M, looked at the songs I'd written the lyrics to and said, "You wrote those words?" He turned me on to an amazing composer named Roger Nichols. "We're looking for a lyricist for him. We think you're it."

Again, an element of my life that helped to create my basic spiritual philosophy is that "no" can be a gift. I wanted to be an actor; that was it, the whole thing. That door was slammed in my face and locked. And because I couldn't get out that one, I opened another and found my life. Found my life's work. Found something that I just loved doing and that was easy for me. It was always easy to write lyrics. I don't know where it came from. I still don't.

Roger and I immediately found success. Album cuts and B-sides for the most part. But we weren't getting the big hit singles. I remember being very frustrated. The impatience of youth. Looking back, I see it as all happening very quickly.

After three years, I traveled to Europe to write lyrics for Michel Colombier's pop cantata *Wings*. The work was commissioned and produced by Herb Alpert. It was my first European trip, and when I returned, I had two songs in the Top 10: "We've Only Just Begun" by the Carpenters and "Out in the Country" recorded by Three Dog Night. Suddenly I found what I was put here to do.

We were the love generation—the sixties. I went to San Francisco with flowers in my hair like everybody else did. I think the first drugs that I really abused were amphetamines and diet pills. I found out I was over the height minimum to get into the Army. I had been cast playing a little boy in a show, *Critics' Choice*, up in Central Valley, California. I'd been given a notice for my physical. This was in 1962 or 1963. And they finally found me, because I'd been all around doing my movie things and all, and it was right in the middle of this play. So I called for a postponement. The last little moment on the phone with the guy I said, "By the way, I'm sure I'm under the height minimum. What's the height/weight minimum?" "Five-foot and a hundred pounds." And I went, "Oh shit! I'm tall enough to get into the Army. I need to get under a hundred pounds." So I started living on dried apricots and amphetamines. And I got down to ninety-six pounds to stay out of the Army. And I surely gained that weight back to a normal weight, but I loved what amphetamines did for me. I loved the buzz. That was my first real addiction, and to deal with it, to keep from coming out of my skin, I drank. That's where it started.

My first toot of cocaine was probably in '65, maybe '66. I know it was like ten or fifteen bucks, certainly fifteen was the maximum in those days. It wasn't a hundred dollars a gram. Cocaine went up a lot in the seventies. Maybe twenty bucks. And it was fabulous. I used to joke that I walked into a bar a pony and came out a mustang. But the real confidence-builder for me was that sense of well-being that I got from cocaine. I think it's the element of spiritual well-being and faith that is the major component actually of my recovery today. Today my faith in my recovery gives me that.

I don't know when I crossed the line from use to abuse to addiction, but from my early twenties for sure, I was out of control with amphetamines. It was more amphetamines than anything else at that point, with alcohol and uppers running partner. Alcohol provided a calm and a sense of well-being while uppers provided the false sense of confidence. Things got nasty when I graduated to cocaine. If alcohol made me feel big enough to take on the rest of the world, then cocaine made me feel big enough to play basketball for money. I thrilled to that strange combination of grandiosity and terror. I suspect some element of being alcoholic is we look at the rest of the world and think that everybody knows something that we don't: They are sharing a joke about me. Some place in the back of our brains or corner of our souls wants to separate from our fellows. That's the "ism."

Being around other people in recovery, in a minute I reclaimed some sense of well-being I missed in my teen years. At the start of my abuse, what kicked in with the drug was a sense of connectedness and belonging. Just as the reward as a teenager wasn't what the substance did chemically. The reward was within the ritual—a rite of passage and earning my stripes as one of the gang.

I remember how I'd feel when I'd score. You've probably heard me tell this story before, but it's important. You'd been up two or three days and nights, you're a wreck, you're falling apart. You're calling the dealer, the dealer's not home, not home. And all of a sudden the dealer's home! And the moment she answers the phone, you know by the way she says hi, something's going on. And you begin to feel better. And I ask her, "Hi honey." And instead of "You bitch" it's "Hi honey, anything happening?" And she goes, "Yeah, want me to come over? Want to come by? Whatever." I'm experiencing a change, a total change. I even look better. I'd remember how it felt to open up an eight ball and look at this amazing white powder flashing and how great I felt. And I'd chop it up, and I'd get out the grinder and get it ready, and I'd have that first toot and feel magnificent. I was bright. I was handsome. I wasn't handsome, I was pretty! I was fuckin' pretty. And I could do anything and I was sexy. And I was already starting to have that little tumescent response, the little edge of a woody. I'm feeling great here.

However, as soon as I begin using this crap, it all falls apart. When I had it in my hand and hadn't used it yet, I was feeling magnificent. What was I experiencing? What I was experiencing was faith, faith in this poison. That this crap that doesn't work anymore is going to fix me. But the faith is so immense, so powerful, that I look better, feel better. I'm brighter, I'm more patient, I'm creative. And it's just faith. The only thing that will work at that point is faith. And if faith in this poison doesn't work anymore, imagine what a faith in this true loving God's going to do for me. What was a big breakthrough for me was when I was in rehab, I read that the spiritual life is not a theory—we have to live it. So I have to have a spiritual life. Okay, how am I going to do this? And that's what happened. I was able to transfer that faith in something that didn't work anymore into something that works every time.

But we've skipped over the time when it did work. There was an accident of parallel beginnings that were lined up. It was either fortuitous or . . . you decide. I was at the beginnings of my career and at the beginnings of my addiction. And so what was pouring out of me as a writer, as a creative spirit discovering his abilities, developing his craft, experiencing his success and having that success compounded by other successes, was happening the same time as my drug addiction. So that's an accident. They're not connected. At the time I'm having the success, I believed they were. God stacked the cards. And this card, stacked exactly this way, makes Paul Williams.

My talent is a wonderful gift, but I transferred that gift that was a gift from the universe and credited it to this little bottle of white powder. I see that now. I see that thirteen years later. If I had discovered cocaine today, I might have come to a conclusion that this crap has got me on a downward spiral. But I don't think so. It was so easy to make creativity and cocaine into Siamese twins. I think it takes what it takes.

You read in Emerson's essay he talks about the artist using mead, drink, tobacco, whatever, that it's the nature of the artist to open up these doors with these substances. Hemingway would get plowed and stand at his mantel and pour out brilliance. So I became really defiant about my drug and alcohol use. I drank and used very much in public. I sat there and smoked and drank on *The Tonight Show* and was glib. But I was not glib because of the alcohol. My ability to entertain people or act/react within the moment was not connected to the drug. The drug was the confidence-builder, but the confidence-builder working hand-in-hand with the success I was having. So how do you separate the two? What's giving me confidence? Drugs or the success?

You're the wave, as Deepak Chopra says. Behind that wave is an ocean. And it's all connected. The ideas are flying around and you can tap into them. And probably thirty thousand other people in the universe could have tapped into that same idea at the same moment. I wrote a song called "Magical Mystery Tour" about the time The Beatles were writing theirs. Theirs actually did better!

As time passed, I became a recluse. I never went out. Chris Caswell, my keyboardist—we were just in New York, and it was the day off before recording a soundtrack we were working on. We were running around and went to the Metropolitan Museum. As we grabbed a cab, I hear Chris behind me say, "God, I can't get used to it. It's so weird to see you out there, Paul, running in front of me there on the street. Because you never left the hotel!"

I mean, I would take the limo to the airport, go up to the Admiral's Club, have a drink, go at the last minute, of course, drink on the plane, go in the limo to the hotel, into the hotel room where I stayed until show-time. This was my MO; I hid out. Sure I went through the hippie years, but I was never comfortable sitting on the edge of the pier naked in the sun with a bunch of people. I was really good in a darkened room, at my best peeping out the venetian blinds at 4 a.m. watching the "tree police." (That's what I started calling my imaginary adversaries lurking in the dark. Life at the edge of hallucination can be exhausting, you know, but seldom boring!)

So the songwriting was an accident. I love the idea that while I'm telling this story, new stuff will happen. And to really see for the first time that those two things happened at the same time—my creativity being born and my addiction. How easy it was to assume they were connected.

As I look back, I realize that I was such a throwback in some ways musically. I wrote dreamy, catchy romantic songs . . . my lyrics were so vulnerable . . . "That's enough for me," "If I can make you cry," "If I can fill your eyes with pleasure just by holding you, in the early hours of the morning . . . when the day that lies ahead's not quite begun . . . ah well, that's enough for me, that's all the hero I need to be," "I smile to think of you and I . . . and how our pleasure makes you cry." And then at the end of the song, "How our pleasure makes me cry." I was saying stuff that I think a lot of guys were not writing at that time. "We've Only Just Begun" was the number-one record in the country around the time "In-A-Gadda-Da-Vida" by the Iron Butterfly was the number-one album. My songs were almost alternative at the time.

Something in my DNA went back to the music that I'd heard and knew. The first rock and roll that I loved was The Beatles. It was a big deal for me to get an Elvis cut when I got an Elvis cut, but I didn't give a rat's ass about Elvis when I was a kid. I didn't listen to rock and roll in high school; I listened to Sinatra. It was a sense of being a part of a movement; there was safety in that. I see now that part of the attraction of The Beatles was the camaraderie. I saw this camaraderie in the band which I never had in my life.

I wasn't the only one who was writing intimacy, but I didn't know anything about having a relationship and yet that's what I was writing about with great intimacy and great identification. When you look closely at my lyrics, it's pretty clear I've written a lot of songs that are basically codependent anthems. The idea of a healthy world and a balanced relationship never quite found its way into my songwriting. Let's face it, "I Won't Last a Day Without You" isn't the healthiest of thoughts. So I didn't know anything about how to have a relationship, but I'm writing songs about relationships—deeply personal, vulnerable. And the relationship that I'm developing is a relationship with drugs.

I wrote when I was high and when I wasn't. What the amphetamines and cocaine were good for was staying up. 'Cause I didn't want to go home alone, so I would stay at A & M and write with anybody who would write with me. And all Chuck Kaye wanted me to do was write with Roger Nichols, to go home, get some sleep, and come back and write with Roger. Roger and I would write, and songs were getting recorded. We were productive and very successful. Roger was my music school. It was an amazing time of growth and learning for me. We'd write our songs, and Roger would eventually do something that I hadn't gotten the hang of: Going home to bed! He'd go sleep and return the next morning around 10 a.m. expecting to write again. In the meantime, I'd survived a twelve-hour chemical experiment that left me looking like the Road Runner had been living in my hair.

I knew I was able to get in touch better when I was in a physically diminished state—when you push yourself and were up all night. The place where we go to as writers that's real open and real undefended, where you don't edit. Sometimes when you're tired and open, it comes easier. In a sense being loaded contributed. But I also noticed that I would stay up all night generating ideas, and then I'd collapse and get two or three hours sleep and write something *after* that was sensible. The way I write now is in complete contrast. I meet someone at ten in the morning; we're done by 12:30. At 12:30 I'm out the door—you know, "I love you, good-bye!" We just jump in. What we're doing is we open up all our filing cabinets of our experiences together as two people. Whatever is going on in your life and mine, let's let it fly! It's much easier to write from a healthy place. You and I could write a song right now. It might not be worth much, but we could do it. Part of this is craft; a lot is trust. A lot not trying to control what happens but just creating.

I think I was born an alcoholic and my addictions were inevitable. But the times certainly nurtured my disease. The sixties and seventies took drug use out of the gutter and into the boardroom. Needless to say, for the creative artist it was as environmental. As expected and accepted in a recording session as flour and sugar in a bakery.

And cocaine wasn't addictive. I remember reading that as I buried my face in a pile of Peruvian enthusiasm. A big toot of cocaine combined with the rush of acceptance as a member of the creative community, and I was higher than I'd ever dreamed of. Again, it's important for me to look at the timing of my exposure to the drugs. The fact they showed up in my life at a time when I was blossoming. In my mind, they remained connected until I had a little sober time under my belt.

The needs to be held, accepted, admired, loved, nurtured—all those basic human needs—they're the source of the strongest hunger I've ever experienced. And to have those needs met by my peers, the public at large, and the industry at the same time as I was experiencing the *illusion* of those emotions created by the drugs . . . It's easy to see how enmeshed the actual and the fictitious become in my past.

The seventies were this incredibly productive time when I had great success, six Oscar nominations, and the win for "Evergreen." Nine Grammy nominations and wins for *The Muppet Movie* and "Evergreen." My career grew. It went from just writing songs for other people to cutting an album for A & M Records and appearing on *The Tonight Show*. Once and that was it! I was so comfy in front of the camera. As scared as I was before I'd walk out. I remember standing behind the curtain—going in—that I couldn't breathe. I saw the red light of the camera and Johnny, and just entering into this parallel universe that was home. It's interesting to see an addiction being born here, one of those clear moments. I went to New York, did *The Tonight Show*, sang the first song, and Johnny called me over to talk to him. I was funny. I did a second number, and I was funny. Denny Bond, my manager, and I were staying at the Sherry-Netherland, and we had a lunch at the New York Athletic Club the next day. So we got up, breakfasted, and walked. We were strolling along Central Park South and doormen were saying, "Hi-ye! You were good on *The Tonight Show*!" And, "That's that little guy who was on *The Tonight Show*." And it was like a first hit of cocaine. It was "I'm on top of the world, man." I was Jimmy Cagney in *White Heat*. All of a sudden, it was that ego-serving self-importance. At that moment something very specific happened. I went from being different to being special in my own perception. Being different is hard; being special is wonderful. That moment may have been the birth of an addiction to celebrity. I was being treated with a level of respect I'd never experienced. And I don't mean better tables at restaurants. I'm talking about a core sense of belonging. Of being "more than enough" in a world where I'd always come up short. It's no wonder I became better at showing off than at showing up. The celebrity was a kind of balm—an ointment for some childhood pain, which was long overdue.

All that energy spent out performing and playing at being a celebrity, making people laugh and love me, and being as good as I was on the talk shows was balm for old hurt I think. Unfortunately, what had been a developing craft as a songwriter was now being ignored. All of a sudden unbridled ego and celebrity took over. For instance, Johnny Williams asked me to write the lyrics to *Superman*. I wrote what I thought was a brilliant lyric and the director had the audacity not to like it. Instead of changing the lyric as many times as necessary until he did like it, as I would today ("let's find a way to something wonderful we both love"), I went, "It's done." Then it was, "Don't you know who I am?" Who I used to think I was!

In a way, the ego is a double-edged sword. The drug is keeping that thing whistling in the air, that ego, that self-absorption. There's a complex relationship between drugs and songwriting, and there's a greater relationship between drugs and career and ego than between drugs and creativity. Drugs ultimately diminish creativity because they're artificial. I believe all of my success came out of authenticity. When I wrote honestly about what I felt, other people related to it. It's interesting that even the parts of my life that I can look back on—and the first reaction might be to say that cultivating the celebrity was a mistake, and it was a failure—evidently it was something that my little soul needed then.

I love it when someone grabs me going down the street and says, "God, I really love what you do." I'm also okay when they say, "And you were especially good on *Laugh-In*," which I was never on. I realize they're talking about Arte Johnson. So my relationship to applause is totally changed. I see it as shared memory now. If someone applauds my performance, it's like we're remembering something wonderful about our lives.

But the damage drugs do is lost in the moment. You live in a maelstrom, a storm, and somewhere along the line, you lose. The drama becomes an element of who you are. Paul doesn't have time to get a driver's license. It's like, Paul always wears an ascot *and* he's always late for the meeting. That's for effect, not the ascot but the being late for a meeting! Or even more absurd, sending my manager to a creative meeting in my place. ABC asked me to write a song to promote their daytime programming. They were using "Let Me Be the One," calling it "Let Us Be the One." A few years later, they came back and said they wanted to promote their daytime soap operas. "Would you write a song for us?" I sent Denny to the creative meeting. How rude! What amazes me is I did not see this at the time. What I had done was make the rest of the world bit players in supporting roles in *The Paul Williams Show*.

I heard Tom, this Englishman in L.A., say that in recovery you start out as a superstar and work your way into the chorus. I had achieved that kind of status: *The Paul Williams Show*, isn't that wonderful? What I think he meant was that the gift of recovery gives you the chance to step into the chorus, become part of the family of man, back away from your own drama, and experience the pure joy of belonging and the greater gift of being a valuable human who can help another. Someone very wise once said, "It's all about love and service." I'm beginning to understand.

Basically I stopped work in the eighties. I was too high to see myself in free-fall. When I finally tried to get sober, it was for a girl, Melissa, a young graduate student. I did aversion therapy for Melissa. They give you injections to make you sick and then alcohol to drink. You throw up and lay there for three hours with a towel around your neck with your own vomit in it. Just lying there thinking about your situation, the smells and all, is revolting. The next day comes a shot of sodium pentothal that knocks you out, like 99, 98, . . . 3. While you're out, they ask if you want a drink. Then you go back for more vomiting. But the therapist said, "We're worried about you, Mr. Williams, because you're the only person we know that's been consistently early for sodium pentothal." I loved it! I wanted another treatment! For seven months, I didn't drink. But I didn't reflect or change on the inside— never cracked a book, shared my problem, or had a support system.

Next I went to Jamaica. Hadn't had a drink in seven months on pure Paul Williams superstar-willpower. White knuckling it all the way. I went to Jamaica for a project called *The Secret Life of Queen Victoria*, a musical I'm still trying to get done. And at two o'clock in the afternoon at the producer's beautiful home, by the pool, a gentleman in a white jacket comes out and goes, "Mr. Williams, would you care for something to drink? Perhaps a rum and coke?" I said to myself, "Wait a minute. I haven't had a drink in seven months. I'm Paul Williams. I have a star on Hollywood Boulevard. I can have one drink." So at two o'clock in the afternoon, I had a rum and coke. Two o'clock in the morning, I was at Bob Marley's grave explaining reggae to a lot of black people I didn't know. Lying through my teeth. I don't know how I wound up there.

At this point, I realize I have a disease and total abstinence is the beginning of how I deal with it. Total abstinence gives me a chance to stay clean and sober and learn. And I had a capacity to learn. But then I was off and running for two more years of uncontrolled using. During that time, I put up a front about getting sober. To hide my use, I became a chronic and habitual liar. Say I was going to some event or to see people, Melissa would say, "I know you're getting high. Just admit it. We'll get you help. I'm not going to leave." And I'd answer, "What the fuck is the matter with you? You have a lot of issues with men, don't you? A lot of trust issues?" I'd turn it on her, and she'd go to bed crying, worried about what was wrong with her perceptabilities to perceive reality. She thought she was dented, broken. Then Melissa would go to bed, and I'd sneak out the puppy door and go score more drugs. 'Cause the real door had a terrible squeak. When I'd been up two days and nights, it was *roar*, the world's loudest door. So I'd sneak out the puppy door and go score. And I remember sitting next to her when she cried, wanting to hold her and be there for her, but being unable to connect with the emotion. Wanting to, but not being able to find the emotion. And eventually she left.

In 1989, right before I got sober, I went to Oklahoma City to do a gig. A doctor had prescribed Antabuse to keep me from drinking. Antabuse is a chemical that causes a violent physical illness if mixed with alcohol. So I was taking Antabuse but using cocaine with it, basically playing with fire as I lived the lie. Evidently the lie screwed me up because I had a full-blown psychotic episode before going on stage. Three o'clock in the afternoon, I'm in a tuxedo walking out of my dressing room with a promoter, never having been out of my hotel suite. And it's like somebody grabbed me and threw me higher than my own head against the wall and then threw me down the escalator stairs. I was dragged by my ears. I experienced an episode—about three-quarters of an hour of pure hell. And in the rear view mirror, as we're driving to the gig, I can see this little monster behind me. And he's twisting my ear, laughing and biting chunks out of my neck. It was like a gruesome monster—a terrifying psychotic episode brought out by the toxicity. So Gary, the promoter, called the psychiatrist and postponed the show for a day and took me to a doctor who gave me something to calm me down.

Two months later, in a blackout, I phoned a doctor. He called me the next day. "I found a place for you," he said. And I said, "What are you talking about?" "Well, you called me last night," he replied. "You said you wanted to get sober and go into treatment." I didn't remember this at all and I started crying. Help was the last thing I wanted, but I went into treatment. . . . Now cut to ten years later. I'm ten years sober and had just spoken at a men's lockdown in Nashville, Tennessee. So I'm full-tilt Gandhi-meets-Jiminy Cricket-Paul Williams.

Back to my hotel. A river to my people, saving lives left and right, I reek with self-importance. I go up to my hotel room, and my key doesn't work, and I'm like, "Son of a bitch!" It's a quick trip from Gandhi to Himmler for me. My recovery's out the window. I want my key, my room, my bed. I go down and get the new room key, and the lobby of the hotel is full of guys with little badges identifying where they're from. It's a convention of talent buyers. And this one gentleman comes up to me and says, "My name is Curt. I booked you once and just wanted to say hi." I noticed the nametag on his chest says Oklahoma City. I went, "Oh my god, are you the guy who booked me when I did my Linda Blair? When my head was spinning? Oh was I possessed!" "Yes, that was me." And I got all puffed up. "I'm ten years sober now. I just spoke at the prison." I was pumped up and shining. "Yeah," he said, "I heard you were sober." I asked, "Are you sober too?" And he reached in his pocket and pulled out a coin from a recovery program, commemorating seventeen years. "Wait a minute." I did the math. "You were seven years sober when I had the psychotic episode? What did you think?" "You scared me to death." "What did you do?" He said they put together a prayer circle the next day in the hopes that I would find a healing for my disease. "That you'd be able to find sobriety, be able to make that choice." And two months later in a blackout, I called that physician.

You can go from that story to that wonderful statement that we show up as superstars and work our way into the chorus. I slid deeply into the chorus. Because I'd been the star of the Paul Williams recovery up to that moment. In some level of my consciousness, I'd taken credit for the effort I'd put into my sobriety. That effort remains strong. So do the pride and gratitude. However, what changed was I saw that every bit of it was a gift. Every bit of my recovery was a gift from the men and women that have gone before and who care enough. And when we hold hands and pray, the prayers are heard and work. Once in the South I heard a woman say, "It always makes me laugh. Worry, worry, worry. Why worry when you can pray?" It was so simple to her. So we can pray and change our actions.

My dad took me to a baseball game when I was thirteen. Drunk as a skunk, he woke me in the middle of the night, put me in the car to drive to see the Cleveland Indians play baseball. Only he drove to Cincinnati, the wrong town. It was a pouring rainstorm, and Dad sat in this empty parking lot saying, "We're going to get really good seats. We're early." Finally he got up and walked to the stadium ticket office and found he'd gone to the wrong city. And I saw his shoulders slump into that alcoholic slump that I've repeated myself with my children through the years. And he came back and said, "Well, there's not going to be a ball game, but it's the thought that counts."

Those words were immense in my psyche: "It's the thought that counts." Because until I was forty-nine years old, I was one of the "thoughtiest" people you ever met in your life. I had the best intentions. I did. I meant to show up on time, or get that song finished for you on time, or give to charity. I said I would. I meant to vote, but I didn't. When I got sober, what was shown to me was that the crux was not the thought, or even my feelings about a matter, as much as my actions.

From the minute I got sober, a friend who supported me would call me up and ask how I was treating the world today. The first time I was like, "You've had a slip of the tongue. Don't you mean how is the world treating me?"

"Well, I do care," he answered. "But I can't do much about that. I guarantee though that if you monitor the way you treat the world, you can change every element of your life. And that's the gift right there. It's magnificent, isn't it?"

We were so affected by the praise. But we so desperately needed it. I don't know all the individual stories of the other people in this book—or little Gary's story. I don't know what they or little Gary were like. But they needed that praise, needed to be held the way that drugs held them, maybe to strike out and get even to what had hurt them. So I needed to be held the way drugs held me, but I found that drugs were not faithful lovers.

I cringe when I remember moments on stage when I was out of control on blow and booze. Tasteless jokes. I think I enjoyed digging holes for myself with the audience, and then trying to climb back out. And I fell, more than once. My record was in Detroit, opening for Joan Rivers. I walked out, and there was an orchestra pit that wasn't there during the sound check. Or so I thought . . . I fell fourteen feet into a concrete-floored pit and survived with no major injuries. Just some bruises and a sprained hip. The years were not wasted on any level to me. And none of it was for naught.

You know you're an alcoholic when you misplace a decade. And the eighties are pretty much a blur. The fast track to my bottom was cocaine. I was using it every day—an eight ball a day by the end of the eighties. A lot of money. But what it cost me was nothing compared to what it cost me. What I mean is the choices I made were almost always selfish and self-destructive behind the drug. And the years of my children's infancy deserved a father that was truly present. Loving and fully present.

I lost so many valuable years to my addiction. But they aren't really lost if speaking about the disease helps reduce the stigma. I went to Florida a couple of years ago to speak at the NCADD. I was briefly on the board of directors of the National Council on Alcoholism and Drug Dependence. I jumped in a cab and the driver said, "Hey, Mr. Williams, what are you doing in town, a concert?" I said, "No, I am speaking for the National Council on Alcoholism." He asked why I was doing that. I told him because I am an alcoholic. The driver remarked on the genetic connection to the disease. I found this heartening. Never touched by alcoholism, yet he knew that. It showed me that the public is educated that we have a disease. We don't have to be ashamed and can be open about recovery.

The brightest, most energetic, and generous group of people I ever met in the world are recovering alcoholics and drug addicts. I have never seen such light as in the eyes of those recovering when someone reaches out to them. To be at this point in my life and have a sense of beginning and use-fulness is more than I could have imagined. If I can stay in a place where I am within God's touch, then every day will be built on a foundation of pure gratitude—or my name ain't Paul W.!

My name isn't on the cover of *Variety* or *Rolling Stone*, but it has not been listed in the obituary column either, which is where I was headed. I have a life today. I'm writing a musical about a decade that I missed, writing of themes like fear and ambition. I'm identifying and kind of kicking through those emotional values.

Melissa, the twenty-three-year-old psychology major, was the first person who reflected the truth back to me and said, "You're an alcoholic and you're going to die, and I'm not going to stick around to watch it." She had a lot of Ernest Holmes books around. He was the creator of the Church of Religious Science, and his whole thinking, like Emmet Fox's, is about the power of thought. If you go, "I'm not going to get that job, I'm not," the universe hears it as a prayer. Emmet Fox goes to the next step that there is no competition, there is no limited supply—there is abundance. If you have a struggling shoe store and a major chain of shoe stores opens across the street from you, you pray for their success.

I used to think such thoughts as "I am not going to do a good job," so the universe hears in the negative. And you can see the fear. I was having fun, but when you look closer, it's like watching someone ducking or waiting to be hit. I was walking up there grabbing the Oscar for "Evergreen," and you would think that moment would abound in life and gratitude. In my acceptance speech, I said I would thank all the little people and then remembered that I am the little people. Funny, but also very revealing that I felt some part of me didn't deserve an award.

It's been said that fear is the activator of all our character defects. The power of fear was the headwaters of my disease. I see the fear in my eyes if I watch videotapes of myself during the years I drank and used. Footage at the height of my disease in the eighties on *Hollywood Squares* or some game show network is hard for me to watch. My eyes were dead. Things were spoken with no restraint of tongue, no editing for social grace. It's as if there were no inner thought. In reading spiritual philosophy, I discovered a new rule book governed by trust. A friend once told me that if the cash went low, he always went shopping. And I love that kind of thinking, 'cause I think like that now. Go shopping, 'cause you're going to get taken care of. God didn't bring me this far to drop me. No way!

I always joke about being master of the codependent anthem. But the joke nuzzles a truth. "I Won't Last a Day Without You" isn't really a healthy thought. But it's reflective of a way I've felt many times . . . and so has the rest of the world. It's odd. I'm less embarrassed about the "neediness" in my own lyrics today, even though I think I'm less needy.

I have a wonderful, magical woman in my life today. It's the love affair

I've always dreamed of—Siamese twin to the kind of friendship I've never been able to maintain. I'm learning to listen. I think that's a big part of my growth. I always said my kids were my best work. The fact is I learn from them every day. Life 101. But it's only possible because I have a relationship with myself and with my Higher Power. There was a time when my lady and I combined made for one healthy person: her! I think that's changed somewhat. I know it has.

I did several years of analysis. That old Freudian "we look at the relationship with the mother" school of introspection. My guess is the first time I was breastfed, instead of getting all warm and fuzzy and secure, burping and drifting off to sleep, I was probably one of those babies that immediately worried that the breast once removed was never coming back. It's a fear-based thinking that may be hardwired into some of us. So at some base level, if I love someone, it's in my psyche that I'm going to lose them.

Overcoming that hidden terror is a big thing. And to deal with it you have to, well, deal with it. That means not medicating it. The gift of recovery begins with clear vision, which means brighter sunlight, more magnificent sunsets, and last but not least, a real clear up-close-and-personal view of your own personalized horror film. Once we get a good look at all that fear, we can go to work on it.

We've only just begun
To live
White lace and promises
A kiss for luck and we're on our way
Before the rising sun
We fly
So many roads to choose
We start out walking and learn to run
And yes we've just begun
Sharing horizons that are new to us
Watching the signs along the way
Talking it over just the two of us
Working together day to day

Together
And when the evening comes
We smile
So much of life ahead
We'll find a place where there's room to grow
And yes we've just begun
To live
We've only just begun
To live

—"We've Only Just Begun"

I believe, if we take habitual drunkards as a class, their heads and hearts will bear an advantageous comparison with those of any other class. There seems ever to have been a proneness in the brilliant and warm-blooded to fall into this vice.

—Abraham Lincoln

Jim Ramstad
(U.S. congressman)

WHEN COMING UP WITH THE idea of writing a book about celebrities in recovery, we decided we wanted to find recovering people in five different categories: music, film, sports, literature, and politics. I was familiar with likely candidates in the first four, but I had no real sense of whom I might find in the political arena. Ann Richards, former governor of Texas, was sober, but she had appeared in previous books about sobriety and was just a bit beyond the age group we were seeking. While watching TV one evening, I came across a program featuring Bill Moyers interviewing congressman Jim Ramstad of Minnesota. I had never heard of Jim, but during the course of the Moyers interview, he started expounding upon legislation he was working on regarding the treatment of alcoholics in this country. He also mentioned that he is in recovery himself, which really got my attention. I sent an e-mail to his congressional office and almost immediately received a warm response. After a quick exchange of messages, I was invited to come see the congressman, and a meeting was arranged.

I was met at the Washington, D.C., train station by Drew Peterson, Jim's well-organized and accommodating press secretary, and given a brief ride to Jim's office in the Cannon House Office Building, passing the Capitol along the way.

I was immediately ushered into the congressman's office, where I was heartily welcomed. Jim was dressed in casual attire: dark-blue crew-neck sweater over a yellow-collared shirt. Khaki trousers and cordovan loafers completed the outfit.

His handshake was strong and firm, and he looked me right in the eyes when I introduced myself. Jim's face is that of an All-American—ruggedly handsome and distinguished by a crease in his lip that makes his mouth appear to smile, even when it's not.

The walls of Jim's office are what you would expect from a congressman. Photos adorn one entire wall. But prominently centered on his very large, dark, wood desk was a copy of *Twenty-Four Hours a Day*. This is a small volume of daily meditations for people in recovery from alcoholism, which he says he reads every morning. He picked it up and held it as if it were sacred.

I could tell Jim was eager and completely willing to tell me his story, one he has told countless times in his twenty-two years of sobriety. The only request I made was that I wanted to hear his *feelings* about the events he would share with me. I was needlessly worried that, being a politician, he might be cautious about sharing his private thoughts.

When talking to another alcoholic about alcoholism, I am almost always struck with how personal and familiar the conversation seems. Talking with Jim was no exception. He was very relaxed and easily recounted his story. I think he felt the same way toward me. We know who each other is and the bonding is rapid.

When he ended our talk, Jim told me he would do "anything" to help me with this book. I knew he meant it.

———

As far as I'm concerned, I waive my anonymity about my alcoholism. Actually the press breached my anonymity for me on July 31, 1981, when I woke up in a jail cell in Sioux Falls, South Dakota, under arrest after my last alcoholic blackout, for disorderly conduct, resisting arrest, and failure to vacate the premises.

I happened to be at the time a young state senator. I had just finished the first year of my first term in the Minnesota state senate. And I went to South Dakota with some Viking football players to roast a former Viking named Neil Graff, who backed up Fran Tarkington as a quarterback for a number of years, to raise money for youth sports in Sioux Falls. I was doing a favor for a supporter who had campaigned for me and was a good friend. We went down to speak and attend a fund-raising dinner.

As was customary for me in those days when I went out of town, when I thought I was safe, I would drink—abuse alcohol—as I did for twelve long painful years. And that particular night was my last alcoholic blackout: I haven't had one for the last twenty-two years, three months, and thirteen days since I got sober. Because I was a public figure in Minnesota, the press breached any anonymity I had. And that was very liberating for me—very freeing actually. At the time when it happened, I wanted to be dead and was sure my political career was over. You know, who's going to vote for a drunk who embarrasses himself and his family and friends and constituents as I did. But instead, it was just the beginning of a whole new way of living. A life of sobriety and a healthy, productive life-style, which I had never known before. A life of honesty, where I am the same person publicly as I am privately. That arrest became the greatest thing that ever happened to me, the greatest moment of my life. It was a blessing, and I believe it was God's way of showing me that I was an alcoholic and that I did need help.

For twelve years, my family and those who loved me had suggested, based on incident after incident, whether it was a DWI, ending up in detox, or embarrassing friends and family at social functions, that I look at my alcoholism. I had two great uncles who had died of alcoholism: one on my mother's side, one on my father's side, both men I respected. One was a doctor, the other a very successful business person. One uncle died on skid row after losing everything, and the other uncle died in a state mental institution.

These were my images of alcoholism, and the last thing I ever wanted to be was an alcoholic. And for twelve years, I was a practicing alcoholic. So you see why it was a blessing that the good Lord brought me to my knees in that jail cell on July 31, 1981. For the first time, I admitted my powerlessness over alcohol. My life had obviously become unmanageable. I couldn't see it until that day in my jail cell. Because I had tried to quit. I had quit for eleven months once. Lied my way through an outpatient and nighttime treatment program. This time was different. In that jail cell, I felt physically lighter. I felt a connection to my Higher Power that I had never felt before.

I always thought spiritual awakenings were fabrications of evangelical spin masters. But I realized that day I was having a spiritual awakening. I had been a crisis Christian all those years I was drinking, and my spiritual life had gone to hell in a hand basket. All I was doing was politics, and then on the side on weekends, I was a binge drinker. And I was afraid of looking bad in those days. Because of political concerns, I would limit my drinking to only in the company of very close friends, or when I was out of town. Well, Sioux Falls was out of town, and I was with some of my closest friends, so I thought I was safe. But I had so many blackouts—just hundreds of blackouts. So I was grateful that I was able to take that first step in that jail cell.

Through high school I was a student athlete, never drank at all, was very straight. Same in college. I was active in student government, president of my fraternity, student senator at the University of Minnesota. I worked hard at my grades. I was very successful in school and graduated Phi Beta Kappa. I wanted to do well to get into a good law school, and so I stayed away from drinking until my senior year. That spring I was introduced to alcohol for the first time in my life. I was at a Polynesian restaurant in downtown Minneapolis with my girlfriend and another friend, and I tasted a Polynesian rum drink and loved it. I drank the whole thing and ordered another and another, and during that first encounter got inebriated. And literally my girlfriend and the other friend carried me out of the restaurant. Thus, the very first time I drank, I blacked out, and for the next dozen years was a binge drinker. There were times I'd drink and function, but towards the end, the blackouts were recurring quite frequently.

The summer after graduation from college, I went on active duty in the Army. During basic combat training, I got back into physical shape. When I left Fort Bragg and basic training, and came to Fort Myers, we had weekend sprees. It was over here in Georgetown, on active duty, that I started on my heavy drinking again in some of the saloons with friends. Again, the pattern was to start drinking and not quit. I could tell my ghastly story but don't want to bore anybody. My story is similar to those commonly heard and to the ones I hear every week.

Yet I wasn't aware I was drinking more than my friends or that alcohol affected me differently. I didn't think of myself as an alcoholic. I thought I could control it. Once I quit for eleven months and was sure I wasn't an alcoholic. I was very ignorant of the nature of the disease. On the plane coming back from Sioux Falls after my release from jail, I asked a former Viking, a drinking buddy, "You mean all those times that we would party, you remembered everything the next day?" And he said, "Yeah." . . . "You never blacked out and forgot whom you talked to or insulted?" He said, "No, I really didn't." And the guy sitting next to him said the same thing. Well, they're not alcoholics. They're still to this day two of my dearest friends, and they're normal healthy drinkers. And that's when it hit me between the eyes—the waking up in the jail cell coupled with that conversation, asking them about their drinking experiences those twelve years that I'd associated and partied with them, that really hit me. "God," I recall saying, "I really am an alcoholic." That conversation brought it home.

I called my predecessor and mentor, congressman [Bill] Frenzel, who held this office for twenty years before my election in 1990. I wanted Frenzel to hear it from me. I had so much respect for him. It was a hard phone call to make, but in typical Frenzel fashion, he said, "Well, the mark of a strong person is what he or she does when they're down on the mat. You're down on the mat now; let's see what you do. Your future's up to you. I'm not going to write you off yet."

That gave me a lot of incentive. Other friends helped me, made arrangements for me to go to treatment at Saint Mary's Rehabilitation Center in Minneapolis—it's now called Fairview Recovery Services—on the west bank of the University of Minnesota. And from that day forward, every day got better. August 1, I came home from South Dakota, and August 2, I was admitted to treatment. Spent the next twenty-eight days in treatment . . . I'm grateful to say, thanks to the grace of God and the fellowship of other recovering people, and family and friends who've loved me, that I've been able to stay sober since. Every day I wake up and get down on my knees before I do anything, before I go to the bathroom, I thank God for waking up sober.

I recently lost my mother. For nine very tough years, she had Alzheimer's. Very early in the disease, my mother told one of her doctors who told me at the funeral that "Whatever my son, Jim, might have accomplished, the thing I'm most proud about him is his recovery, that he's been able to recover from alcoholism." Nobody could have given me a bigger, more appreciated gift than to tell me that. My mother respected and appreciated my recovery. I know I hurt her, my father, sister, and significant others a lot when I was drinking—caused them embarrassment, shame, and worry. Pain that while I was drinking I wasn't aware I was causing my family and parents. No. I was in stubborn and intractable denial, because of the images that I had as a young boy about alcoholics. I didn't want to be like my two uncles, who died tragic deaths from this fatal disease. I didn't feel guilty at the time, or think of myself as an alcoholic. My self-image was of someone who worked hard and played hard.

Eventually though the consequences became greater. It wasn't just headaches and stupid drunken behavior. It was a DWI. It was embarrassing a friend at his wedding. It was embarrassing my own sister at her wedding. It was ending up in a jail cell. The consequences started coming after I moved back to Minnesota in 1978. I'd lived in Washington from 1970 to 1978—went to law school here, practiced law, and taught as an adjunct professor at American University. Taught five years, starting at Montgomery College and then at American University. From 1979, drinking wasn't fun anymore. I was worried more about the consequences than I was carried along by the fun. And the consequences became more significant.

I never intended to drink to blackout proportions. Sometimes I'd succeed in my resolve: "I'm going out tonight. I'm only going to have two beers." And I only had two beers. But then the fifth or sixth time I was only going to have two beers and woke up not knowing where I was the next morning. It was unpredictable behavior. Part of that was the excitement and contagion that some alcoholics feel, but any excitement was more than offset by anxiety, fear, worry. Going out to my car the next morning, checking my bumpers for blood and dents. This is how crazy my alcoholism got. Especially given the Minnesota roads in the winter, I consciously feared that I would end up in a car accident, killing myself and others. In fact that's the first thing I asked the jailer when I woke up in that cell. I said, very respectfully, "Would you please answer three questions? Was I driving a car last night?" He said no. "I didn't kill anybody? Or hurt anybody in any other way?" And he said, "No. No, you didn't hurt anybody." I was greatly relieved because of the insanity of this disease, which I've learned about in recovery. The disease is a form of insanity, and the more it progresses the more insane a person becomes, and certainly my drinking was insane.

That night in jail was really the night I was led out of the wilderness. I was literally brought down to my knees that next morning. I knelt down in the corner in that jail on that cement floor and folded my hands and sought my Higher Power. I totally admitted my powerlessness over alcohol. I said, "Oh Lord, I know now what I am. Please help me. Wherever you lead I'll go. If it's treatment, resigning my state senate seat, doing something else with my life, whatever." I quit trying to control things and let it happen. I had advisors telling me when I returned to Minnesota the following day—I'll never forget the buzzwords were "unfortunate misunderstanding"—just tell the press and your constituents that it was an unfortunate misunderstanding between you and the Sioux Falls police. After my experience that morning in jail and turning it over, I said, "No. No. No more. I can't. That's . . . No. This time I'm going to tell the truth about my drinking. I'm going to let it all hang out, be totally honest, and let the chips fall where they may. I can't deal with this any other way. I can't continue with it anymore."

I knew I needed help and wanted my alcoholism to stop. I knew I couldn't do it alone. I needed treatment. So instead of hypocrisy, I told my story. About twelve years of abusing alcohol. What happened in Sioux Falls. That I really didn't remember the details—I was blacked out as I commonly experienced it in those days. Being in a disco with loud music and drinking, and that's the last I remembered except flashes in the hotel lobby across the street—the hotel where we were staying, and the security guard who came by and asked if I was a guest. I said, "No, I'm not." Well I was. Apparently I didn't have a key. I have no independent recollection of the rest of this, no firsthand knowledge. This is what I was told by the authorities, that the guard said I had to leave. I was sitting in a roped-off area which was a coffee shop during the day and in the evening, because it was two o'clock in the morning, and I refused to leave. "Are you staying here?" he said, and I said, "No, and it's none of your blankety-blank business. Leave me alone. I'm not moving." The guard called another security guard, and when I wouldn't budge, they called the police. Then I again refused to leave and was charged on three counts. I was on probation for a year with the condition that if I didn't get into any further trouble, the charges would be dropped. There was never a formal adjudication. The plea was as a first-time offender. And going into treatment was not a condition. I didn't need a judge to tell me I needed it.

Treatment was a scary proposition, going into the unknown, the uncertain, not knowing what to expect. Every day, though, improved over the previous. I learned about my disease; things like the pattern of it started making sense. It seemed that I personified the disease concept. Speakers and small groups during the treatment reinforced my understanding and provided tools for recovery. I made a commitment during my stay that I would put recovery first for the rest of my life, as long as the good Lord gave me on this earth. And I've been able to maintain that—one day at a time.

The more truthful I became with people, the more they embraced me. The more honest and open I was, the more people responded. The first week I got out of treatment, I went to my American Legion post for a luncheon meeting and saw a gentleman who frequented it but was no friend of mine. In fact, he did everything to foil me. I had just won the election that previous November and finished my first year of my first term. It was a hotly contested campaign. I beat a popular Democratic incumbent, strongly supported by this gentleman. Even though we were both members of the legion post, he hated my guts! He came up to me and said, "You know, Ramstad"—and I figured he was on the verge of asking me to resign my state senate seat or something negative, something involved in politics and very critical given what had just happened. But he said, "You know,

Ramstad, I always thought you had three strikes against you. First of all you're a damn lawyer, and I hate lawyers. Secondly you're a damn politician, and I hate politicians. Thirdly you're a damn Republican lawyer, and there's nothing worse." And then he reached up his big arms. (His forearms were as big as tree stumps. Was he going to hit me or what?) And he got this big smile on his face and said, "But now that I know you're an alcoholic, you're one of us. Welcome to the club, brother." And he gave me a hug.

I started crying like a baby. The tears kept coming. I felt, wow, this guy was one of my worst critics. He did everything he could to defeat me in the election and here he's welcoming me to the club. He's my friend and he gave me a hug! . . . And the more I opened to people, the more I was embraced.

By and large, people gave me support and encouragement through the rough time, after my problem was exposed. I think of a couple in Plymouth [Minnesota], very devout churchgoers who were active in the Republican Party. When I saw them, I felt so bad because I cared about them and I'd fallen from their standards. I felt they would be judgmental and withdraw their support. But this couple surprised me when they too surrounded me with a big hug. They had struggled with substance abuse also. These people were right off caring about me as an individual and encouraging my recovery. It's been a whole new world, the life of recovery. No more doublespeak in any area of life. A feeling of being real with everybody.

Now I feel that my political persona and private persona are one and the same. What a great feeling it is! I don't have to be somebody else when I go out to give a speech or when I meet constituents or speak to a campaign rally. I see many of my colleagues who are kind of split personalities. They are one person privately and another on the stump. Because honesty is a cornerstone of recovery, my life has become a lot easier and more fun, a lot healthier. I don't have to pretend. I quit pretending on July 31, 1981. I quit worrying about the ramifications of what I said. I just try to be honest and open. I try to apply the principles of recovery to all aspects of my life. I've not been perfect, but I feel as though every day I make progress.

I force myself every single morning of my life, when I first wake up and get down on my knees, to remember exactly what it was like in that jail cell. I can tell you where the plaster was chipped and where the drainpipe was that I knelt by and where the bars were to the outside. I can still picture that jail cell vividly. I can draw it for you exactly as it was. I never want to forget that turning point, that epiphany in my life. That's how I stay sober. It took me twelve years to get to the admission of my disease, and it was crucial for me. The first step was 90 percent of the battle. Because I didn't want to be an alcoholic. I was taught and wanted to be as nearly perfect as I could be—in school, sports, politics. I didn't want my flaws known. The recovering enabled me to feel human and to recognize that nobody's perfect, no relationship is perfect. Everyone has flaws. Everyone is dealt problems. My life's not perfect; I have problems every single day, but it's how I deal with them that counts. Any problem would only be exacerbated, would only get worse, were I to revert to drinking. And of course I'm absolutely convinced that if I hadn't had that experience with those police officers and that jail cell that I'd be dead now because I was drinking such large quantities. I've learned about the disease the more I've gotten into it, not only from my own recovery standpoint but also from the standpoint of a policymaker trying to provide the same access to treatment to the 26 million Americans out there who still suffer the ravages of this disease.

My counselor at Saint Mary's Rehabilitation Center said the first day of treatment, August 2, 1981, "Jim, the only time you're going to be a *recovered* alcoholic is when they put you in your casket, when they put you underground. Because you're never out of the woods. Nobody's safe from relapse. We're recovering one day at a time." I was disappointed at the time I heard that because I wanted to call myself a recovered alcoholic. You know, I'm fixed. I've got the *Good Housekeeping* seal of approval that I'm well and can now be normal. I'm not normal, I'm an alcoholic. And I've got to deal with my alcoholism every single day of my life so I don't take that next drink.

Whether you're a successful writer, great athlete, or wonderful First Lady—I think of Mrs. Ford in the photograph on the wall there with her husband, who have become dear friends of mine—this is an equal opportunity disease. It doesn't matter your socioeconomic status or your position. We're all in this together. I like all my groups, but my favorite meets at the House of Charity in Minneapolis. About half the members are in the long-term treatment center there for indigent people, most of whom are off the street. A lot come from other cities. That's really their last chance between this world and the grave. I've made many friends over the years going to that Thursday night group with those men who are really down on their luck. But there for the grace of God go I.

I can't think of any group I frequent where there haven't been relapses, and that's important to see. One of my groups had a guy with forty-two years of sobriety who got in a big fight with his wife and went out and was dead in three months. Because of the progressive nature of the disease, that could be me. So my point is that addiction is an equal opportunity disease, and I just love the people in recovery. I'm just so grateful for every one of them because they help me stay sober. They're the most wonderful people in the world. I just wish this place, I wish Congress could become like a recovery group where people say what they mean and mean what they say. You know this would be a lot better institution. We could make a lot better public policy, a lot better laws, if it weren't about spin but about honesty. If it were a requirement that Congress adopt a program of recovery—like the Twelve Steps—we would all benefit. Certainly the American people would benefit.

Nobody can really measure the indirect cost of alcoholism. All the absenteeism in the workplace, the lost productivity and injuries, and of course the 100,000 people who died from alcohol and addiction last year. That doesn't measure how many lives failed and how many people died of liver failure because of alcohol, or how many died of heart disease. That's just those that we know the direct cause was chemical addiction. Eighty-two percent of people in our jails, according to a Columbia University study, are there because of drugs and/or alcohol. So I just wish this place would turn into a big recovery group. Then I know we could get a good treatment parity bill passed. But all we can do is carry the message in our lives. I feel very blessed and fortunate to be a recovering alcoholic. There is no way I could be anything else—a good uncle, son, or partner for

Kathryn, a good friend, let alone a member of Congress if I hadn't been able to treat my alcoholism. That's who I am fundamentally. It's so basic. I'm first and foremost a grateful recovering alcoholic.

A lot of people my age are dead at the present time.

—Casey Stengel

Dock Ellis
(baseball player)

LIKE DOCK ELLIS, I'VE LOVED the game of baseball for as long as I can remember. It was almost as important to me as the procurement of drugs, at the zenith of my years of addiction. The choice between watching a Dodgers game live or even on TV versus scoring the next batch of whatever I was going to smoke, drink, or snort was difficult to make. Intoxication would win out, but not before I'd think long and hard about the game I might miss. Ideally I would score, get high, and then melt into my sporting pleasure.

I remember fantastic sun-drenched afternoons at Dodger Stadium watching my beloved "Bums" while high as Tommy Davis's batting average. Smoking a couple of joints on the way to the game, washing down a few beers to keep the buzz at the proper level, and disappearing into the slow-dance rhythm of the game. Most often the worlds of baseball and drugs didn't blend, each having its own demands and considerations, but occasionally I'd finesse them onto the same page in exquisite harmony.

Which brings me to Dock Ellis, who married these two endeavors better than anyone I'd ever heard of. Dock Ellis, the guy who unbelievably pitched a no-hitter on acid, for God's sake. It can't get any more bizarre than that.

As soon as Jane and I started formulating the list of subjects for this book, Dock's name surfaced in my mind. Of course I wanted to interview this legendary screwball, but weeks of Internet and library searches got me nowhere. I found a couple of addresses on the Internet but received no response to the letters I wrote. I was getting the sense that this guy just didn't want to be found. Persistence finally paid off, however, when a friend of a friend told me Dock was working at a correctional facility in the desert town of Adelanto, California. A little additional searching came up with a name and phone number.

Elated to be finally reaching this renowned character on the telephone, I blurted out about how hard it had been to locate him. "You found me, didn't you?" was his terse reply. "Yeah, I guess so," I said. He laughed. "Well, I guess it couldn't have been that hard."

It took but a minute for Dock to hear my interview request and agree to see me. "One condition though," he said. "If I'm going to tell you my story, you're going to tell the inmates of my facility your story."

I'm always willing to share my experience, strength, and hope with anyone wanting to hear about my recovery, so this was an easy stipulation to accept.

What follows is, in essence, the morning I spent with Dock at the Marantha Correctional Facility, smack dab in the middle of the California high desert.

I showed up early on a typical sun-baked morning, temperatures already pushing triple figures. The reception room is a no-frills deal with security glass protecting the reception desk. Dock took about ten minutes to come for me, and I was getting a bit antsy. Through the glass, I could observe lots of activity, with prisoners in blue overalls coming and going, along with the expected array of uniformed guards. Suddenly the door to the reception room opened and out sauntered Dock, as casual as could be in his Nike warm-up suit, looking more as though he were headed to a fitness club than to work at a prison. His greeting was warm, like that of an old friend. For him, just another day at the office, but for me, it was going to be an experience to remember.

Dock Speaking to Inmates
Marantha Correctional Facility, Adelanto, California

Dock: I signed to play baseball in 1963, right after I was released from jail for stealing a car. I played baseball all over L.A. We used to play out in Glendale, and I thought I was on a road trip to San Francisco or something, because we stopped and ate breakfast. We thought we were going a long ways, but it wasn't but thirty minutes from home. I played all up and down the West Coast. That's when I met Bobby Bonds, Dusty Baker, all them guys.

I got involved with drugs when I was young, playing around in the alley on 135th Street. I was a California hot dog, smoking marijuana, talking stuff. I was fortunate enough to be in baseball for twelve years, eleven years more than I was supposed to, because during the first years I was into all kinds of things I shouldn't have been into. Drugs was taking me to all kinds of places. I had but one good year.

Inmate: I thought you said you had one good *ear*!

Dock: Oh come on, man, I'm talking about all those Gottis I used to run into. I thought one of them would kill me. I got away with a lot of stuff. I met a lot of crazy people.

Inmate: You played with Babe Ruth, right? [much laughter]

Dock: Naw, I didn't play with Babe Ruth. I was before him! Did I tell you I got a call yesterday from a reporter wanting to know about Barry Bonds and steroids? I told him if you want to know about some dope, you might have to go into the Hall of Fame from about 1963 till now and take everybody out. So leave Barry alone. The bottom line is they got to get these steroids off the market. If they are around, people are going to buy them. They're going to use them.

Inmate: You mean some of that over-the-counter shit?

Dock: Right. They got stuff out now that'll turn you into the Incredible Hulk. . . . How'd I get onto this?

Inmate: Dock, go outside and come back in and start over! [laughter]

Another Inmate: Hey Dock! If you had to do it all over again, would you?

Third Inmate: He just did! [more laughter]

Dock: I just wanted to see if you were paying attention. Now where was I? Nobody's listening. So let me get back to the drugs. You see, I got involved with drugs real heavy when I got to the major leagues, because when you get to the big leagues, you start getting big league dope.

Inmate: I thought it was because you got a big league check!

Dock: Naw, the only dope I ever bought was some heroin, one time. And I flushed it. I don't count that as buying it, 'cause I didn't use it, so I never bought any drugs.

Inmate: Did dope mess up your game?

Dock: Definitely.

Inmate: Hey Dock, did you ever hit a home run?

Dock: Oh come on, man, you know I hit two! One in batting practice, and one in spring training.

Inmate: That's all Dock ever talks about! [more laughter]

Dock: So here's what happened to me. I was functioning as a baseball player, but I was addicted to drugs and alcohol. I want you to understand that my life was no different than yours—my arena was just different. I was in baseball, but I was in the streets too. Like I was saying, it's all the same. We experience the same kind of stuff, some more than others, but it's all the same.

I was seen at this time as a militant, a black militant, with braids in my hair. No one knew what that was, so I rolled with that. Then there were curlers. I had curlers in my hair. Some of y'all aren't old enough to remember Superfly. I was the OG [original gangster] Superfly . . . on the mound with pink curlers in my hair!

Inmate: Now you got the Shaq look.

Dock: Chemicals killed all my hair. Chemicals and drugs. But I was fortunate to have played ball for twelve years. I played with some great ballplayers. I played in a great era. I met a lot of people, traveled to a lot of places, and I had a chance to do a lot of things.

If you stay clean and sober, you're going to meet people from all walks of life, so don't be afraid to get out there. I even got jobs in movies because of baseball. I also met many influential people.

After I got out of baseball, I ended up in treatment. My son had a lot to do with me getting there. When he was a baby, he was playing with some of my jewelry, and I tapped him a few times, tell him, "No." Then years later I was watching TV and saw this story about a father hitting his kid and breaking his arms, and it flashed in my head, "How hard was I hitting my son, or one day how hard *would I hit him*?" And that caused me to accept going into treatment. Also my friends were telling me, "Dock, you got a problem with drugs and alcohol."

I played baseball from 1964 to 1979 [includes time in minor leagues]. I was in two World Series. We won in 1971 against Baltimore, and we lost against Cincinnati in 1976 when I was with the Yankees. People ask me where my rings are? I left one in the bathroom on Highway 10 in Arizona and the other on top of a car that my nephew was washing. I could call the people who make the rings and get new ones to replace those, but I really don't care. Remember I told you that the materialistic stuff isn't going to mean that much when we really get clean and sober, 'cause it ain't about that.

I left a lot of friends in baseball that was all screwed up, and I said, "I'm gonna go to school." So I went to school, the University of California at Irvine, to become a substance abuse counselor. When I graduated, I went to work in a drug program in Beverly Hills. I soon decided that I liked this kind of stuff. I met this guy named Bill, the head of special education at California Youth Authority [CYA] in Paso Robles. He started calling me and saying, "What are you going to do, Dock? Don't stay down there in Beverly Hills. Come on up here and start saving some lives." Every day he would call—same thing. "These guys need you, Dock, they need you." He said, "Stop fooling around with all those rich people down there. Come on, Dock." So after about three weeks I gave in, and I went to work with him at the CYA. That was about sixteen or seventeen years ago. Bill and I started a new program there. I continued to work in and out of institutions and juvenile halls. Then I took a job in Texas to get back with my son, who I had lost through a divorce. He was calling for me, so I went down there to Texas. I was there for seven years and finally came back to California with him so he could go to school. We settled here in Victorville, and I got this job at Marantha. I called Bill and told him I was working at a penitentiary called Marantha, and he said, "That's where I'm at!" So there you go, we were back together again. Now I tell people, "I'm locked up and that's where I'm supposed to be, and where I want to be." As long as they'll let me stay here, this is where I'll be. I ain't going nowhere.

Inmate: Hey Dock, you in the Hall of Fame?

Dock: Yeah. You go downstairs, make a left, go all the way to the wall, make another left, and I'm right there. The no-hitter section. But I wasn't *voted* into the Hall of Fame.

Inmate: You pitched a no-hitter?

Dock: Yeah, I threw a no-hitter for the Pittsburgh Pirates against the San Diego Padres in 1970, under the influence of LSD! Want to hear the story?

Inmate: Yeah Dock, tell it!

Dock: Well, I didn't know until six hours before the game that I was going to pitch. I was in Los Angeles, and the team was playing in San Diego, but I didn't know it. I had taken LSD . . . I thought it was an off-day, that's how come I had it in me. I took the LSD at noon. At 1 p.m., my girlfriend looked at the newspaper and said, "Dock, you're pitching today!"

That's when it was $9.50 to fly to San Diego. She got me to the airport at 3:30. I got there at 4:30, and the game started at 6:05 p.m. It was a twi-night doubleheader.

I can only remember bits and pieces of the game. I was psyched. I had a feeling of euphoria. I was zeroed in on the catcher's glove, but I didn't hit the glove too much. I remember hitting a couple of batters, and the bases were loaded two or three times.

The ball was small sometimes, the ball was large sometimes. Sometimes I saw the catcher, sometimes I didn't. Sometimes I tried to stare the hitter down and throw while I was looking at him. I chewed my gum until it turned to powder. They say I had about three to four fielding chances. I remember diving out of the way of a ball I thought was a line drive. I jumped, but the ball wasn't hit hard and never reached me.

The Pirates won the game 2-0, although I walked eight batters. It was the high point of my baseball career.

Inmate: Man, sounds like you was going faster than your pitches. [laughter]

Dock: Let's settle down. I'd like to talk a little about my father. Remember that I once told you about how if I lost a game, my father was there to pick me up, and if I won a game, we would celebrate together? But when he died, I got mad at God, because I had just started letting my dad into my life again. Even today, I can't remember my father being at my early baseball games, yet I've seen film of some of my old games and there he is. But I still can't picture it. I've blotted it out. Something happened when I was a little boy. My father was taken from me, and I blotted it out. To keep him alive, I blotted out all of my early memories.

Inmate: So how does that affect you with your son?

Dock: I came and got my son when he was fourteen, and he stayed with me until now.

Inmate: He still with you?

Dock: Yeah, he ain't going nowhere.

Inmate: How old is he, Dock?

Dock: Twenty-four! But I spoiled him like my father spoiled me. I've gone to every one of his games. He'd say, "Why you here?" And I'd say, "'Cause I want to be, now get out of my face." Even when he got into college in Bakersfield, I'd fly to every game. You see, where I was missing my father, I won't allow me to be missing his life. But I sure do spoil him. I'm trying to break that spoil cycle, but my son is still messing around. Failing to pay his child support. I told him, "You do that and you'll be over here [prison] with me!"

But I'm trying to be there for him when my father wasn't there for me. You see, my father was in the hospital a lot, and I hate hospitals. My friend Big Daddy went to see my father more than I did. He had a good relationship with my father. He was there with my father more than I was. He brought that to my attention when I got out of treatment.

But anyway, here I am . . . where I'm supposed to be.

Inmate: Hey Dock, you originally from Pittsburgh?

Dock: No man, I'm originally from Beverly Hills. My father lost an $800,000 bet and we had to move to Watts! [laughter]

Inmate: If you had to do it all over again, would you change anything?

Dock: No, I wouldn't. 'Cause I wouldn't be the person I am today. Coming to this place is a blessing. A godsend.

Interview with Dock Ellis at Marantha Correctional Facility

Lets see . . . my first memory of drinking was when I was three years old, drinking vodka, thinking it was water. My parents were looking for me, and I was down in the basement, drunk. They thought I was asleep, but I was drunk. I was just three. I can go that far back. I can remember my grandfather drank Boilermakers: Brew 102 beer and vodka. I thought it was water. He caught me a couple of times and told me, "Boy, don't drink that water," so I thought it was water. That's my earliest recollection of drinking.

My father didn't drink. My mother didn't drink. I might have seen my father take two sips of beer when I was a kid, so I didn't have no influence for drinking from my parents. It was in the streets, trying to belong, being part of the group, in the alley on 135th Street. That's where it started.

Growing up, I graduated into drugs, smoking dope. We used to use bean shooters. Kids don't even know what those are, so I tell them straws. We used to put cigarettes in them so we didn't get the smell on our hands. Tricking our parents. We also used those bean shooters with weed. And always drinking alcohol. I always talk about Harvey Wilson started me drinking rum. Rum and coke. I found out I needed drugs to do certain things and alcohol to do other things.

When I began competing in sports, we drank wine and took Seconal. We called them Red Devils. To dunk a basketball or to run with a football. I remember my sisters telling mother, "Junior's high, he's fooling with drugs." My cover was always to act crazy. "Junior's crazy, Momma. Look at him. He's on drugs. Look at him. He's eating his beans and rice off the floor." I had dropped the plate, so I just sat there and ate off the floor. I was loaded, so I didn't care. My sisters were aware of what was happening but not my mother. My father was always gone. My mother never knew. Even up until I went through treatment. She just thought I drank a lot. I remember lifting up the mattress and puking once and then just putting the mattress back down, rather than go to the bathroom. I told my mother I was sick, but I was just drunk.

Once my mother had a doctor come to the house. My friend and I had drunk a half-gallon of scotch and taken some Dexamil. We wanted to stay up all night. Dr. Murakami came to the house and he tells my mother, "Oh, Mrs. Ellis, don't worry, he's just got a hangover." I thought I was dying.

I was into alcohol pretty good until I really got into baseball. Then I started with cocaine. That was around 1965 in New York. From there I was off and flying. By 1968, I was gone. A lot of things were happening. My father wasn't around, and I was going through a period of hating God. I learned in treatment that I had a built-in excuse for my using. I always had my father patting me on my back when I won or lost, and he was gone, so I had my excuse. When other guys' fathers would visit me when I was in baseball is when I went on some terrible runs. I was mad, 'cause my father wasn't there. I was really hurting.

Drugs got me in a lot of trouble in baseball and in the press. Having to deal with them every day. They would pick at me, and I would pick at them. Many people in Pittsburgh took a liking to me when I played there, and if it wasn't for them, I'd be dead because I went to places I was not supposed to be. See, I had never run in the streets of California like I was in Pittsburgh. I had never been in a club. These streets became my stomping ground.

The turnaround came for me when I left Pittsburgh. That's when I went into treatment. I had hit my bottom, because I didn't know what to do. Baseball was over. Cocaine was over. But I kept drinking, trying to reach that high. I went into treatment because this woman kept telling me I had a drug problem. That, and the scenario with my son. So I said, "It's time to go." This was September 30, 1980, which is my sobriety date.

The first person I met in treatment was Dr. Hernandez, a psychologist who told me I was suicidal. I told him he was a damn fool. But then he handed me back a piece of paper that I had given him listing all the drugs I had put in my system. He told me that anyone that would take all of this stuff is trying to kill themselves. Right then I said, "You don't ever have to worry about me and drugs and alcohol again, 'cause I ain't no damn fool." That's all it took for me to get it. That was it!

And in more than twenty-three years of sobriety, I never looked back. I'm not suicidal. I know that if I ever use again, I'll kill myself, and that's the bottom line.

We're goin' down to the bottom
There is another world
Spinning inside of this one.

—"Freefall"

Anne Lamott
(writer)

I WAS INTRODUCED TO ANNIE Lamott in the late eighties by my friend John. I was told that Annie was down in Los Angeles from her home in San Francisco to write a review for *California Magazine* of a new restaurant in West Hollywood called Chaya Brasserie. An extra body was needed to order additional food to be sampled by Annie. I readily agreed, loving new culinary experiences. I was curious to meet Annie, whose writing I admired. I also heard she had incredible blond dreadlocks.

Annie and John were fairly new in sobriety, and the conversation, as it often is among recovering people, focused on war stories about our days of uncontrolled consumption. I knew John's history as a drunk matched mine, and I had heard that Annie had done a bit of drinking and using in her day as well. We had some good laughs and conversation. The only other part of the experience I remember was Annie continually sampling food off our plates, for her review.

Over the years, I've followed her writing closely. I've become a fan. When I asked her to contribute to this book, she didn't hesitate. Listening to her share her story with me over the telephone, I could just picture those creative wheels spinning in her extraordinary head. I wondered whether she still has those dreadlocks.

I had been a very shy and worried child, with a lot of feelings of not fitting in or being pretty enough or being too smart or more-than or less-than. An egomaniac with an inferiority complex. I had a tremendous amount of pressure on me scholastically, 'cause I was good at it. I was a tennis champion, and I really couldn't hardly enjoy anything like winning. I couldn't bear losing because I had such a fragile, fragile sense of myself, all based on how I was doing, which was never quite good enough. And at about the age of twelve . . . I skipped a grade, I skipped the fourth grade, so when I was twelve or so, in junior high school, I was already a year younger and much less developed, and I had this crazy, wild hair and just didn't weigh anything at all and felt really ugly and just so desperate to be loved.

Some girls brought some beer to a dance. This was all in Tiburon, California, and we went out back to a baseball field and drank it. I'd had beer before. My older brother and I had already started drinking. We always snuck sips or were given some. I remember chugging part of a beer once and getting really tipsy. But the first real intentional drinking I remember was at twelve, and I slugged down a beer as fast as I could with these popular girls and I went back to dance and I felt like I had been given a new lease on life. I felt like I could breathe. I felt like I was prettier, and I just felt that the real me had finally arrived. And after that I just always knew that there were girls that drank and girls that didn't drink. There were good girls and there were popular girls—bad girls, and by the seventh grade, we were all drinking and smoking dope.

I was born in 1954, so this was all taking place in about '66. I just loved it and couldn't wait to do it again. From the beginning, I always drank differently than the other girls. We'd get beer and wine that we'd steal from our parents. Sometimes we'd get older kids, who had ways of scamming it, to get us six-packs and red wine, which we'd mix with 7-Up. The other girls would have a drink and maybe a little bit of a second one and they'd be high and want to do all these slightly girlie things: brushing each other's hair or putting on the soundtrack to *Hair* or doing these kind of vaguely mystical teenage girl things. And I would just want to have another drink. I remember always wanting another one. I remember getting the whirlies at this girl's house a couple of times, and I wasn't even embarrassed. I would just lie down on the bed to try to get the whirlies to stop, and all I'd think about was how to get another drink without the girls judging me.

It escalated. I started doing more of everything. Mostly at home on the weekends. I started smoking dope. I'd practice tennis really hard every weekday and often was in tournaments, but there were always kids at tournaments that drank. Everywhere I went there were people like me. I call them "The Sevens" now because somebody once said that maybe one in ten of us are alcoholics, and before we come down to Earth, God has everybody who is going to get a human body call off from one to ten. After that's done, he says, "All the sevens step forward." And these are going to be the alcoholics.

I started developing a taste for hard liquor—very disguised hard liquor. It was not discouraged at my house to have wine in front of the adults or at a party. There were all these blender drinks going around. Mostly the women were given the whiskey sours and could always pour a glass right from the blender.

I loved it. It sort of gave me a chance at a real life. A feeling like I wasn't a piece of shit. Those first couple of sips felt like the oxygen tube had been untangled, and I could breathe again.

So I was off and running. I got into a lot of trouble, not with the law or anything, but by often disgracing myself. Passing out at parties, doing stuff no one else would do, doing things with boys I wouldn't even remember having done. Never wanting to stop. Even as a girl, I had that feeling of loving to get high. I just loved to get drunk. And then I started to find more interesting drugs. This was all in the late sixties in high school.

I went to this little hippie high school, and there were a lot of drugs available. Cocaine was very rare back then. People were taking acid, but I wasn't. There was hash you could buy for five dollars a ball, wrapped in a little silver foil, but it had been soaked in opium, and it was so unbelievably delicious and good. It gave you that feeling of floating, that kind of amniotic feeling. So a girlfriend at my school had made me this little hash pipe out of clay. I had it in my pocket. We'd been smoking hash with opium in it at lunch, and we came back to my very favorite class, with this teacher I just adored. A literature course, and I really lived for him. He was really an important figure in my life. He drank but he wasn't a doper. He was actually disgusted with all the dope at this school. I was seen as a good girl because I was a tennis champ and because I wasn't ostensibly "out there."

Back in the classroom, I remember him asking me a question and I realized I couldn't get my mouth to work! I'd gotten too stoned, which is basically the story of my life . . . too drunk, too stoned, too often! He asked me a question, and I was concentrating so hard on getting my lips around the answer that very slowly the hash pipe slid out of my pocket and crashed to the floor and shattered. I got a big shot of adrenaline and my friend tried to pick it up. There were only about eight kids in my classes and everyone knew what it was, but I'm not sure if he did. It didn't matter though, because I went into such a terrorized state of paranoia from being stoned and also the hash pipe being broken in front of my cherished teacher that I felt like I had completely lost my mind. I had to sit there while everyone around me cleaned it up, tried to get rid of the evidence. My teacher looked at me like . . . oh, God! All I could think to do was to try to win back his love—after I could think again.

It never occurred to me that I should think about the fact that I was so stoned that I couldn't answer a question, that I couldn't form an English word. What I thought was I just had to find a way back into his heart, 'cause it made me feel of value. That such a cool teacher loved me.

I had to try to get the schedule right. Get the levels right. I remember a number of times being way too stoned to function or to pull it off. I really liked getting impaired. I tried to find that edge where I could still sort of function but have that wonderful feeling of no feeling. That sort of vague stoned floating and the energy and the music. And being with other stoned and drunk people. I really drink to get impaired. I don't like to get "a little drunk." Many, many, many times, beginning in high school, I would get so that I couldn't walk, couldn't get up off the floor, and it didn't bother me that much. I just learned to sort of sit it out. Somebody would come by with cocaine or methedrine or a nice diet pill and get me going again. And I wouldn't even think, "Gee, that's scary. I couldn't even get off the floor." I would just think, "Thank God for crank!"

I went off to college in Baltimore for a couple of years and sort of loved it but really wanted to be a writer. While I was there, there were the girls that I hung with and many of them were hippie feminists. I went to a women's college called Goucher. They were older girls who could buy alcohol legally for us, and I just always gravitated toward the type of people who liked to get drunk and who liked to be alone. We all started smoking by then, and there would be five or six of us listening to Carole King or whoever we were listening to and getting stoned and drunk. Talking about life and then going out and doing really silly, goofball, dumb things together. I was not able to stay in college, although I loved English, philosophy, and literature. I think I scheduled them later in the day because there was one bonehead science class that everyone took . . . astronomy, and everyone took it because no one had ever failed it in Goucher's history. I failed it because I was just so sick in the mornings. I'd get there okay, but I'd feel like the journalist in *Bonfire of the Vanities* when he'd describe his hangovers and how he'd feel like there was a mercury sack in his head, like a yolk sack, and the nausea would kind of roll back and forth increasing the nausea. Oh man, I just always got bad hangovers. I had a number of blackouts and disgraced myself a number of times. Showing up at parties where there were teachers, just shit-faced.

I dropped out of school when I was nineteen. Wanting to be a writer, I moved back to San Francisco and worked in a nuclear quality assurance department, as a clerk typist. I got food stamps and my best friend, Pammy, who I've written a lot about, lived on B Street and I lived on Bush and Leavenworth, which was this fabulous upper tenderloin with lots and lots of bars. We just always had alcohol. My dad would buy me booze, a nice bottle of Tangueray. He'd come over, and we'd have a couple of martinis. Then he would go home, and I'd drink the rest until I passed out. I got these terrible gin hangovers.

I would disgrace myself always. I remember there was a Christmas party, and I just got so bombed that I could hardly stand up. I was dancing with the boss and it was getting very erotic, in front of everybody. His wife was there, and a couple people came over and told me that it probably would be better that you weren't dancing with the boss that way. Maybe you should go get a cup of coffee. That was the last thing I remember. I came to at my apartment on Bush, very sick, like I'd been food-poisoned. I didn't have a car. It turned out that I'd driven it onto the sidewalk, and the police department had towed it. I just kept thinking alcohol is not the problem, I have a pacing problem. I don't pace myself right. I tried to switch to just beer and wine, and, you know, I didn't really want to quit.

My father and mother had split up when I was in college, and my father really liked to drink. He was a very functioning, high-bottom alcoholic. I would say he loved to drink. Now he's dead, so I'll try not to hurt his feelings. He had a number of drinks every night and sometimes got quite drunk and sort of passed out early every night. He was glad for me to be drinking. We were best friends, and we smoked and drank. He had a girlfriend, and we all would go out and drink martinis, but I was always on my best behavior with my father 'cause I just loved him so much.

My mother was living in Hawaii then. I remember going to visit her and saying I wouldn't come over unless she got me some dope. So she bought some pot from her friends. It was the first time I ever smoked pure Hawaiian sinsemilla, but of course I smoked it like it was from San Rafael, and I started tripping as if I were on acid. Tripping out of my mind. And I remember crawling down the hall holding on to the wall trying to get to my room, and my mother sort of being aware of what was going on but we couldn't talk about it. Of course I didn't throw it out, I just learned to take one hit and then drink a lot, which I could control better.

I ended up working at Billie Jean King's sports magazine, which was called *Women's Sports*. It was my first great literary job. I was nineteen and there were all sorts of fantastic writers there, and we all drank. Just like they do at a literary gathering, but it was so enveloping. I felt like I found my spiritual home. I was off and running. I moved out to Bolinas and then we all quit one day, a political issue, and by that time I was just a falling-down drunk with absolutely no borders.

I started trying to make it as a writer. I made a new friend in Bolinas, and we drank together. We also did coke, acid, and methedrine. I preferred meth 'cause I was always broke and it was so much cheaper. Also, I always had eating disorders, and you didn't have to eat while on methedrine. I could go for about three days on just milk.

Just lived with no boundaries, anything, with any man, any time. I stole drugs from people who had cancer. I had elective dental surgery just to get Percodan. All the while, I was putting away close to a fifth a day. I was a real bar drinker. This friend and I were there almost every night. We were just legendary. Everyone loved us, and we were both hilarious women, with no boundaries and just devoted to each other.

Then, when I was twenty-three, my dad got sick with brain cancer, and the world just came crashing down on us. It gave us total license to begin each day with a drink if we needed it. We were eventually living with my dad, taking care of him. My younger brother and I alternated taking care of Dad, so if it was your night on, you stayed with him in this little cabin we had, and if it was your night off, you got to go to the bar. We had a little trailer outside. It was so disgusting. It was about the size of a queen-size bed, and we took all of our boyfriends and girlfriends there. We were so drunk and hungover, but it was like an oasis because inside the cabin our very, very beloved father was losing his mind. He basically had cancer of the everything. So he died and my consumption continued, even grew. Seriously hungover, in blackouts. I tried to quit drinking with my friend sometimes, and we'd go for a couple of weeks and we'd feel so great. Our minds would be clear, and we'd be horrified. We'd count up what we might drink typically, and the calories involved. Once we figured that if we were drinking a fifth each day and a few beers, we figured we could each eat a chocolate layer cake with the same amount of calories.

I had two books out by the time I was twenty-nine: *Hard Laughter* and *Rosie*. I had supplemented my writing by giving tennis lessons and cleaning houses and doing whatever jobs I could get. My books had done great critically but hadn't sold enough for me to feel secure. *Rosie* did pretty well. It sold ten thousand copies, which was pretty great back then, but I couldn't get any self-esteem going. My dad died when I was twenty-five, and I don't really remember a lot of the next five years. I was writing. I was becoming famous. I was still in horrible relationships with men who mostly didn't love me but found me mesmerizing, and who discovered that I loved to use and drink just like they did.

I started disgracing myself as a writer. The worst experience I can tell you about is at the age of thirty or so: I was doing some sort of benefit in the city at a Basque restaurant. I believe it was a library benefit. The restaurant had long tables with green generic bottles of wine and family-style eating. I was supposed to speak as soon as dessert was served, but I started getting bombed. I'd gotten stoned before I got there on some really good pot. I was stoned and floating and good, and after two glasses of wine, I was fabulous. Then I had six, seven, eight, and I was wasted. All the people at my table were getting very worried because I was getting loud and kind of weepy. I started thinking about my dad. I hadn't written a speech. I just thought that I'm at my best with a crowd and a few too many.

There was a problem, though, when I wanted to order one last bottle of wine, and people around me were getting that very nervous, slightly angry look that I became very familiar with. The waiter said, "Do you guys want a bottle of wine or don't you?" They all said, "No," but I said, "I would. Please bring a bottle." That was humiliating in itself. The waiter poured me a glass. I raised it to my lips, and it was the last thing I remembered. I went into a full-fledged blackout. I came to on stage, barely able to keep my balance, like Truman Capote at the University of Maryland, when he was staggering around saying, "I'm an alllcoholic."

Apparently I was in the middle of saying the sentence that "I dreamt of a colorblind world," like I was channeling Dr. King or something, and I came to and there were two hundred people looking at me attentively, and I had no idea what I was talking about. I didn't know whom the benefit was for. I had no speech. I didn't know what I was supposed to be talking about. So I said, "How'm I doing on time?" This brought the house down 'cause the first and only sentence I said was "I dreamt of a colorblind world!" Then I started staggering around trying to talk about how much I loved writing and reading or something, and I was just stunning! To this day, people still talk about it.

So then I had another book come out, *Joe Jones*, which was just a devastating flop. I couldn't really work by then. My mind was getting sort of spongy. I always worked really hard. I sat down at the same time every morning, which was 8 a.m. I would always wake up early. Pretty sick, I would go for a run, take a shower, have a lot of coffee, and have some speed.

I might smoke a little bit of pot to just get going, and I wouldn't drink till the afternoon. I would try to get my work done. It was like I was on an elevator and kept going down, one more floor, and trying to make it be okay. Then I would try to set limits. I would only drink beer and wine. Night Train, wino wine, or Mickey's Stout Malt Liquor, the "green death." So I'd say, "I'm only going to drink beer tonight," but I'd drink six or seven 16 oz. Mickey's or Ranier Ale, which is even stronger, get shit-faced, take a bunch of sleeping pills, and go to sleep.

I remember my one effort at sobriety. It was called going "on the wagon." I was kind of aware that there were sober people out there. Communities with people not drinking, and some of them were very hip. There were a number of musicians that I loved, and writers, who had crashed and burned and were sober. I would hear stories about them and think, "I'm not that bad" or "I was still so young." I was thirty. I was thirty-two when I quit on July 6, 1986. So I tried to go "on the wagon," so I could have some control over my drinking, and this is what it looked like.

I decided I would go "on the wagon" and not have anything at all to drink. This was on a Monday. I would just take some Valium. I had a Nike box filled with Benzos [Benzedrine], opiates, and speed, so that all bases were covered. So, I would have a couple Valium and maybe go for a walk. Well, I had a couple Valium and realized it was ludicrous, and that the new rule on the first day of being "on the wagon" was that I would only have two beers at night, come rain or shine. So, I went and got two 16 oz. Ranier Ales and drank one very quickly, to get off. Then I took a Valium, and then I tried to sip the second one. (I had to take a Valium and a number of Halcyons just to get the night to end.) It was about 6:30 p.m. I woke up the next morning at 6 a.m. I got about twelve hours sleep because I had taken those Halcyons, which is a very potent sleeping pill. They were deadly, with lots of terrible side effects. I felt great 'cause I had slept for twelve hours. I loved this! I loved being "on the wagon."

I thought, "Two beers and pills. That's all." People would call and say, "How you doing?" And I'd say, "Great, I'm 'on the wagon.'" I'd always call people in the morning when I was hungover and try to figure out how badly it had gone. I wouldn't remember what had happened at the bar or in the car. I'd call and say, "How you doing, Gary?" And you'd say, "I think we need to take a little break from each other, and not talk for a while." And I wouldn't have any idea of what had happened. So I would get on the phone trying to piece together what happened.

I was living on a little tiny houseboat in Sausalito, on San Francisco Bay, and it was very beautiful. There were tons of drug dealers on the docks—lots of bohemians, hippie types, and we all drank together, but I preferred drinking alone. I'd go to North Beach, steal everyone's cocaine. People would buy me drinks 'cause I was funny and sweet. Then I'd have sex with people in the bathroom. Everyone seemed to like that in a girl! People would give me their little bottles of cocaine, and I'd go into the bathroom and I'd do a couple of huge lines, like Sherman cigarettes. Then I'd put a little aside in a bit of toilet paper and put it in my pocket, so by the end of the night, I might have ten, twelve little packages of coke. I'd be able to go home and be by myself with it and a fifth of Bushmills, and come down slowly. That's what I was doing when I *wasn't* "on the wagon."

When I *was* "on the wagon," on day two, it was just two Ranier Ales and all the pills, and I fell asleep about 7 p.m. and I felt great. On the third night, I wanted to stay up longer, so I got a third Ranier Ale and had all the Valium and Halcyon and woke up and felt *pretty* great. Then on the fourth day, I thought, "This is just ridiculous," so I got four Ranier Ales, took a bunch of Valium and Halcyon. On the fifth day, I thought, "This really works," 'cause I wasn't vomiting, I wasn't sick. I didn't have the yolk sack from *Bonfire of the Vanities* rolling in me. I was drinking so much less. So the fifth day, I went to the store and got into an alcoholic rage of "Who do they think they are trying to control me?" So, first I got my four Ranier Ales. I was so angry I was going to get a couple more. Then I got a fifth of Bushmills and went back to the room and got plowed. That was my week of being "on the wagon."

When I was thirty-two, the elevator had gone down one more floor. I had finally reached a place where I couldn't bear it. I screwed something up very badly. Right around the Fourth of July, I had to pick up a package for a family that had a child that was mentally damaged. A beautiful child. They needed for me to be on the dock by 9 a.m. to pick up something that was being delivered that had something to do with their kid. And I slept right through it. Oh my God! It wasn't a toy for the kid; it was something serious. I don't know 'cause I never even got it.

Then on the Fourth of July, 1986, I was right off the docks of San Francisco Bay with my publisher, Bill Turnbull of North Point Press, who published my third book to really devastating reviews, which had really plummeted me down the chute. You know, my alcoholism was like the game Chutes and Ladders. I went up a little bit. I might get something written, got published somewhere and read widely. I'd think, "Oh this is the new me, really on top of things," and I'd take three steps forward. Then I'd go further down the ladder than I'd ever been. Then I'd haul myself up again.

I had gone down a bad ladder when my third book came out. I was with my publisher and his wife, and we were on this little boat watching the fireworks across the bay. We had been drinking all day at a Fourth of July party and I had been smoking dope, the non-habit-forming marijuana, and I couldn't stop thinking about climbing off of the side of the boat. I was in a good mood; that was what was so troubling. I was with two cherished friends, but I was very drunk, watching the fireworks. I could not get this tape loop to stop. I imagined myself climbing off the side, bobbing up and down in the water, and then going under. I couldn't stand the thought of getting up again in the morning, 'cause I knew what it was going to be like. I knew I would be sick. Would I have taken someone to bed I didn't know, or even worse, did know and shouldn't be with? I would feel rocky and scared 'cause I wouldn't know what happened.

Our dad died long ago, about seven years, and my younger brother was still feeling very fragile. That was the last thought I had. I wasn't going to climb overboard because Steve couldn't handle it.

Bill and Mary walked me home and put me to bed. I woke up in the morning sick as a dog. Vomiting. I called Bill and Mary, and they were really worried. Bill, who I was very close to, said, "Oh Annie, you were really, really in a state last night." That was just the worst thing anyone had ever said to me: "in a state." Because that just suggested real madness—Joan Crawford sort of madness. He said it with such grief. I said, "I know, I just need to take it easy." So I wasn't going to drink that day, and my kidneys really ached. I was experiencing that more and more because I was drinking a lot of gin. But it didn't mean I would stop drinking martinis, under the right circumstances, which was like . . . if it was evening, and I had a bottle of gin! I learned I could flush my kidneys with cranberry juice. I wouldn't think, "Maybe we should just lay off the gin." I would think, "I need a cranberry flush."

Now I decided to just drink beer again. Beer and Bushmills. So, after like three beers, I was off and running again. I ended up in the city, buying cocaine at one of the bars in North Beach, getting totally wasted. Stopping off at the bars on Lombard Street to get even more of everything, getting home after two in the morning, in a blackout.

The next morning, I realized I had two blackouts the previous night, which I'd never had before. I hadn't gotten hardly any sleep because of the cocaine. I was very scared, so I was just going to drink wine. I took a bunch of Valium, and then I drank a pint of Bushmills and didn't feel drunk. Sometimes I couldn't get drunk and sometimes just a little bit would cause me to black out, or after two glasses I'd be impaired. I'd have to take some drugs to get stabilized.

Anyway, my boyfriend brought over two bottles of really expensive pinot noir, and we went up into the loft and went to bed. We started drinking and I blacked out. The third time in a row. I woke up around midnight, and the man was gone. I don't know what happened at all that night, not that it matters. I guess we finished a bottle 'cause there was one left, but I felt a despair come over me like a niacin flush. A full-body flush of terror. I felt like I would have a blackout every night now, and I was truly scared to death.

That was the Sunday I agreed to pick up the important parcel for those people's child, and I had overslept. Midnight that Sunday, as it was becoming Monday, I opened the last bottle of pinot noir, took three or four Halcyons—sort of flirting with suicide I think—threw 'em down like peanuts, drank half the wine, lay down, and overslept, so I couldn't get up for my friends. And that was my bottom.

I woke up on July 7 and it was just over. I don't know why it wasn't over July 6 or five years before, or the morning after the Basque restaurant. I ran out of gas, and I knew I was going to die. Either deliberately overdose on all these pills I had or on bad methedrine. I knew I was going to die. I just couldn't stand being alive, and the funny thing was that I was warm and truly loved. I didn't have clinical depression. I could get going. I could pick myself up.

So I called a friend who had been clean and sober for about eight years. A really old, beloved friend of my family. He never tried to con me into not drinking, or joining a recovery group, but he was always there for me. So I called him and said, "I really think I'm done." And he said, "Oh, great."

Well, it wasn't great! He started introducing me to a number of people who were clean and sober and sticking together, and who had helped him get sober or who he had helped get sober. They kind of took me under their wing and told me what they had done. And I just thought, "What a fucking joke. You have got to be kidding." I was religious. I couldn't believe that I was ever as bad as they were 'cause they would tell me their stories, and I also couldn't believe that I was anything like them. It was very different to be me. I'm a writer, an artist. People love me. A lot of people I was starting to get to know, who were helping me get sober, had real jobs, and they ended up losing everything. I had nothing to lose, sort of like Bobbie McGee.

I didn't have a cent—was $12,000 in debt. When I got sober, I rented a houseboat for $300 a month. I didn't have a car. I asked myself, "Do you want the car or do you want to stop drinking?" I had so many blackouts over the years; I had one time where I drove the car up on the curb in a blackout. I had dents in my car. I won't ever know if I killed anybody with my car. I know I hit a dog once and kept going. I was in some sort of white-light terror flip-out. It was dark and I hit something and I know it was a dog. I hit a deer once and wrecked my car.

And three years before I quit drinking, I said to myself, "You either have to quit drinking or you have to get rid of the car." Well, that was a no-brainer. I got rid of the car! I took cabs to North Beach, and I stayed home. I like to be alone when I drink. And people would just sort of take me places, for coffee or we'd go to the movies or we'd go shopping at Longs.

I had a friend who was the main person that supported my sobriety in the first couple of years. She was this junkie who was also an alcoholic. She got clean in Synanon. She and I were always broke. She was older than I was and *hilarious*. I loved her more than life itself. She had what I wanted. She was hilariously funny and had been sober for ten years. I knew that she was as bad as me and that I was as bad as her. So we'd take like $30 and go to Longs or Walgreens and we'd each get a basket and make $30 go so far. One of the first things we got was the *Graceland* album for about $10 and $20 worth of stuff that made us really, really happy. All the cleaning stuff we needed and a new lipstick, a pad and a really great pen. You could get a ton of stuff for $20. I started to have simple, dumb joys and just kept hanging out with all these sober people.

I didn't have any contact with my North Beach friends, and a couple of them had gotten sober too. I had lots of people to mentor me, and little by little, I started to learn how to bear being a human. I started to have better self-esteem 'cause I was doing esteemable things. If you wanted to have loving feelings, you did loving things, and that I could get out of myself and help somebody else. That i-s-m of alcoholism—I, self, me—I, self, me—I, self, me. The solution was God and service. Caring for other people, and so I just started healing slowly. My friend Jack, who was this person who helped me, who I called in the very beginning, said, "You are just going to want to tip over the fifty-five-gallon drum of shame and mess and failure and disappointment and terrible episodes of self-loathing and all the awful things you've done. All the ways you've hurt people. And you're just going to want to tip it over, but it's not going to work that way. But if you don't drink, every time you tell the truth, every time you reach out to help somebody who is also trying to get sober, every time you try to make things right with somebody you hurt or fucked with, you take out a tablespoon. Every time you sit quietly and do your prayers and meditation you take out another tablespoon. Every time you move towards the light and solution instead of the problem, which is this terrible alcoholic mind and this inability to stop drinking once I started. Every time you do something else, you take out another tablespoon." That's proven to be true for me.

So what's happened for me in the seventeen-and-a-half years since then is that I've had a child. I'm a single mother. I learned to trust that all of my needs would be provided for, although all of my wants would not be granted. And that God was not some cosmic bellhop, and that God was the source and the relationship upon which I can most depend, and to whom I need to turn in order to remember who I am—which is an alcoholic and drug addict. Somebody who was dangerously close to dying and who is given a daily reprieve based on the healing in community that goes on with brothers and sisters who are on the same path.

I know that no matter what, I don't pick up a drink. And if my ass fell off, I call somebody else who is sober and who is working a spiritual path, and they help me get through my crisis, without picking up a drink or using.

My best friend died a couple of years after I got sober, and I thought that was the end of the world, 'cause she was sick with breast cancer. But I had learned this way of life where I could show up for people. It's like Woody Allen said, 90 percent of life is just showing up. I was taught to show up and listen and for everything not to be *The National Annie Lamott Crisis Hour*, but to bring some healing and some quiet and some faith where I was needed and to be there. That laughter and confidence and crying and just being together would be its own healing. So I was finally able to be the kind of friend I'd always wanted to be, but couldn't.

It took me a long time to get my career started again after the devastating failure of my third book. It took me awhile to be able to write again. So I just started again and ended up with this incredible career. My first sober book, *All New People*, is one of my most favorite, favorite books. It was kind of small in scope and sold steadily. It wasn't a big success to the world, but it was a gigantic success to my soul because it was finally the book I wanted to write. My windows felt like they were washed and very clean, and I had a new perspective on the world.

I always felt that I couldn't write without alcohol and a little bit of dope, because I relied on the myth that most of the great writers were alcoholic and many of them drank when they wrote. Many of them started out the day hungover, and many, many were alcoholic. My father was a writer and all of his friends drank a lot. It just seemed like they went hand-in-hand with each other, and I wasn't sure I could unlock my unconscious and sub-conscious to tap into that dreamscape and soulscape and memory bank that you need to in order to write without alcohol. My mind was damaged by all the drugs and alcohol, and it took awhile of just health. When I was liv-ing on the houseboat taking lots of walks and trying to eat better, it was like an ambulatory psych ward, and I couldn't be expected to bite off much creatively.

Then this thing started forming in me. This piece of work, the prologue to *All New People*, and it's the best thing I've ever written. I let it form and bob up to the surface. It was kind of a lava lamp moving slowly, but dis-tinctly, and I just started getting thoughts down, but didn't have any confi-dence in myself, especially because I had just gotten the shit kicked out of me with *Joe Jones*. It got devastating reviews and people thought it might end my career, and I believed it to some extent. All of a sudden, again I don't know why, I knew that when I got up that first sober morning, I was going to go for a run, take a hot shower, have a cup of coffee, and get back to work.

It came flowing out, but it also took me a long time to get my chops back. So this one piece, which is probably twenty pages, which I wrote for Bill Ryan, who was an editor at *California Magazine* and a very dear friend of my dad's—it was just wonderful. It was exactly what I always dreamt of writing and it remains one of my favorite pieces. What happened was I took out enough gunk and slime from the fifty-five-gallon drum that I could now see these creative visions that come to me.

There's a priest who once said that he believes heaven is just a new pair of glasses. By then I really loved being sober and I felt like I could see again. I could understand myself in a whole new way. That I wasn't "better than" or "worse than." That there was this terror and grief and rage inside me from my earliest days.

It must be this feeling of deprivation and self-loathing that led me into this journey of self-destruction, and I tried to medicate the pain. Little by little, as I was rediscovering parts of myself that were sealed off because I couldn't manage that much pain or disgrace. So lots of the prologue of *All New People* is recovered memories, like Christmas ornaments.

People started teaching me that amazing lesson that you didn't think your way back to healing, you didn't think your way back by dealing with your alcoholic mind, and you couldn't solve your problems *because* of your alcoholic mind. It was like opening up boxes that were sealed off like in an Edgar Allan Poe story. Understanding why my parents had done or hadn't been able to do what I had been so starved for. It was wonderful.

It was like those Chinese gift boxes, where you open it and there's lots of beautiful shredded paper or newsprint, and then you come to a ball and you open it with anticipation and very attentively, and find this funny little thing in it. It might be a beautiful thing. Might be a gag thing. It might trigger your memory. But you're attuned to it 'cause you're not obsessed with drinking or getting the next batch of methedrine. You can pay attention. I started writing everything down and then I'd go to the next Chinese gift box, and it would be stuff about my childhood or be stuff about these new dreams I had of having a life with a family and a child.

All that crying I did in therapy and feeling things and getting it down on paper softened my heart. I'd always had a tender heart, but I had a tender *drunken* heart. Now I had a heart that became a tide-pool where I could take in more of life and just be with it. Deal with it spiritually or creatively. The tide-pool would flow back out to the visible world and maybe into other people or people who were trying to get sober. Give them a little bit of water with a little algae and nutrition and love and breath and whatnot. I was much more permeable, much more honest, because I started telling my secrets.

So those are the most important things about being creative. The softness of heart, taking the walls down, watering the ground in which we're growing new seeds. Learning to pay attention and learning to tell the truth. How exhilarating the truth is.

At that point I started writing incredibly truthful books. My first books were really truthful but these were sober truthful books. I wrote a journal about being a mother, a sober mother. How crazy and what a mixed grill it was. So I could offer my experience, strength, and hope to other sober mothers. And fathers. To say it's okay to be angry a lot of the time and really bored. Here's the solution: leave the room or call a friend. Then I started

writing books that were total, radical truth-telling, because I was so exhil-
arated. All these people would tell me the truth of their sobriety or their
drunkenness, and it would give me life.

I wanted to give people permission to tell their own truth and to live
in it, and to let those deep wounds in us be healed and shred and cleansed
out instead of just sealed over with more scar tissue.

The last five books I've written, the work of a sober writer, are just
huge gifts of my sobriety. I had a gift, a certain gift, not a huge gift, but a
good gift, and it was just being poisoned by alcohol and self-loathing and
narcissism. I still have all those things, except I don't have the alcohol, so I
can use the narcissism and all the mistakes I make and self-doubt. I either
use it as creativity or to help other people stay sober. It's like alchemy. It
goes from dross to gold.

> Call it iron discipline. But for months
> I never took my first drink
> before eleven P.M. Not so bad,
> considering. This was in the beginning
> phase of things. I knew a man
> whose drink of choice was Listerine.
> He was coming down off Scotch.
> He bought Listerine by the case,
> and drank it by the case. The back seat
> of his car was piled high with dead soldiers.
> Those empty bottles of Listerine
> gleaming in his scalding back seat!
> The sight of it sent me home soul-searching.
> I did that once or twice. Everybody does.
> Go way down inside and look around.
> I spent hours there, but
> didn't meet anyone, or see anything
> of interest. I came back to the here and now,
> and put on my slippers. Fixed
> myself a nice glass of NyQuil.

Dragged a chair over to the window.
Where I watched a pale moon struggle to rise
over Cupertino, California.
I waited through hours of darkness with NyQuil.
And then, sweet Jesus! The first sliver
of light.

                              —Raymond Carver, "NyQuil"

Give me my whisky, when I be frisky
Give me my rye, when I be dry
Give me my reefer, when I be sickly
Give me my heaven, my heroin, before I die

—"Junko Partner—Traditional"

Mac (Dr. John) Rebennack
(musician)

DR. JOHN, THE "NIGHT TRIPPER," sashayed into my life at an after-hours party in Los Angeles sometime in the late sixties. Musical wizardry is what we were told to expect, and the good doctor didn't disappoint.

The club was packed with music-industry insiders, all filled with great expectations, when all of a sudden bells, whistles, and sundry other rhythm noisemakers joyously announced the band's arrival. Its magical leader was decked out in a floor-length black velvet robe adorned with small bones and other odd trinkets. On his head he sported an enormous multicolored feather headdress. His face was eerily sprinkled with patches of sparkling glitter. Light up a joint and let this party begin!

Fronting a group of New Orleans exiles, Dr. John performed a rich gumbo of blues, cajun, funk, and dance hall, seasoned with Caribbean rhythms; music based on voodoo myths of the Crescent City. Gris-gris they called it. Weird, spooky songs with psycho-voodoo chanting that created images of imaginary places. Dr. John, strutting and in command, appeared like some kind of hip, exotic medicine man.

They call me Dr. John
I'm known as the Night Tripper
Got a satchel of gris-gris in my hand,

Got many clients that come from miles around
Runnin' down my prescriptions
I got medicines, cure all y'alls ills,
I got remedies of every description

—"Gris Gris Gumbo Ya Ya"

Dr. John's arrival in the psychedelic sixties was right on time. Unfortunately, heroin addiction was his closest companion and refused to leave the party.

A decade or so later, I met up with Dr. John (the "Night Tripper" name had been abandoned some time earlier) at a recording studio in New York. I had recently been hired to handle his public relations, so I thought I'd drop by and see how he was doing. One thing led to another, and when the conversation turned to drugs, as it always did in those days, I informed Mac that I was newly clean and sober. He mentioned that he too was trying to clean up, and I told him that he could call me if he ever wanted some help or just to talk about it.

Over the next couple of years, we spoke a few times about sobriety, and I heard rumors about his attempts at getting clean. It was very good news to one day learn that he had finally had enough.

According to Joel Dorn, my friend, "Mac is the most complete musician I know, a student and teacher of New Orleans tradition. He's one of a kind. Our generation's Louis Armstrong." I couldn't agree more. It's hard to imagine that his musical gift almost died from drug addiction.

I interviewed Mac at his remote log cabin home, located up a long and winding dirt road overlooking a beautifully placid lake near Woodstock, New York. It reminded me faintly of bayou country. An old hound dog greeted my knock at the door with half-interested howling, but no one answered. Finally, after what seemed like several minutes, Mac stumbled to the door, mumbling apologies for having overslept. It was just past two in the afternoon!

He finally got his bearings, fixed a pot of coffee, and we went outside. Surveying the panoramic view of the lush countryside, we pulled

up a couple of rocking chairs on his front porch and began the interview.

I've never heard anyone speak as Mac does. He has a unique
vocabulary and speech pattern, and similar to Mark Twain, is known
for his creative use of language ... "Mississloppy River." He says things
like "edjamacation." You always have to be aware of his underlying
humor. "Tigerette syndrome," for instance, is a play on Tourette's syndrome, and "bisexual polar bear" is Mac's way of saying bipolar. I once
reminded him of something he told me on the telephone, to which
he responded, "I wasn't aware that I wasn't awake the last time we
spoke."

During the course of the interview, I tried to stay out of his way
as much as possible, as he had such a great rhythm going. Regarding
his references to treatment, Mac is very vague about time. He doesn't
delineate chronology. For some reason, I enjoy this interview more
with each reading, as I pick up new insight into his wondrous psyche.
I hope you will find it as compelling.

———

Hey Gary, it's good to see you. I'm sorry I don't see you better, but that's
another story. Shot eyeballs, you know what I mean?

So, you want my story, huh? Well, let's see what we got here. My father,
he taught me good stuff and he hated people who was activated [drug
users]. When he was around people, sometimes he drank, but he never got
drunk. He got straight. He was never, in any kind of way, drunk. That was
not true of most of the people around him though.

When I was a kid, my dad owned a little record shop. He sold what
they used to call "race records." Gospel records, jazz records, rhythm and
blues records. The shop was right by Dillard University, which is a black
university in New Orleans. My dad had all these 78 records that were
stocked into small jukeboxes and we delivered to hotels and stuff. Even as
a little kid, he would let me play them. As long as I didn't break one. The

A-side was always scratched, so I would listen to all the B-sides. My daddy had a whole collection of dirty records that were stashed in a liquor cabinet. I would get into them and play 'em for all my friends. He would sell them records in brown bags in his record shop. They weren't really the dirty songs. They were the risqué songs.

Anyway, I remember as a little kid, my Aunt Andre taught me how to play boogie-woogie on a piano. My Uncle Joe showed me a little stuff too, and for years I was learnin', but my hands was too little to play the left-hand part. Finally they was big enough, and I started learnin' stuff on my own. My aunt said I had a gift. I never really studied piano. I studied guitar, because early on, I decided that there was so many killer piano players around. Everybody in my neighborhood played.

My daddy also fixed PA systems, and I'd go with him and listen and everyone I heard was killer. And so I wanted to be a piano player. When I was young, I heard Pete Johnson playin' some stuff with Big Joe Turner, and I wanted to be Pete Johnson. I didn't care nothing about the singer. Just wanted to play piano, but I thought I'd never get a job, so I studied guitar. I studied with three guys. Al Guma and two guys, Papoose and Ron Montrell, who both played in Fats Domino's band. It's funny. My pa knew everybody. Just from his little record store and from fixin' PAs and amplifiers and everything electronical. He knew stuff.

My daddy also knew a lot of prominent New Orleans musicians. He knew Al Hirt. He used to fix Louis Prima's TV set. Everybody knew my daddy. He knew the prizefighters. We used to get free tickets to the prizefights 'cause my daddy fixed the PA system at the Coliseum. The wrestling matches was there too. We'd get a lot of fringe benefits.

So after I studied guitar a little while, somebody told my daddy, "This kid can't read music. He just memorizes stuff. All he really wants to do is play the blues." I'd go home and I'd learn Lightning Hopkins or something. So that's when my dad got me to Papoose, and Papoose told me, "You'll never get a job playing the outta-meter, foot-beater crap. You got to learn to play something like T-Bone Walker." I loved T-Bone Walker, but I couldn't figure out how to do any of that shit, from what I was studying with my guitar lessons. So Papoose started me on that, 'cause he was my teacher and he was also a damn good studio musician.

At this time, I was already smoking a little weed, popping some goof-balls. I don't remember exactly when I started. There was always a lot of weed floating around. There was guys who actually shot dope in our base-ment when I was a kid. It was easy to get in 'cause it wasn't locked. Guys from the neighborhood would go down there and I'd see them and think, "These guys is stupid to do that shit." But somewhere down the line I asked somebody if I could try it.

The first time I did it I got beat. Somebody gave me a water shot, and I didn't get nothing out of it. I'm sure the guy did it to keep me from doing dope, but I was on a mission to get some real shit. I remember going into the high school, the first time I really got loaded, and I walked up these stairs and puked all over this trophy case, and I thought, "This is what being high is all about." I felt so good. And that was the high I chased all of my life.

Sometime later, I met this girl, who was married to my bass player at the time, and I really dug her. Both of us was chipping. We wasn't really strung out yet, but we progressed from being chippy dope users to getting a real habit.

My daddy found my works one time. I told him it must belong to somebody else. I was, by this time, becoming a lying dope fiend. My girl and I was trying to support our dope habit. Sometime before my pa passed away, he started busting me. He was finding works all over the place. My poor mama had like eighty cajillion heart attacks behind the fact that I was using dope. Me and this tenor sax player—he's doing three hundred years at Angola right now for narcotics—we was selling peyote buttons. They was legal, but nobody knew that, and so we was getting grand-theft money sell-ing this crap. My mama didn't know what the hell we was doing, but then the narcotics squad came to our house looking for somebody. It was me, the bass player, and the tenor player. We panicked and was flushing these peyote buttons down the turlet, clogging the damn thing up. My mom completely freaked out, the poor thing.

So anyway, the tenor player escaped to Baton Rouge. The tenor player got a gig in a pharmacy and got popped working there, 'cause they had an

APB [all points bulletin] out on his ass. The bass player went to another state to get away from the police.

Dope was a real inconvenience to my music. The police was always picking us up on seventy-two-hour investigations. It was all we ever talked about. When we were high, we said we got to get out of this fucking game. This shit sucks. It just became a big trap. Go make the gigs, the recording sessions. I was doing good with my music on one side, supporting a don't-quit-dope habit on the other side.

I was even trying to run a whorehouse on the side. Me and my first wife. A little bitty operation. It wasn't shit. Chump change. A friend of mine gave me a book of tricks, and we found some girls and put 'em to work. It was just another way to support our habit. I also started a little abortion business. Back then, in the fifties, abortion was illegal. I knew a guy who was in a concentration camp in Poland. He knew how to do something beside coat-hanger abortions. I had friends in the church down in New Orleans that took in girls that was pregnant and tried to save them. It was a bad time though, because of the abortion laws. Everything was a bust. It was a losing battle. We'd get picked up on a seventy-two-hour investigation. We'd have a good lawyer, who'd get us bonded, but we'd get picked up by the police as we was walking out and they'd put us right back in. We'd have to go through the same shit all over again, and get really dope sick. It's amazing. We'd go through all that, but we'd forget how much shit we just went through and that we were that close to being past it all [dope sick], and the first thing I'd do was get some codeine cough syrup till we could cop. Then we'd get loaded and it was the same ol' shit. "Man, we got to get outta this game." Over and over and over.

Guys told me this, old-timers said, "You fuck with dope and all you're going to do is just chase your sick off." And that's what I did. Just trying to feel like normal, whatever the fuck that is.

Dope made me feel like there was this big wall. I used to play in these bucket-of-blood clubs, where you didn't feel exactly safe. I'd be playing guitar in places where I'd always try to stand by a slot machine. All these clubs had slot machines, even on the bandstand, and I'd always try to play next to one, so that when they started popping caps in the joint, I could duck behind one. I knew a bullet ain't going to go through all them slugs and money in those machines. I was always high in these clubs, but I had to pay attention. All of a sudden you'd hear *pop, pop, pop.* These were mostly clubs on the west bank of New Orleans, Algiers, Jefferson Parish, all the way down through south Louisiana. They had a few on the east bank. When you first crossed the Mississloppy River, you were still in New Orleans in Algiers. These were dangerous clubs I'm talking about, just plain danger-ous. The club owners made sure the bands were safe, but there were some of them where the club owner was crazy as the customers. There was a guy out at the Weego Inn on the hill in West Weego, and this fucking guy, he'd shoot up his own damn club. Empty it out, then blame us for the joint hav-ing no business. The guy was dangerous.

At a lot of those gigs, I shot dope and took goofballs on top of it. Red Devils, any kind of sleeping pills. I got into fights under the influence of sleeping pills. That's what made me stop taking them. I'd get into fights and get my ass kicked. I even hit some pedestrians with my car, and I started thinking, "What if I hit a little kid?" So I quit taking those fucking things.

During this time, no matter what I did, I would still shoot dope. I had to go to various institutions with the hope of cleaning up, but when I got out, I always did the same thing. I'd get a bottle of codeine cough syrup to get balanced. Codeine to me wasn't like heroin or any of the opiates that I really liked. I also didn't know that one of anything is too many. I didn't understand that it was the first one that gets you started. I thought I was just doing this to take the edge off. It went on and on, till at some point in the game I felt like I'm never going to get out.

When I first heard that there were ways out, some old-timer told me that if you're going to be a bullshit artist, you have to believe your own bullshit. And when I first started trying to regroup my life, I couldn't tell you where the bullshit ended and the truth began. It was all fucked up in my head. And that was a problem.

The first time I was getting detoxified from methadone. I'd been on that crap a long time. I hated methadone. It was a fucking nightmare. Somewhere in the eighties I went into my first rehab, or I should say, rehabs. All of them around the same time. I got detoxified offa methadone and went back to shooting dope, which was better than drinking methadone. My mother made novenas all the time, my sister constantly worried, and my daughter would panic every time I went to the bathroom.

After that, I started getting some heat on me 'cause I was dealing a little in New York. I didn't want to take a fall, and I talked to this friend of mine. The motherfucker had regrouped his life [gotten clean] in New Orleans and he said to me, "I'll tell you, Mac, you're too old for the game. Your crippled old ass ain't goin' to outrun one of these young kids with a Mac 10 or an Uzi or a sawed-off shotgun. You're too old for the game." So I went to another rehab, and this time, some counselor said to me, "You can't smoke here." And I said, "What are you telling me? I'm outside! I'm a nicotine fanatic! You telling me I can't smoke? Outside?" So I ended up flipping out a few times there. And the next thing I know, I'm in a cardiac ward, laying in a bed next to a guy on a morphine drip. A nurse walked in. I hadn't held nothing in my stomach. The only thing I could hold down was Gatorade, and I hate Gatorade. So this nurse says, "Here, try some of these tangerines." After she talked to me, they shipped me back to rehab and I met her old man. He was a sweet guy. He'd take me outside in the desert there and prop me up against a cactus or some shit, and then he'd make these nice sand paintings. Then he'd start playing this little homemade flute, and while he played, the wind came up and blew the painting away. I said, "Wow, that's pretty cool." One day, I watched him kill a snake with this nice stick. I looked at him and said, "I'm gonna beat you for that stick." He said, "You don't have to commit no felony for this stick, I'm gonna give you the motherfucker." I still got it.

Anyway, them people really helped me. It was a nice place, if you like deserts, but I'm not a desert kind of people.

So this is where I got clean. Period. I made a decision in my head that I wasn't gonna get caught up in this shit anymore. . . . That was in December 1989. From there, I was put in a psych ward, still pretty flipped out. While I was there, three croakers [doctors] decided to put me on psych meds. Each one thought the other ones was monitoring me. I was slowly being poisoned. Lithium poison. It's called diabetes insipid. This was in California, where a lot of people were trying to help me. So eventually I get back to New York and end up seeing some psych-pharmacologist. This guy tells me I'm being poisoned from lithium and he wants to get me off of it. So now I'm off psych meds and I'm starting to flip out again. All this shit keeps piling up on me.

I'm also with this woman that's driving me crazy, so I try to throw her out of my pad, but she has extra keys, and when I come home off the road, she's back in my pad and I'm getting crazier by the minute. Now I'm ready to kill this bitch, but I don't go back to dope.

I hang on to praying and doing things these people in rehab taught me to do. I moved into the Carlyle Hotel in New York, so I didn't have to go to my pad, 'cause I knew I'd kill this woman. I was really getting crazier. I had herbs hanging everywhere and candles burning. The maids wouldn't clean the room. I had incense burning and all kinds of weird shit. Nobody wanted to talk to me. Even the people that worked for me stayed away because I was so out there.

I didn't know I was still flipped out. I was diagnosed as having Tigerette syndrome and being a bisexual polar bear. Every night I'd walk all the way from the goddamn Carlyle Hotel on Eighty-something Street down to below Houston. I'd go to my friend Shane's joint and hit on this chick that worked there. I'd walk along the river every night. I'd call people on the phone all night long. Anybody I had a number for I'd call. Some people would stay up all night talking to me, and finally they'd say, "I got to go to work." I'd never let them get a word in the whole time, and they would put up with this crap.

I didn't know what the fuck I was doing, but I knew I wasn't gonna start using. I had really started flipping out in California. I had did a song for a Walt Disney movie about dalmatian dogs, and I started really flipping out again. I started singing, "You motherfuckers, technicolor, Cecil B. DeMille wannabees" . . . insulting everybody and everything, telling them this is the city of Saint Francis the Sissy, in the state of fruits and nuts. There ought to be a video of this gig! I'm insulting everybody. I'm just out there!

I got back to New York and kept doing weird shit. I couldn't stop cussing. My managers, my shrink, my accountant . . . everybody was on my case. They had me go back on these psych meds, and I'm still on them today. I don't flip out no more.

So from that point on, I started learning how to take better care of myself. At that time, I was weighing about 350 pounds 'cause this bitch that I wanted to kill was feeding me ten tons of food each day. I was close to blowing up! I still had this water retention from being on methadone. I started seeing an acupuncturist and doing all this stuff. I also started seeing this shrink. I was starting to get positive about things. And most important, I was staying clean. It was not no bed from roses. During all this time, I was making records for people, getting dumped from record companies—typical musician stuff. I was still able to work gigs, but I was trying to take better care of me. I'm still not good at it, but my life started to shift.

Since I've been offa narcotics, I just know that that ain't the way to go. That's a slow version of self-suicide. Some people it might not affect that way, but I ain't one of them. I'm proud of the fact that I flipped out twice in recovery without picking up.

It's very funny that all of the things my pa told me when I was a kid proved out to be exactly correct. "Kid, if you smoke weed, you're gonna take goofballs. If you take goofballs, you're gonna shoot dope." He always called dope fiends, back in the forties, "junkers." Junkers. I don't know where that word came from. There was a lot of things he told me. My pa always approved of me playing, even in these low-down strip joints, 'cause I was with the older guys. He knew they were good musicians and I'd learn how to play music. Ain't nobody in that crew did anything like try to turn me out. I got turned out on my own. Wasn't like anybody gave me my wings. Nobody gave me shit. I went out with whatever rebellious stupidity my head was into and I went that-a-way, and I couldn't get out of it. That was another thing. I heard that from a million people. They'd all say, "Once you're a dope fiend, you'll die a dope fiend." Even I used to say, "Yeah, Daddy, I'm a hope-to-die dope fiend." There was a dope fiend toast I remember: "To all my dope fiend friends, we'll be dope fiends till the end." What the fuck was all that stupid shit about? It's like all them codes of the street. "Fuck them before they fuck you." All that dumb shit. And I'd buy into it, 'cause it's all you need to know in the game.

When my daughter passed away recently, a guy pulled my coat and asked me, "You know why they call it the game?" I thought about it and said, "No." And he said, "Because nothing is real. The only thing real in the game is death." That was pretty profound.

I feel like I'm blessed now. It beats whatever I had in a million ways. Every day I wake up and you know the first thing I'm grateful for? The ability to take a crap! To make my daily deposit. All them years on methadone, living like a toxic waste dump. Sounds stupid, but to me it ain't. When you ain't used the turlet in two months, that's a big deal.

You know, anything I tell you is shit I heard from some other mother-fucker. I hang on to a lot of stuff. I been around a lot of good people all my life. There was things people told me I didn't understand till I was clean. You know, getting away from that life-style gave me time to think.

Deacon Frank's wife, in the Spiritual Church in New Orleans, told me, "You got to be in season, in order to catch the right season when it come. You got to be in order, all in order." Now she was passing down words she learned from Mother Catherine. The Book of Ecclesiastic. If it's your time, you get it, and when you ain't, you ain't. Simple.

Nothing that is, or lives,
But hath his Quickenings,
and reprieves.

—Henry Vaughn

Pete Hamill
(writer)

ONE OF THE THINGS I've asked myself in determining who I'd like to interview for this book is "Would I like to drink with this guy?" Pete Hamill, an author with enormous range, is a guy I'd most definitely like to have gotten drunk with.

Throwing back a couple of cold ones in some dark, seedy pub, while we shared stories of the good old days . . . I can just hear the argument that would have ensued over the Dodgers' move to Los Angeles. For Brooklyn-born Pete, it was a travesty and an act of unforgivable abandonment. For me, a native Angelino, it was joyous. The dream of seeing guys like Koufax, Drysdale, Pee Wee, and The Duke in person was more than I could imagine. We could have easily come to blows over that one.

Or how about politics, boxing, or women? I'm sure we would have spent hours working our way through those meaty subjects. I'd have bought a round for any guy who loves the fight game as much as Pete does. I know we could have shared a story or three about Muhammad Ali or any number of former champs, arguing their prowess or lack thereof while consuming a few whiskeys and a couple of good cigars at a local fight arena. And how about his knowledge of New York City? I'd try to outdo him with tales of intrigue about L.A., but I'm afraid I'd be no match for him. A restaurant I used to frequent, called Musso and Frank's, billed itself as "Hollywood's

Oldest Restaurant—Established 1919." "In New York, that's considered a new restaurant," Pete would have chided.

I've been told by the women in my life that I'm a "guy's guy." I've always taken that as a compliment. Pete would have to rank as one of the great "guy's guys," and so it was with great appreciation that I conducted this interview.

I never crashed and burned. I began to deteriorate and had other things I wanted to do. I knew that drinking was the most destructive path for a writer, because it attacks memory. You wake up in the morning and say, "Man, I had a great time last night," but you don't remember where you were. It wasn't that I lost a job or crashed a car and killed two people. I didn't even drive in those days. Nothing like that happened. In my book [*A Drinking Life*], I didn't want to make what was going on with me worse than it was—for the entertainment of readers or for some moral lesson. It wasn't a moral problem to me; it was a practical problem. I was a writer who wanted to be a better one.

Working on newspapers and drinking, I could always squeeze enough out of my talent to get into the paper the next day, but the attempts to see what the limits of that talent were couldn't be determined with drinking. In other words, could I write novels? Could I write movies? Could I write extended essays? I had no idea. I had already written one novel when I was still drinking. A thriller, which helped me figure out the form. It's like starting with sprints and then saying, "Can I run a marathon?" So it was partly that—my work—but I also had custody of my two daughters at the time, after a divorce. That added a very simple reason: I didn't want to look like an asshole in front of my kids. There was real responsibility to bringing them up . . . and not in the context of semi-consciousness! That was a factor too.

When I got to the end of my drinking life, I said, "I can't do this anymore. I don't even like this anymore." It was reasonably easy to stop. I don't mean that it was *completely* easy. It wasn't like saying, "That's it. I think I'll go to the ball game." It involved certain alterations in the way I lived. I emphasized in my book that it was not about the drinking life, it was about a drinking life. There could be ten thousand other reasons why people drank. This book was about how it got into my life, and how I started to get it out. It was also why I didn't go to AA [Alcoholics Anonymous] or anything like that, although I have great regard for AA. I've brought people there, but it wasn't a thing that I could do. I couldn't get up there and say, "I'm Pete Hamill, and I'm a drunk." I couldn't do it! For whatever reasons—upbringing or personality or whatever.

It all depends on which way you emerge from this place where you're lost. Some people climb a tree and look out to see where the hell the road is. If they're lost in the forest, some people have to retrace their steps to get back. I had to retrace the steps.

The first year of sobriety was the hardest in terms of readjusting the patterns of my life. Particularly in the newspaper business. And particularly in a world where the Lion's Head—the great Village saloon in its day—was still alive. This was a world that was still very turbulent with Vietnam and Watergate and the rebellions they helped create. So it took some adjustment. How to walk into a saloon and order—of all goddamn things—a Diet Coke, which I would have laughed at a year earlier. Afterwards, I didn't have any problems with cravings or anything. I wish I did so I could make it sound like *Under the Volcano*. But I didn't. The only problem I encountered was this amazing sweet tooth. I began to eat ice cream and other stuff I hadn't done since I was a teenager. I had cravings in that way, which was obviously not solely in my brain but in my physiology. "Where's the sugar?" But I had by then learned that I was going to have to live my life without anesthesia, and that meant accepting the pain along with the laughs.

As a writer, since I've stopped drinking, I published nineteen books. If I kept drinking, I wouldn't have written as much as I have, and at the highest level I could reach. I'm not suggesting sobriety turned me into Balzac. But it helped me become the best possible Pete Hamill. In a certain way, the sense of renewed, more focused life came from the realities of death. There were a few people whose deaths showed me the consequence of continuing drinking. They were friends. And the consequences were visible. I saw them in my life. I saw them in Brooklyn when I was a kid. People get drunk and fall into a snow pile in winter and get taken out in the morning. It wasn't that somebody died and I suddenly said, "That's it, I'm stopping drinking." It wasn't like that. I wish it were. It would be a better story. As noted, my decision was based on a combination of factors. I didn't stop drinking because Buddy Greco was a terrible singer. That was like the way people get divorced because their spouse burns the English muffins. There's obviously something preceding that kind of moment.

By the way, I almost never drank while I was working. If I had to write a column or go out and report on something, I didn't do any drinking till after the work was over. It was a classic repetition of the patterns of my father's generation of blue-collar Americans. You rewarded yourself with drinking . . . later. For them it was too physically dangerous to drink on the job. You couldn't be an iron worker and go up to the thirty-ninth floor with a load on. I think one of the things drunks do, and I was certainly one of them, is find situations in which they feel normal. You know, your friends are all at the bar and it feels normal. You think the whole world is drinking, and it's not till you stop that you discover it's mostly sober. I didn't choose my life on the basis of drinking, but if you go into the Navy as I did, sailors drink. They still do. All you have to do is watch a bunch of sailors on parade. Sailors are expected to be drunk.

Certainly the newspaper business, when I went into it in 1960, was dominated by guys who had probably started in the last years of Prohibition and then had come through the Depression, where there were all sorts of vestiges of Prohibition, and then into World War II, where the culture of drinking was very much alive.

In my new book, I talk about the kind of party mentality that prevailed in the Village in the late fifties, when I first set up in Manhattan. It was perfectly normal to go to somebody's place for a party and find seventy-five people standing around like it was the "D" train. All in various stages of getting loaded. I was at parties where it was perfectly normal to stand there and discuss Krazy Kat, the comic strip, with LeRoi Jones, or explain the affinities of Willie Mays and Fred Astaire, or drink eleven bottles of

Rheingold while arguing about Jackson Pollock. You didn't feel you were doing something daring, or defying the bourgeoisie. It's how people grew, given the previous twenty-five years of American culture.

To be Irish American meant living in the same kind of culture of normalcy, even though all the collars were blue. You drank when you came home from work. You drank at weddings. You drank at funerals. You went to wakes and everybody got loaded. It was normal. We had no way of knowing that that's not the way William Butler Yeats handled himself. Or, God knows, any number of other Irish characters I came to love. It's hard to imagine getting loaded with Samuel Beckett, although I'm sure he did his share. I came to recognize that, aside from your own physiology and psychology, a lot of this stuff is environmental. It was how you grew up, and where you grew up, and how the larger world taught you the rules. The rules were based on what seemed normal.

I think of my friend Carl Hiaasen, the wonderful Florida columnist and novelist. I've known him for many years. He once went off to do some reporting on the Cayman Islands, and when he came back, I called him up and said, "How was it, Carl?" And he said, "It's the kind of place where they *point out* the honest people." In certain New York neighborhoods when I was young, they pointed out the guys who had "taken the pledge" and didn't drink. They would remind you sometimes that Hitler didn't drink either.

After I stopped drinking, I still kept going to places like the Lion's Head because that's where my friends went. I made the ultimate sacrifice: I ate there! Even the owners went out to eat. So I stayed in touch because I loved those guys, and the women too (there was a fairly good percentage of female drinkers at the time in the Village). I was more conscious, so I became, at once, one of their friends and also a kind of spy in the world. I would carry these index cards in my pocket, and when I'd hear a good line, I'd retreat to the john and write it down. I couldn't write it down in front of them. So the world I knew was still feeding the part of my life that was about writing, even though I was detached from it. Writing became more important to me sober.

I often thought of a line from . . . I'm almost sure it's from Henry James, and I'm almost equally sure I'm misquoting it: "To become one of those people upon whom nothing is missed." I certainly never got there. I missed a lot of things—sober, and still do. But I missed less. Less actually did become more, in that case, in terms of consciousness.

As far as my friends were concerned, I didn't become an object of suspicion because I was sober, but probably an object of some mixture of pity and weirdness. The one good thing about the Lion's Head and some other saloons that were part of the same culture was that all sins were forgiven, except cruelty. So yes, even sobriety was forgiven. If the guy next to you threw up on your shoes, that was forgiven. So was this weird thing where you decided not to drink. I didn't make any big pronouncement. I said, "I'm laying off the sauce for a month" so it didn't look like some sort of permanent conversion. The road to Damascus running through Sheridan Square . . . it wasn't that. But then it became a habit. They got used to me being sober.

Something I noted sober was the amazing amount of repetition. One person would tell a tale, and I would have heard it four times before. In that sense, I lost a certain amount of benevolent patience. In a more important way, I realized that we drunks perform our lives instead of live them. You have a tale that once got a laugh. You want the laugh, so you tell the tale. Almost like an actor. That makes life easier. You don't have to pull something out of your guts. Or think of something new. A lot of what happened in a weird way was a continuation of vaudeville. Which is why I had so much fun. I had an amazing number of laughs, and I learned a lot, in my own drinking years, from old newspapermen. Not just the Lion's Head, but bars near the old *New York Post*—newspapermen's bars. They were serious craftsmen, these people. They would look at the papers, and find your story, and say, "How the fuck could you write that?" And you'd learn something about craft. Even though there might have been more vehemence than you would get at Columbia School of Journalism, it was also a school.

Many things were of great value. There was a thing characteristic of newspapermen and other kinds of writers. I think that writers start off fairly shy, many of them, and become writers to overcome this shyness. I'm sure if you could really get into the brain of Ernest Hemingway or William

Faulkner, there would be some shy sixteen-year-old in there someplace. Nora Ephron once said, "The writer is the guy who thinks of the great line on the way home from the party." All these writers created ways to live, to enjoy themselves, to feel like they were taller than they were, wittier than they were, and maybe more talented than they were. And in many ways, drinking was helpful. It allowed them to live lives instead of being buried in some boardinghouse somewhere.

The hard thing to figure out is where the tipping point is. Where you go from being a social animal to being a goddamn fool. Where drinking, which helped release you, becomes something that starts to destroy you. It's very hard for people to determine that point.

I think the most dangerous drunk is the functioning drunk. It's one thing to be some poor soul huddled in a doorway somewhere, having lost everything. But the guy who goes off to work, has a cocktail or two before he heads up to the office, and then some at lunch, and then goes home and whacks his wife around—he's a much more dangerous guy. He forces the people who like him to become co-conspirators. They cover for him as long as they can. Although now, I think, there is much less tolerance of this stuff. In those days, everybody knew somebody who was fundamentally decent, who was turned into Mr. Hyde by drinking. I remember I met Robert Mitchum a couple of times and liked him very much. He was intelligent, self-deprecating, and had a real sense of irony. But if you stayed with him to the point at which he became drunk, he became a nasty piece of work. So that even in the movies, the directors knew that they could only get a performance out of him in the morning. After lunch it was impossible.

One advantage of being sober for the last thirty-two years is that I've lived long enough to see how different stories turn out. I had some friends that stopped drinking but died anyway. In some cases, in the world that I'm in (and it's not a normal world)—the world of talent—you see people who start out bursting with potential and ability, but they burn out like shooting stars. I'm convinced, more than ever, that drinking did it to them because it cuts memory, which is the mother lode of every writer, and it cuts into physical energy because this is hard work. If you work the way I do, or any good writer does eventually, you get up in the morning, have your breakfast, and then you go to work. And maybe late that afternoon you stop, but at night you're tossing and turning with the work. All of which comes flowing out, for good or bad, the following morning. And you do it seven days a week even though there are days when you do no writing at all. Your consciousness doesn't go away.

I'm walking down the street here in Mexico, yesterday, and I have a scene in my mind from the North River in 1935, part of my novel, a long way from where I am. And it's vividly alive. That is why so many writers' marriages collapse. It takes a rare woman or man who realizes that when the person they're married to is looking out the window, the person is working!

The people who stay conscious derive amazing benefits from it. They're aware of the only life that they are going to have, and without it, they end up lying in those hospital beds with tubes up their noses, wondering, "What the fuck was it all about?"

No, when the fight begins within himself,
A man's worth something.

—Robert Browning, "Bishop Blougram's Apology"

Gerry Cooney
(boxer)

I ALWAYS HATED WHITE heavyweights like Gerry Cooney. Aside from there never being an outstanding one that I could remember—Rocky Marciano was a little before my time—I always felt embarrassed for them. They seemed to be offered up in hopes of knocking off whatever reigning black champion prevailed. Ingemar Johansson, Jerry Quarry, Britain's Henry Cooper and Brian London, U.S. Olympian Duane Bobick, Randall "Tex" Cobb, and Tommy Morrison—all "great white hopes," all heavyweight bust-outs.

From my perspective, Gerry had another problem. He had the most despicable group of managers and handlers I've ever observed in boxing. Arrogant guys with smug faces and loud mouths who seemed to think they owned the sport. Poor Gerry looked like a lost child when surrounded by these jerks. I always rooted against him because I didn't want his managers to succeed, but when Gerry put up that gallant performance against Larry Holmes for the heavyweight championship in 1982, my opinion of him changed. This was some courageous fighter.

I met Gerry at his modest, colonial-style home located in a New Jersey suburb. He greeted me at the door wearing a black wool beret with a small brim turned to the back, like a jockey might wear, black sweat pants, and a plain, gray, long-sleeved T-shirt. My first impression was that this guy looks in great shape, probably could still go a few hard rounds. Gerry has a huge welcoming smile and a soft-handed handshake that I've often experienced with prizefighters.

Entering the house, I couldn't help but observe that it is in a state of complete disarray thanks to his two rambunctious children: two-and-a-half-year-old Sarah and her doting six-year-old brother, Jack. Led to the sunken family room, I immediately noticed the enormous photo wall, the highlights of which Gerry quickly pointed out to me. His favorites are not of his fights, or of other fighters for that matter, but pictures of Gerry with Bob Hope and another with Frank Sinatra. Toys dominate this room, in sharp contrast to the many pictures of the pugilistic wars Gerry has been in.

His children were omnipresent, often wanting his attention, which he gladly gave them. Our interview was interrupted several times by the kids, but Gerry didn't seem to mind. He truly loved them being around. Sarah hopped on his lap to tell Daddy she loves him, and not to be outdone, Jack does the same. Gerry assured his son that he knows he loves him, but Gerry reminded him that he wanted to be dropped off a block from school so that the other kids wouldn't see his dad kiss him!

Gerry eats from a large porcelain bowl containing an entire cut-up roasted chicken. As he speaks, he waves a drumstick for emphasis.

While telling me his story, Gerry occasionally paused, wanting to feel the experience he was re-creating for me. His eyes closed for a second as if he were being transported back in time. It didn't seem difficult for him to share with me hurtful events from his past, so confident is he now in his present.

———

I grew up in hell. My father was an alcoholic and my mother enabled him. He was a strong guy, physically very abusive. And I grew up basically learning five things: you're no good, you're a failure, you're not going to amount to anything, don't trust nobody, and don't tell nobody your business. That's what I learned in my house growing up.

I swore I was never gonna be anything like him, and I became just like him. Except I wasn't physically abusive, but boxing helped me out with that. I spent a lot of my childhood hiding in the basement, because if I hid down there he couldn't see me and he wouldn't hurt me.

I remember he wanted us kids to be marines, so one night while drunk he woke us up and shaved our heads. He would wake us up in the morning by pouring cold water over us, pulling us by the hair and ears, horrible things. I found out later a psycho does those kinds of things. So the last nine years of his life, he didn't drink and I swear I'm never gonna be like him, and at age thirteen, I started drinking. Boone's Farm apple wine. I used to hold my nose and drink it down. I liked how it felt. It took care of the hole that I felt. I had a deep hole here [pointing to his stomach], and those five things I learned growing up, that's how I felt, how I learned to feel.

My dad wanted to control me I suppose, and that was a way to do it. Make me not feel. But when I drank, all of sudden I became attractive, I became funny, spontaneous—and I fit in. Once I had some Boone's Farm apple wine . . . I remember getting so sick the first time I drank it. I was crawling around the backyard saying "I'm never gonna do this again." But there was something about those five or ten minutes when I was alright with the world. I'll never forget that, and so until I got sober and stopped drinking when I was thirty years old, I drank to get to that high. The bad part about my drinking was I was pretty good at it. I learned how to mix and match. I didn't have to work, just train. I was a young kid. I didn't have to train until three or four in the afternoon, so I would sleep until two, grab a bite to eat, and catch a train into the city to go spar. I always knew I was going to be a fighter.

At sixteen, I won the state championship in New York, in front of 21,000 people at the Garden on Saint Patrick's Day. And then I won the New York Golden Gloves heavyweight title in 1976. My father got sick, so I didn't go to the finals of the Olympic trials. I didn't go because, you know, I say because my father was sick, but basically I had low self-esteem. I thought I wasn't good enough—all those things had an effect on me. I really regret those days that I didn't pursue the opportunity, even if I didn't succeed. I was afraid of looking bad—things that hit me at my core. I wasn't worried about upsetting my father; I was angry at him. My father was a mean, nasty guy. It was his way or the highway. That's how my life was around him.

In some ways, I think I became a fighter because he learned how to control life around him, and he was strong. I went to the gym to express my anger. Next thing I know my picture is in the newspaper, so I was somebody. I remember going to the store when I was sixteen and looking at that paper and saying, "That's me!" Anger fed me and kept me alive. Amazing. I anesthetized the pain all those years, drinking and hiding and later with drugs and not feeling. You know, I say that if I would have not drank, I would have been heavyweight champion of the world. If I would have become the champ while I was drinking, I'd probably be dead today.

When I was young, every night there were parties to go to, different clubs to hang out in. I could drink pretty good and I could handle it pretty well, or so I thought. I didn't have somebody in my life that would say, "Hey, Gerry." They didn't know how to reach me. You know, I try to work with a lot of guys now. You can tell them things, but most of them can't hear.

Fortunately, boxing kept me in line. I did take halfway decent care of myself, but as I got older, I started taking less care of myself. After knocking out Kenny Norton in 1981, I don't fight again for thirteen months, and in that period of time, I started drinking. I started doing some recreational drugs and then I'm fighting for the heavyweight championship of the world.

I lost to Larry Holmes in 1982. I think I drank and did drugs during this period of time to have an excuse in case I failed. I could blame the drink: "It wasn't me." Now I realize that in life I have to go for that nut. I got to do everything I can to get that nut. And if I don't get it, it's okay because I did everything I could.

I remember the old guys in the gym telling me, "Don't get caught up," and I'd say, "Thanks, but it's not going to happen to me" and then everything happened to me. The thing about life is that it keeps repeating itself.

You know, I do a lot of work in prisons and with troubled kids and gangs, and I'm thinking, "Am I really helping anybody?" And somebody told me that if you help one person and that person doesn't go back to jail, he changes the lives of many people. Like in *It's a Wonderful Life* with Jimmy Stewart. And that's a great way of looking at things.

I go to an orphan program a couple times a week and work with kids and I love 'em, but they've been mistreated for so long that it's hard for them to open up. Just like me as a kid. I can relate to them and talk to them in a language they can understand 'cause I was there.

Anyway, going back to my career, I used to drink after every fight and would go wild. In 1981, I fought Kenny Norton and knocked him out in fifty-four seconds of the first round. That night was the first time I did some cocaine, and I started drinking twice as much as usual. Coke numbed me out and covered the hole up. Coke also helped me reach my bottom a lot quicker, so I'm grateful for that.

The pressure was building. Here was a kid with my background on the cover of *Time* magazine and *Sports Illustrated*. Everyone was focusing on me, and it was a very frightening thing, especially with the set of tools I had. No skills. The only thing I knew was not to trust anybody. I couldn't trust my father, my mother, anybody. So there I am, in the spotlight. I go from "You're no good. You're a piece of shit" to "Everybody loves Gerry Cooney." What the hell is that all about? I couldn't understand or trust it.

My old man died in 1976, but he never learned how to live. He never enjoyed his life. I went through life with blinders on till I stopped drinking. Then I could finally see. I'd fall down, dust myself off, and move on.

The night I fought Larry Holmes for the championship, I had a phone line to President Reagan installed in my dressing room. If I won the fight, the president would call to congratulate me. It was unbelievable, but I was so afraid of failing. So in the fight, I got stopped in the thirteenth round. Now, I want to tell you, during this time I got all this shit going on. My managers hate each other. They are also fighting with my trainers. I have this high level of insecurity, dysfunction. Chaos is everywhere, and I'm trying to deal with it all.

I had this girlfriend at the time who got into a terrible car accident. It was very depressing. I felt some guilt about it because the day of the accident we were supposed to go out, but I was drunk and didn't show up. She goes out and gets in a car wreck. Alcohol was perfect for me, helped me get rid of the guilt. All these things, you know . . .

I went to a party in the penthouse of Caesars Palace hotel. Everybody I ever wanted to meet from sports, movie stars, Frank Sinatra was there for *me*. Kareem Abdul-Jabbar, Muhammad Ali, everybody. I was on top of the world and I couldn't feel a thing. Couldn't feel it. 'Cause I knew it could be taken away from me.

I think I was overtrained for the Holmes fight. I had a trainer who was a good trainer, a good man. I love him, but I trained a little too much. I learned since being sober: balance, work hard, but play. So I worked too hard for the fight. It was 115 degrees in Vegas. I got every kind of excuse you can imagine. Holmes was a great fighter. That was my biggest excuse! He was a great fighter. The press kept telling me I couldn't go the distance with him, so I tried to go the distance instead of just go out and fight. And you know, Holmes is ranked the fifth greatest heavyweight in history, and that's the guy I had to fight that night. I hadn't fought in thirteen months 'cause Don King wasn't letting me. King owned everybody, and I wasn't signed with King, so he was keeping me out. He didn't want me to gain the experience I needed in order to beat Holmes 'cause I wasn't signed with him. So I was only fighting once a year. Not nearly enough.

This fight was the first time that I wasn't nervous. I just wanted to hit him. I'll tell you a story: I'm fighting Jimmy Young in Atlantic City, and I'm in my dressing room on the third floor, all by myself, and I'm thinking, "This guy's gonna kill me." So I start thinking about jumping out the window, but I didn't. I went out and beat him. Knocked him out in four rounds. Flash forward . . . 1981, I'm fighting Kenny Norton, and three nights before the fight, we're on *Warner Wolf Show*. Warner says, "How you feelin', Gerry?" Kenny is sitting next to me, and I look at him and say, "I wish I was fighting you right now!" I was full of shit, you know what I mean? I couldn't wait the three days? See, I had that fear, but in some ways it made me work so much harder. They made me out to be a monster, but I was just a man.

I didn't have that fear when I fought Holmes. I wish I had! I just wanted to hit him. I didn't like him as a man. So I go twelve rounds with him. I get three points taken away for low blows. I go out for the thirteenth round saying, "You can't hurt me." And I let him hit me instead of saying, "Let me go out there and take him out this round." Then he knocked me out.

After that I really crashed and burned. That was really a tough time, for a couple of years. I didn't want my mother worrying about me, so I'd go over to her house once a week, sit in front of the television for a couple of hours, then leave.

I kept thinking of John Lennon's "I'm just sitting here watching the wheels go round." That's where I was at the time. I regret it. Nobody cared about me and I didn't care about them. I was just existing, surviving, and that's what my old man did. Paid bills, drank when he wasn't working, and drank while he *was* working, and so I didn't have any options. I couldn't stand my managers. They hated each other. I was the hero to my family, so I'm fixing everybody with money: "Let me fix this problem, let me fix that problem." It got to the point where my family expected it, and so I finally had to cut them out of my life.

So I needed to go through all of that. I had a couple friends I stayed in touch with, but that was it. I also stayed close to women. They would hold me and tell me I was okay. And even that eventually stopped working. Then I don't fight for a bunch of years. All of a sudden Spinks beats Holmes and they're calling me to see if I want to fight Spinks, and I say, "I'll take it tomorrow!" So I go to training camp and the fight doesn't happen for two years. I'm in training camp for two years for a fight that's supposed to happen in six, seven weeks. It was postponed 'cause of this lawsuit or that thing. So I start drinking again. "This fight ain't ever gonna happen," I tell myself. It's on, it's off. Even when I'm walking into the ring I'm thinking, "This ain't gonna happen." I was drinking right up to the night of the fight. Not taking care of myself. And I got stopped in the fifth round.

I was fed up. It's all bullshit. That's the only fight that I really regret. Spinks didn't belong in the same ring with me. And I cut him up pretty good. If I cut someone, he's finished, but I was a walking dead man that night and didn't know it.

I did know it, I did know it. I remember telling a friend of mine before the fight, "I don't know what I'm doing here." And so that was the beginning of the end. I moved out to East Hampton, and I met this old guy out there, and we went and drank every day. One day I woke up and said, "I got to give this shit up. Who's in charge, man? What's going on?" The next day I woke up the same way. I turned on the TV and there just happened to be an infomercial for this rehab out there. I call them up and say, "Listen, I might have a problem," and they say, "Why don't you come on down?" So I go see this guy and he walks me around the place and says, "You don't have to stay here, but if you can't make it out there, you can come back." I'm thinking, "I don't want to be here," so I gave it up. I just gave it up on my own. No rehab.

I remember someone telling me, "You got to be careful. You get three, four, five months, you're gonna think you're all better," and I said, "Not me, man, not me." And two months later I'm back out there drinking again. For me it was the best thing that could have happened, because it had to be proved to me that I was not in control. So I drank for two months, and then one day I'm going to my office. I say, "Let's go have breakfast," and I see an IHOP over there. This guy I knew was there and we start talking. He tells me he hasn't had a drink in three years, and that's when I heard it. That was sixteen years ago, and I straightened out right then. April 1988.

It's been a long journey. I tell this story all the time. You can be anything you want, but you have to put your hand out. It's been a miracle, magical. I've been to Africa, watched the sun rise from a hot air balloon, sailed to Central America on a giant sailboat, traveled through the rain forest, been to Trinidad, to Europe on my honeymoon, and I live "one day at a time." And I love my life.

I have a friend who's seventy-five years old. He's getting weak. He's thirty-something-years sober. He has to go get iron taken out of his blood once a week, and I'm seeing him lose it a little, and it's killing me. You know, I'm really feeling for him.

I wish that I had known back then what I know now, so I could have fully appreciated it. I would have been heavyweight champion of the world! And I would have handled things differently. I had this friend, Bob

Waters. He was a great writer for *Newsday*. He told me, "You know, Gerry, if I knew I was going to live this long, I would have taken better care of myself!"

So I'm a work in progress. I'm a blessed guy. I've got a lovely wife, two great kids, and I roll with the punches. Aside from hearing bells now and then . . .

What though the radiance which was so bright
Though nothing can bring back the hour
Of splendor in the grass, of glory in the flower;
We will grieve not, rather find
Strength in what remains behind.

—William Wordsworth, "Ode"

Richard Pryor
(comedian)

ARE THERE WORDS TO tell you how much I love Richard Pryor? He made me laugh, he made me think, and he often scared the shit out of me. I thought I had a special appreciation of black people and their plight while I was growing up in the late fifties and early sixties. Integrated schools, equal-housing opportunities, "one man, one vote," freedom marches, integration of sports, "would you want your sister to marry one?"—hell yeah, I married one myself. These were all issues of great importance to me. However, Richard told me that unless I were black, I didn't have a clue. Whitey could appreciate all he pleased, but he couldn't walk in a black man's shoes. This was the kind of thing that Richard talked about and chewed to the bone.

I first met Richard in 1975 when I was producing my first motion picture, *Car Wash*. A character in the film was patterned after the legendary Reverend Ike, who once proclaimed, "The best way to help the poor is not be one of them!" We tried to get the good reverend to play himself in the movie, and it appeared as if he would do it. But after a lengthy negotiation, he informed us at the last possible moment that God had instructed him not to be in the movie. I think it had more to do with our refusal to pay the fee he was asking, but I could be wrong.

We were scrambling around to find someone to take his place, when someone suggested Richard Pryor. "Wow, what a great idea!"

we all responded. Aside from being the funniest man alive, I knew Richard to be a legendary cokehead, so I got word back to him that if he would do the movie for a reasonable fee (and we promised it would only take one day), a nice surprise would be waiting for him in his dressing room. Richard quickly agreed, and a day or two later, we shot what turned out to be one of the highlights of the film. Richard played Reverend Ike better than Reverend Ike would have. And man did we get high. Just watch Richard's performance in the film sometime, and you'll see the manic energy that coke gave him.

The one-day shoot extended into a second day, but Richard was enjoying the experience so much that he agreed to come back without charging us. This is pretty unusual, in my experience, because actors or their agents will almost always take advantage of a situation like this to get as much money as they can. Not Richard though. At least not in this movie. Maybe it was all that good coke floating around the set, but Richard was back the next day and did a hell of a job.

Richard now suffers from multiple sclerosis. His disease has progressed to the point where it was impossible to interview him for this book. Jennifer Lee, his life partner, suggested that I find existing material from his albums, films, and books. This composite, I believe, reflects the best of Richard's riffs on his drug use and the culture he helped create. He has been clean and sober for several years.

**From *Pryor Convictions: And Other Life Sentences*
(New York: Pantheon Books, 1995)**

You can't tell nobody not to snort no cocaine. Mother fucker's gonna snort it anyway. It took me a long time to learn that shit'll kill you. Once a big booger came out my nose. A mother fucking black one this long. Scared the shit out of me. I said, "Goddamn, please, I'll quit. Just let it stop." (139–40)

Then I fell in love with the pipe. It controlled my very being. This mother fucker say, "Don't answer the phone. We have smoking to do." Or the pipe's talking about "Now come on, don't put me down anyplace where I might fall. It's two in the morning and it's hard to get one of me." (183)

Somebody told me if you put coke on your dick you could fuck all night. Shouldn't have told me. My dick got a Jones. Six hundred dollars a day just to get my dick hard. (78)

Neither Maxine [former girlfriend] nor I had tried LSD before, so we didn't know what to expect. We started out at a rock concert, but by the time that shit kicked in we had made it back to the safety of our home. Thank God.

I can't imagine what it would've been like had we stayed out, because once I started tripping, I got into a thing with our kitty. Ordinarily, me and the cat didn't have much to do with each other. We put up with each other.

"Hi, kitty. How ya doin'?"

"Don't talk to me, asshole. I see how you treat women."

Suddenly, this cat follows me around as if we were attached, as if the cat was my shadow. Real close. Too close. Particularly for somebody on LSD. Wherever I went the cat crept right beside me, rubbing, touching, meowing. I thought the cat was fucking with me, you know?

"Get the fuck away."

"Fuck you, Rich."

I swear, me and that cat got into an argument. (79)

I remember Redd Foxx and I spent an entire night and most of the next morning at a little table in his club, battling each other for the attention of a sexy waitress, listening to jazz, and snorting cocaine by the spoonful. I kept asking for more, more, more and Redd kept giving it to me, until finally I was too tired to inhale.

"Hey Redd, why do I always want more?" I asked.

He laughed as if to emphasize my ignorance.

"Because you're a junkie."

Then it was my turn to laugh.

"Bullshit."

I just didn't see. (101)

Needless to say, going over to [dope dealer] Dirty Dick's house meant I had one thing on my mind, and it was no secret to anybody, because I was so God-damn open about using cocaine that it had become a cornerstone of my act, such as it was. When I walked into his place one afternoon, I saw him going through this complicated process to fix up a fine rock of 100% pure coke and then smoke it.

It transfixed me. My feet might as well have been in cement blocks. I stared and tried to comprehend the nuances of the ritual. It was like watching someone do a new dance step. It looked cool, the expression on his face, total bliss, real out there, and when the mother fucker came down from that rocket blast, he looked at me like he's just come.

"Oh, man," he said.

"Yeah?"

"Yeah, Rich. You know, I just seen God."

"God?"

"Mother fucking God."

When I first did it, I knew it was going to fuck me up, but I had to do it. Had to be hip. Mother fucker said, "You ever try this?"

I thought, He's going to string me out. He's a dope dealer who needs me to get hooked so he can get some freebase. This dude used to snort a little coke. But I saw him and said, "What's wrong with you?"

He said, "Have you ever freebased?"

"Say what?"

"Freebased?"

He told me he saw Jesus.

Dirty Dick didn't have to ask if I wanted to try it. From the look in my eye, he just started to cook the rock.

"I'll do everything," he said. "You just suck on the pipe."

Honest to God, I was scared that first time. I thought it was going to be something else. But it was nice.

That was the worst part.

That it was nice. (179)

It started out innocently enough. Every now and then. A little bit. "Naw, not now. No base. Fuck it." Pretty soon, I noticed I wasn't walking as far away from the pipe as I used to. I used to put the pipe down and go.

If you're unlucky, you sit and wait for someone to fix your rocks, and that's all you think about—when am I going to get my turn? The person who cooks has got all the power. I was fortunate. I had money. I cooked it myself. I was fascinated with shaking up the shit, cooking it, watching it bubble down, you know?

I was like a kid watching magic.

Performing it myself.

Spellbound by the power of turning powder to rock.

You put it on the paper end and—*dink*—it turns into a rock. (180)

After freebasing without interruption for several days in a row, I wasn't able to discern one day from the next. Night and day became shades of gray. Nor did I care about such details as time. But after waking from a short, unrefreshing, troubled sleep I drove into Hollywood, where I entered my bank and demanded all the cash from several large accounts I had there.

My brain was strung out. That morning's smoke-a-thon rekindled my paranoia that people were stealing from me.

I wanted my money.

While I was ineffectually arguing with the bank manager, who explained that he needed prior notice for such a transaction, Jennifer called my house and pleaded with my Aunt Dee to get me help. She'd never seen me so wasted and sickly. When Aunt Dee reassured her that I was fine, Jenny made a beeline out to [my home in] Northridge in order to confront me herself. But the sight of me in the dark, clutching my pipe, told her it was useless.

"I know what I have to do," I mumbled. "I've brought shame to my family. I've hurt you. I've destroyed my career. I know what I have to do."

Shortly after she frustrated herself out the door, Deboragh [former wife] phoned me. We hadn't spoken for almost a year, but she felt compelled to check in and see how I was doing. It was as if she and Jenny, the people who didn't give a damn about my power trips or being cut off, sensed it might be time to say good-bye. They knew it was a scary time.

"You're the only one I trust," I told her. "They're trying to get my money."

"Who is?" she asked.

"It's not fun anymore," I mumbled.

"What's not fun, Richard?"

"I don't think I can get out of here, you know?"

The house was full. From Rashon [bodyguard] to my cousin and Aunt Dee, not to mention the housekeepers and cook, people were doing their thing. They were trained to leave me alone. Oh, Mr. Pryor, he's in his bedroom. They didn't mention that the door was locked. By late afternoon, the only reason to suspect I was present was the continuous smell of acrid smoke and the foreboding vibes that sent into the rest of the house.

Nothing changed as darkness took the heat out of the beautiful spring day. Hovered over my rocks, pipe, cognac, and Bic lighter, I smoked and soared and crashed and smoked again, repeating the deadly cycle over and over again as if I was chain smoking Marlboros. But I didn't allow time even for cigarettes. I'd never felt more paranoid, depressed, or hopeless.

Hopeless.

As if I was drowning.

Voices swirled in my head so that I wasn't able to tell which came from me and which were hallucinations. My conversations became animated, like those crazy people on the street. I heard people who had worked for me talking outside the bedroom window. They were loud, rude, laughing, angry. They made fun of my helplessness. I yelled at them, louder and louder, and still they refused to answer.

"What the fuck are you doing out there?"

As that craziness went on, I continued to smoke until I ran out of cocaine. By then, I was experiencing serious dementia. Stuck in a surreal landscape of constantly shifting emotions. No weight. Floating at the distant end of a tunnel. Miserably alone. Frightened. Voices growing louder, closing in. Wave after wave of depression. Needing to get high. Real high.

No more dope.

Unsure what to do, I panicked.

"God, what do you want me to do?" I cried. "What do you want me to do?"

I didn't wait for a response.

"I'll show you." I said with the giddiness and relief of a certified madman. "I'll show you."

More laughter mixed with tears.

"I'm going to set myself on fire."

Hysteria.

"Then I'll be safe. Yeah, then I'll be okay."

Now here's how I really burned up. Usually, before I go to bed I have a little milk and cookies. One night I had that low-fat milk, that pasteurized shit, and I dipped my cookie in it and the shit blew up. And it scared the shit out of me. Not the blowing up, but the catching on fire.

Imagining relief was nearby, I reached for the cognac bottle on the table in front of me and poured it all over me. Real natural, methodical. As the liquid soiled my body and clothing, I wasn't scared. Neither did I feel inner peace.

I was in a place called There.

Suddenly, my isolation was interrupted by a knock on the door. A bang, really. My cousin opened it and looked inside at the moment I picked up my Bic lighter. I saw him trying to figure out what I was doing.

"Come on in," I said.

He zeroed in on the lighter in my hand.

"Oh no!" he exclaimed.

"Don't be afraid."

Then I flicked it. The lighter didn't work. I tried it again and nothing. Then I did it a third time.

WHOOSH!

I was engulfed in flame.

Have you ever burned up? It's weird. Because you go, "Hey, I'm not in the fireplace. I am the fireplace!" (186–89)

Deep down, I knew the truth. Lying in my hospital bed, I let my mind wander back to the time when I'd asked Redd Foxx why I always wanted more, more, more cocaine, and how he'd looked at my ignorant face and told me it was because I was an addict.

An addict.

I didn't tell anyone.

As if it was a secret. As if it wasn't true.

But who were you fooling, Rich?

Even then you wanted more. (204)

You go through changes in your life and you just fucking change. Something happened in my life just fucking changed my mind about all the shit. I used to think I knew everything, man.

I'd be fucked up and I knew it. I knew all the shit.

And all of a sudden I didn't know shit.

I was one of the dumbest mother fuckers that ever lived. If you catch me on the wrong day and ask me my name, you're gonna get trouble. (206)

Several weeks later Richard got a call from a friend in a rehab. She wanted him to help her in recovery by participating in her therapy. He reluctantly agreed. As he remembers the situation: (207)

One day, caught in the fervor, I stood up and admitted that I, too, was a drug addict and alcoholic. It wasn't anything I didn't already know. Amen. Or hadn't known for years. Sing it brother. But to say it loud, in front of strangers, without adding a punch line, man that was like saying adios to the greatest, funniest character I ever created. My best work, you know. And it scared the hell out of me. (208)

From *Richard Pryor: Here and Now* (Columbia Pictures, 1993)

I stopped drinking.

It's really strange.

I stopped after twenty years. I'll probably die tomorrow.

I got tired of waking up in my car driving 90.

You ever go home drunk, trying to get to your bed, and your house starts moving?

You know you're fucked up when your dog won't come to you!

And where does that breath come from? Did someone just come and shit in your mouth?

I couldn't stop drinking until the bartender would say, "We got no more liquor!"

I went for a job once, and the guy told me I couldn't have it because I wasn't dependable. I told him, "I got a $200-a-day habit. Tell me that ain't dependable."

I can remember when I was just off drugs. I noticed that my dick was a lot smaller than I thought.

I get scared when I'm out on stage sometimes. I want to run. If I had some drugs, I wouldn't give a fuck. But then I come off stage, and I still wouldn't give a fuck. Then, by the time you're fifty, you've had a lot of don't-give-a-fucks. You miss a big part of your life that way.

Before enlightenment, chop wood, carry water.
After enlightenment, chop wood, carry water.

—Zen saying

Malachy McCourt
(writer, actor, entrepreneur)

POOR AS CHURCH MICE were the McCourts of Limerick. Starvation and death all around and sexual molestation by priests were the order of the day. Two brothers, Frank and Malachy, shipped out as soon as they could and struggled to make a better life in America. Malachy worked as a longshoreman and became an actor and saloonkeeper. He owned New York's first singles bar, Malachy's, a hangout frequented by the likes of Richard Harris, Peter O'Toole, Richard Burton, and Grace Kelly. As an actor, he played in a half-dozen movies including *Reversal of Fortune*, *Bonfire of the Vanities*, and *She's the One*. He has also had many television roles, including that of a priest on HBO's prison drama *Oz*. Frank told the story of his boyhood in a book, *Angela's Ashes*, which became a hit movie. At sixty-six, Malachy became a published author with *A Monk Swimming*, an account of his adventures as a young immigrant in New York. This became a best seller and was followed by *Singing My Him Song* in 2002.

Transforming desperate straits and madcap adventures of their real lives into art has been the brothers' stock-in-trade. In several productions of their autobiographical stage play, *A Couple of Blaguards*, Malachy even played himself.

Frank was more the literary brother, Malachy the happy-go-lucky one who lived it up. A regular in the Hamptons bacchanals that were wilder than F. Scott Fitzgerald's by far, he was a gadfly of the sixties-seventies rich at play. Signs of political conscience began to surface, and today he is a political and environmental activist.

Meeting him at his cluttered apartment on the upper west side of Manhattan, I was greeted by his warm and friendly wife, Diana, who explained that Malachy was off getting a haircut and should be home shortly. In the meantime, she told me all about the breakfast they had both just attended that morning to hear new presidential candidate John Kerry and his running mate, John Edwards. The McCourts are heavily involved in politics and freely shared their liberal ideology with me.

Malachy arrived full of energy and spoke to me as if we were old friends, even though this was our first meeting. We began the interview in his cozy den, seated across from each other in two overstuffed chairs. His readily adapted to its occupant's shape almost as if it does so automatically. Books and bookshelves fill three walls, the fourth allowing for a couple of windows that provide nice morning light. Malachy is dressed in a simple, white, long-sleeved shirt rolled up to just below the elbows, and a wrinkled pair of white linen trousers. Add the shock of uncombed white hair, which contrasts nicely with his bright red Irish complexion, and you have the basic picture.

As we begin the interview, I sense that even though Malachy has told his story countless times, he still enjoys retelling it for my benefit.

There was always an acceptance in Irish society of drinking alcohol and drinking to excess. Brendan Behan said, "To get enough to eat was an accomplishment, but to get drunk was a victory." Getting food was grubbing, but getting alcohol, not just stout or port or beer, but getting whiskey . . . you made it! Under the cover then of drinking, all sorts of terrible things were done to people: assaults, violence, murder, assaults on women, and the most horrendous of all, abuse of children, both sexual and otherwise.

If you looked at any of the Irish newspapers, the defense lawyers, or solicitors as they are called, would say, "The way it is, Your Honor, my client had the drink taken." . . . "Ah, was that the way it was? So the poor man must not have known what he did." I remember one case, it struck me so forcibly, they're having these traveling people in Ireland called tinkers, and they had animals that would wander grazing. They never fed them, so their horses and donkeys or mules were all over the place. I remember one of them; he got six months in jail for letting his horses roam. Another fellow had raped a young girl and he got off 'cause he had the drink taken and didn't know what he was doing. So with that sort of a background, I looked on alcohol as something to aspire to. That you would grow up and be able to drink like the men.

And the men, of course, congregated in pubs, and the women had snugs, little areas in the pub that were walled off, like the Taliban does. Like little speakeasies with sliding doors. They looked like a confessional.

A lot of people didn't drink and a lot of people drank moderately. They would have one or two pints and that was it, but the disease of alcoholism is always after people.

One day my friend and I, at the age of eleven, talked about getting drunk. He said, "Let's do it," and I said, "Fine, but where are we going to get the money?" And he said, "I know where my brother keeps some money, some savings." So he stole it. We went to a pub and we ordered some cider first, and we got drunk. That was the first one. And I found it to be absolutely exhilarating. I had never felt like that. Coming out of poverty—there are a couple of things that accompany poverty just like those that accompany alcoholism. The sense of shame. You're ashamed of being poor. As an alcoholic, you're ashamed of what you did and what you are. So it was the business of escaping, always escaping what we are. Shame takes care of the past, and all fear is future based. Fear is always in the future. In our own heads we project what is going to happen, and it almost never does. It's like coming attractions, but my God doesn't make coming attractions. I do, because God is far too busy.

My friend Father Michael Judge, who was killed on 9/11, was a recovering man too. A decent, terrific man. I was moaning to him about what was going to happen to me. "My life was coming to an end," I thought. I couldn't make any money. My career was in the dumps and I was depressed and all of that. Things were not going well. And he said to me, not once but several times, "My God does not deal with the future, and I don't think yours does either. You see, God is extremely busy dealing with today, and consequently he has not yet made tomorrow. That's the future. Nor has he made next week, next year, or any time, really. As infinitely all-powerful and infallible as God is, as much as God knows, he has not yet made tomorrow. He does not know what's going to happen, so who the fuck do you think you are?"

And when you think about it, it's quite logical. So anyway, back to my drinking . . . I didn't drink again as a youngster 'cause I took a pledge at my confirmation, and I didn't drink again until I came to America at the age of twenty. People here said to me, "Oh, you must drink a lot. You're Irish." And I said, "Sure I do!" but I didn't. What a people pleaser! So I started to drink.

I had no education, so I was always ashamed of that. I left school at thirteen, but I was always a good reader. I loved reading and still do, and that saved my arse. I faked my way about my education so I would speak knowledgably or eloquently. I could recite a list of poetry and they would think, "He's educated," but it was still bullshit.

Through a series of events I got myself hired as an actor, though I was only a dockworker and dishwasher. And then a friend of mine, Tom O'Malley, who died of this disease, Tom got me on *The Tonight Show* 'cause he booked the show. So I got famous for about fifteen minutes. Then somebody offered to back me in a bar, so we opened Malachy's, and it became a very famous singles bar. I was just having the grandest time, drinking and carousing. There were lots of young, nubile women who were willing to share my bed, and I was not at all discriminating. Then I met this young woman who said, "We should get married," and I said, "Oh yeah, we should do that."

Then after three months, we discovered she was pregnant and we had a baby. Then a short time later, we had another baby. And I'm still drinking, and she's getting annoyed because she can't go out. She's got to take care of the babies. So she dumped me, much to my astonishment. As I said before, everybody loves me. But she said, "I don't!" That was it and it drove me nuts.

But I kept drinking, and I was still trying to win her back. Crazy, crazy drunkenness, belligerent and threatening. I never, ever hit her though. Never violent, just a threatening, nasty person. Here's the thing. Here I was doing exactly as my father had done. My father had deserted us. Although I was here physically, I wasn't here. I wasn't a father to those children. I was this sort of lunatic whirlwind. I amused them a lot, but I was not a caring father. I always said I wasn't like my father. My father took off. This is the alcoholic denial thing. What I *don't* do. I'm not like . . . I don't drink gin, I don't mix my drinks, I don't drink before five o'clock, and I never do this or that. And it's all bullshit you see, which we are. Bullshitters. And that, of course, is the denial. I *don't* do . . .

So here you have me, the Great Egyptian, living on denial!

I had one saloon and then another and another. My fourth saloon was called Himself. Richard Harris, who was from Limerick, the same town as me, was always coming to see me when he was in town. One time we were drinking and Richard said, "I'm fed up with all this Hollywood shit, and I'd like to work for you." And I said, "I already have a full staff." He said, "You don't have to pay me." So anyway, he got behind the bar and started pouring drinks. He didn't know a damn thing about bartending, but he would pour and pour. One day these two little old ladies came up to me and said, "You have the nicest bartender. He gave us a bottle of Dom Perignon champagne and didn't charge us. He's so nice." I said, "He sure is." I couldn't naysay anything Richard did because people were flocking in to see him. After a couple of weeks, Richard decided "bartending is not for me" and packed it in. He left and off he went. He was heading back to London, so I saw him off at the airport. I then went back to the bar, and my other barman says to me, "Here, Richard left this note for you." So I open up the envelope and inside is a check to cover everything he had given away during those weeks.

After my wife and children left me, it was all downhill. It was like watching the whirlpools: slow at the top, then sucked into this hell of despair of hopelessness. As a retired Catholic, I recognize only one sin: the sin of despair. No hope and no forgiveness. That's a thing about alcoholism, you see. "No one will forgive me." The fact is, I continued to drink. I met Diana. She was a bright light that came into my life. And through this agony of this awful disease, I saw Diana's face and the beauty of her soul, and I thank my God for that.

It didn't stop me drinking though. For the next nineteen years or so, I was not the most faithful of husbands or partners. We got married. She had one child and I had two. Her little girl was retarded, and that got me very involved in the movement for the retarded. And that, for once, got me out of myself and out of my own selfishness and self-centeredness. I still drank but, at the same time, got involved in doing some kind of good, you see. For me, the good finally started encroaching on my soul; it sealed the evil within me. Evil goes when the light comes upon it. At the same time, my disease was being forced out into the light and I began to see what it was.

I traveled to Ireland with my brother Frank to do a show there. I was very angry at that place because of the horrible way we were treated as children. The humiliation my mother suffered over there. Being on welfare. The deaths of three children. The deaths of eleven classmates. Constant sickness and death. Fear and this rigid Catholic society. God was always threatening to beat the shit out of you. It was always sin, sin, sin. Never to talk about a loving God. You were told that if you were very good you'd get something at Christmas, so you assumed you were bad. There was never any credit for trying! No acknowledgment that you were essentially a good kid, a decent kind of a little fellow. So what you did was take refuge in booze.

When I came back from Ireland, I went to a doctor because I was feeling sick. Physically ill and mentally ill. He said, "You're drinking too much, you're smoking too much, and you're eating too much." So I asked this physician, who's a friend of mine, would he give me some medicine for those conditions? He said, "I'll give you medicine. I'll give you a boot in the arse. Now get out of here 'cause you know what to do." And I said, "Yes, I know what to do." And I knew. I knew what to do. I knew about the Twelve Steps. God knows I had recommended them often to other people. I didn't need them, but I knew people that did.

So here's the odd and embarrassing thing about getting into recovery. I said to myself that drinking was no problem and smoking, well, I can't stop smoking till I stop drinking, but the real problem is that if I stop smoking and drinking, I'll start eating way too much. So the eating is the problem. Somebody said to me that there is a program for overeaters, and I said, "What do they do, give you diets?" And he said, "Why don't you try it and find out?" So I did, thinking this would solve all my problems. I wound up listening to people talking about the toxic and fatal effects of chocolate chip ice cream and lemon meringue pie. While in the room, I started substituting the word "alcohol" for "food." So I just figured that my God has a peculiar sense of humor. It wasn't long before I said, "Fuck this, I'm an alcoholic. I'm also a food addict and a nicotine addict and I have other addictions: being judgmental and a finger-pointing asshole." And I said, "Yeah, go to an alcohol recovery program, jerk-off." And I did.

At first it was terrible. I was also a debtor, horrendously in debt. I had borrowed over $200,000, which I couldn't possibly ever pay back. At this recovery meeting they said to me, "Keep coming back." I told Diana that I would stop borrowing and try to get some kind of work that would keep us afloat. No matter what kind of work it was. But somebody offered me a large sum of money, a loan, and I took it and didn't tell Diana. Then we split up for a while. I was living out in Queens here in New York, living on somebody's floor. I couldn't get any work, so I ended up on welfare. So here I am at the age of fifty-four going into welfare, like my mother used to do. Something I said I'd never do in my whole life. That's where I learned the difference between humiliation and humility. I said, "I'm not being humiliated. I'm learning to acquire humility." That's what it was. I did it with my heart, mind, and brain. I had been a fairly successful actor and a fairly successful saloonkeeper, and I used to have quite a bit of money, and I was recognized by some people in the welfare office from being on a soap opera. . . . That caused a bit of a stir in the welfare office. Here I am signing for welfare and signing autographs. A most bizarre situation. They were so nice to me there. They were mostly black folks, and they kept saying, "You'll be okay. We have seen people like you who have taken a hit, and we know you'll be fine." They were very sweet and nice. I thought they would stomp on my head and say, "Yeah, look at you, you big deal asshole." But they didn't at all.

So I kept in touch with Diana over that period and learned how to say, "I'm sorry. I'm sorry for what I said and for what I did, and will try not to do that again." And I said to her, "Would you see me again?" And she said, "Yes, but I don't sleep with men on the first date." So we started seeing each other, and I was able to say that due to this recovering program I'm on a path, and hope to stay on it. A day at a time I don't drink. A day at a time I go to a meeting. A day at a time I stretch out my hand to help another alcoholic. A day at a time I try to remember those I injured and make an amend. Making amends isn't always about forgiveness. Some people have told me, "What you did is unforgivable." And I say to them, "If you don't forgive me, I will be your burden. You think of me with anger, which means I have the power to make you angry. You shouldn't give me that power."

Sometimes my God pisses me off and I say, "What the fuck are you doing to me?" You know God always answers your prayers, and many times the answer is "No, asshole!" Then you find out it wouldn't have been good for you anyway.

In recovery I have laughed and cried. I have buried friends, 'cause there's no guarantee that they're not going to die. I've suffered prostate cancer. I've suffered heart disease. I've suffered very, very deep depression, and I've seen some pretty horrible things, but a day at a time it is certainly better than it is bad. Because I don't think of myself as bad anymore. I'm not too bad at all, as a matter of fact! So life gets better. I tell Diana every day that I love her, no matter where I am. I like using the word "love," you see. Like when you use the word "hate." People use the word "hate" all the time. I said to Diana one time—we were watching the first President Bush on television, and he said he hated broccoli—I said, "He won't get re-elected." And he didn't, 'cause you can't use that word. "Hate" and "hatred" are two words not in my lexicon. It's amazing, you can use the words "kill" and "hate" on television, but you can't say "fuck," which could connote the sexual act of love. If you're doing it right! But anyway, that's another matter.

The change in my life has been remarkable. There's been so much laughter. Not jokes either. It has to do with absurdity. The appreciation of words and observing. I used to think that all life took place in these shoe-boxes we call saloons. I didn't drink much at home, but wherever I did drink, I could not just stop. I never said, "I need a drink." I always said, "I want a drink. *I want it.*" I didn't need it. Nobody does.

So now I'm in love with life. I've had some health things, but I'm able to handle them. Like recently I went for a physical. Part of it was a colonoscopy. All of a sudden my heart began to race, like Indianapolis: *boom, boom, boom, boom, boom.* And they couldn't do the procedure. It was up to 150 beats a minute. So they sent me to emergency, where they try to stabilize it and all that. Finally they gave me these defibrillators—*ba-boom, ba-boom*—to get my heart back to a normal rhythm. They thought I was going to have a heart attack. I could hear them talk. They told me that maybe because of the preparation for the exam, I drained myself of these various nutrients that the heart needs, like electrolytes and stuff like that. So I'm lying on the gurney and this very serious young doctor is listening to my heart go *biddy-beep, biddy-bump,* and I said to the doctor, "Do you sing?" He said, "No." And I said, "You really should sing." Trying to get a smile out of the guy, but he was deadly serious. I said, "Everybody should sing." And he said, "Well, I don't." So I turned to Diana and said, "This is what comes from not paying your electrolyte bill!" I got him, I made him laugh. I just thought, "Isn't this absurd? Here I am on the verge of a fuckin' heart attack, and I'm telling jokes to make a doctor laugh."

So life is fun and sometimes sad. I go to funerals and all of that, but for now, I'm staying on the right side of the grass. As an alcoholic I was a liar, a swindler, a thief, a deceiver, and just about anything else that a person can become when his defects are allowed to run wild. Getting sober did not mean I suddenly became a haloed saint, or all the defects took a hike into the wilderness, never to be seen again. Not bloody likely! You can take the brandy out of a fruitcake, but you still have a fruitcake. Getting sober has allowed me to work on those defects and bit by bit get better. It's fairly clear to me now that if I stay clean and sober, I've got a good chance of acting right and having a peaceful day, and then tomorrow, if there is one, I won't have to lie about what I did the day before.

A Benedictine monk named Father Basil once told me there's another life after this one, and when I reach it, the only question the deity will ask me is "Did you have a good time?" While I'm in no hurry to get there, I'm ready with a "Yes, I did, thank you very much. I particularly like those parts towards the end."

It seems to me that this world
is beginning to pick up speed
and is hurtling past me so quickly
that it is on the point of disappearing.
But no I tell myself, it is I
who am picking up speed and am
almost on the point of disappearing.
This is one of those basic illusions,
e.g. the sun rising and setting,
that dizzy you when you try to dispel them
or lead you to punishing truths.

—Harvey Shapiro, "It Seems to Me"

There is a rhinoceros
in this poem. It is stamping
around, trampling things. In
this poem, it is crazed. These
things happen only in
poetry, you know. No
such beast exists
in reality.

—Richard Morris, "The Rhinoceros"

Chuck Negron
(musician)

CHUCK NEGRON WAS the long-haired, mustached lead singer on the Three Dog Night superhits "Joy to the World," "Old Fashioned Love Song," "Easy to Be Hard," "Pieces of April," and many others. His band had twenty-one consecutive *Billboard* Top 40 hits between 1969 and 1975. The song "Joy to the World" alone sold 12 million copies. In 1972, *Rolling Stone* magazine's cover story called Three Dog Night "the top of the rock & roll heap," with "more gold," "bigger crowds," and "fatter purses" than any other rock band. Other people may have dreamed about a life of sex, drugs, and rock and roll; Chuck Negron lived it.

Chuck was a multimillionaire by age thirty—talented, rich, and famous. A few years later, he was living in a corrugated cardboard box on Fifth Street on L.A.'s raunchy skid row. I thought I was the king of reckless drug use who could handle more drugs than anybody. Then Chuck became my client.

Handling public relations for Three Dog Night was a dream gig. I was getting paid big money to hang with one of the hottest groups in the world. Almost every kid in America had a TDN record, and almost every publication wanted to tell the group's story. TDN was the first rock-and-roll band in America to play large stadiums, with the exception of The Beatles, who had appeared at Shea Stadium in New York and Candlestick Park in San Francisco on their U.S. tour in 1966. Promoters had been afraid that a rock-and-roll act wouldn't fill the seats. TDN's management promised that if a promoter took a loss, the band would make up for it with another concert.

During the summer of 1970, a series of twenty-two summer concerts were booked at outdoor stadiums across the country, where TDN performed in front of audiences numbering in the tens of thousands each night. The massive undertaking included large video screens behind the stage that projected images of the band members as they performed. This technology, new at the time, is still prevalent at large rock concerts. Deals were negotiated whereby the promoter had to pay for limousines, food, and other perks. This too was a new concept, and it blazed the trail for other rock acts.

At home and off the road, the members of TDN needed a place to feel like regular people. So to relax, Chuck hung out at the infamous Rainbow Bar & Grill on the famed Sunset Strip. The Rainbow was built to accommodate people like us. I was one of the original owners. There was a sense of a new rock community brewing. Musicians could feel isolated and separate in the outside world, but here they hung out with other rock stars. It wasn't about the food, which was mediocre at best. The booze poured freely. The sweet odor of marijuana filled the air, and cocaine was snorted at semiprivate booths. People got high and weren't bothered. The waitresses wore jeans and funky tops. Wall Street guys, movie moguls, and bankers had their special restaurants—this was our place.

The six-block-long Sunset Strip is located in West Hollywood, a separate incorporated city within Los Angeles. It has its own sheriff's department. In the old days, unlike the Los Angeles police force, which was known to be among the strongest in the nation—a no-nonsense, incorruptible, hit-first-ask-questions-later outfit—the West Hollywood sheriff's department at that time was a more "reasonable" group. Thanks to good relationships, no one would complain of fights or if the sex and drugs got out of hand. We could pour after hours and indulge in our pleasures.

The place was homey, paneled in dark wood with lots of big, leafy plants and large, stained-glass windows. Rock music pulsed throughout. Upstairs was Over the Rainbow, a private club where we continued the party after hours. An office the size of a phone booth had holes drilled in a wall separating it from the ladies' room. A piranha swam in a large tank over the bar. We fed it 250 goldfish a month. You could flip them into the water from your seat at the bar.

Just about every touring rock star came to the Rainbow. If the Rolling Stones, Elton John, or The Who were in L.A., they would go to the Rainbow. It was also the haunt for hip stars like Jack Nicholson and Dennis Hopper. They could be themselves, undisturbed by the "squares" or reporters. The Rainbow's character combined sophistication with silliness. And it gave us seven owners great cachet. I could get you a table at the Rainbow or entertain you at my table. I eventually got tired of the business—being called by everyone I knew with requests for tables or other considerations—so I sold my interest. The scene has changed, but the Rainbow is presumably still a gold mine. This was one of the places where I often saw Chuck. As TDN's PR guy, I sometimes traveled on their private jet as they went from city and arena to city and arena and gave concerts to audiences of phenomenal and unprecedented size. The tours were completely hedonistic. One of their managers would hire groupies, contracted as one-day flight stewardesses, for the entertainment of the stars and their entourage. Chuck and I also shared drug dealers and sometimes saw each other at various dens of iniquity and party palaces.

A year or so after I got sober, I started seeing Chuck on the edges of recovery, making halfhearted tries in what seemed like a record number of rehabs until he got a grasp on his life. We decided on the Rainbow for a meeting place, and based on our conversations, here are some of Chuck's reflections and memories.

Unlike The Doors and the Rolling Stones, who had bad-boy images, Three Dog Night was perceived as All-American boys. It was ironic because we messed with every drug known to mankind.

I started singing in the fifties when rock and roll started. I made my first record in 1958 and then made another in 1959 with a group I formed called The Rondells, and it got some airplay in L.A. and New York. We got to play the Apollo, which was a big deal back then.

My life was beginning to work itself out. I got an athletic scholarship in 1961, and at this time, I still didn't drink or use. I went to college on a basketball scholarship. It was one of the best times of my life. I made records my first, second, and third year in college. Columbia Records then signed me, and one thing led to another, and I ended up leaving college to give this music thing a shot. The record company wanted me to be involved in the L.A. scene, so they took me to premieres and things. One of their producers took me to a party, and I walked in, and it was like being in another world. I had short hair and was very well groomed—I'm sure all these people thought I was a narc. They were all hippies—beautiful young people—women, guys. It was wonderful. Frank Zappa and The Mothers of Invention were playing. There were all sorts of drugs around, which I noticed, but it wasn't my thing.

It was such an exciting, glamorous setting that when the drugs came around—stuff I'd turned down for years 'cause it was not like me, I was a world-class athlete and so forth, the kids in the neighborhood in New York City did it—I didn't want any part of it.

The interesting thing was I had been talking about the stuff I had heard my friends talk about. They were doing Romilar cough syrup, so I boasted it was really a good high, although I never did it. Even if my friends had asked me, I'd think, "Why would I do that? I don't have a cold." It wasn't actually the Romilar cough syrup that they sold over-the-counter. It was a behind-the-counter pharmaceutical they had to special order.

I made a decision in a heartbeat that I was going to do something with total naiveté, with no sense that this could be a problem, because these new people were so cool and they seemed to know what was going on. I was at a table upstairs in the Rainbow one night, and two tall, gorgeous girls were selling Quaaludes and I bought them all. They invited me to a party in the Hollywood Hills. So I got loaded. I started fooling around, and a girl came over and kissed me and dropped something in my mouth, and it ended up being a combination of peyote and LSD. Apparently I was standing near a glass-topped table in the living room, and passed out, and fell face-first onto the table, because the next morning I woke up with my face ripped up and blood all over the couch. I became the guest from hell, and I was on my way.

From that time on, I got high just about every day, unless I was sleeping or arrested. Boom! I was just an accident waiting to happen. I started with Romilar and had done most of the other stuff, but heroin became my love. It had been offered to me countless times and I had refused, but one time I said yes. I loved it! I'd never felt anything comparable to that first heroin rush. All the emptiness and fear inside vanished. Everything seemed fine. Even throwing up felt good. Soon I was devoting my life to heroin. I stayed faithful to it for ten years, seven months, and two weeks. I didn't care about anything or anybody. I just wanted my dope.

Soon we were touring, and life was unbelievable. I remember that sex at this time was wild, and so were the women. Our first real orgy came on tour in Tulsa in 1969. B. J. Thomas was in the Top 10 with his song "Hooked on a Feeling." He was our opening act. After the concert, we went to a club filled with guys with crew cuts and cowboy hats. We got drunk and were carrying on. Eventually B. J. Thomas, guys from Vanilla Fudge, and Three Dog Night got up on stage to jam with the house band. The girls were staring at us, and those country guys were mad as hell to have us take over their territory. The evening progressed to our wing at the Holiday Inn. There was sex going on in the hallway, in the bathtubs, and on the floor, everybody switching partners. It was gruesome and unreal. It was rock and roll!

I started out as a shy kid. Now I'd have sex several times a day with different women. It seemed like every time I looked around, they were there. I even worked out a system to handle the overflow. I would book a suite with a couple of bedrooms. I'd have sex with a girl in one bedroom, then another. By the time I finished with her, a third one would be waiting in the first bedroom. Sex became a meaningless game, but it was all incredible fun.

Often I'd leave the stage after our encore while the audience was still chanting our names. Shortly I'd be back in the hotel with nothing but dead silence. It was spooky. Sometimes I promised myself I wouldn't go out and party. I'd stay in the room, eat, maybe watch a little TV, and go to sleep by myself. Soon I'd hear women in the hallway, and I'd inevitably check it out—more good-looking girls who'd pour into my hotel room, take off their clothes, and be ready to party.

I see my addiction as a forest fire that burned through everything in its path and left only charred remains. That's a curious thing about addiction and the consequences. Some people get to walk away; they're just not predisposed. Most of the people who were in our group were using drugs, although several moved on and didn't have a problem. But it just filled me up with a wonderful feeling of warmth that I knew I was going to do this. This was having a youth, a childhood that I never had. As a child, I spent time in an orphanage and it was tough. That drugs filled me up and was wonderful was an experience that little by little consumed more of my day and my time. And the next thing you know, by a casual progression, that was all our focus for the day: getting high, going to a party, getting high, going to a party, getting high, getting high . . .

I always loved the chance to perform and create music, from the very first, when we—Danny Hutton, Cory Wells, and I—got together. We were really very lucky young guys. We kind of tweaked the interest of Brian Wilson of The Beach Boys, and he wanted to make us the first act that he produced on Brother Records, and we go in, and he writes two songs for us. Brian brings in the L.A. Philharmonic Orchestra. Huge tracks, and he's going to make it happen. And we'll be on our way. Unfortunately, the other brothers were feeling Brian was moving away from them. Doing his projects. It put in a lot of fear, and they really kind of bullied him into coming back to the fold and doing their thing. So it didn't work out.

We moved on, and about a year later, we had put our own band together. And all this time Danny and I are hanging, doing drugs recreationally. It was basically downers and some psychedelics and pot. I had found two trees in my yard. They were about six feet tall and had already fallen over. There was a female and a male plant of marijuana. I gave it away as Christmas presents. I gave kilos of marijuana away to about twenty people—that's how much this female tree produced. I smoked pot until I couldn't smoke any more pot, because I was getting paranoid. I was standing in the line of a movie theater once, and the next thing I know I was in the front, and the ticket seller said, "Can I help you?" and I said to her, "Whaat, whaat?" It had been so long I walked away, and the girl I was with said, "Why did you wait in line so long if you weren't going to the movie?" and I said, "I don't know, bad vibes or something." So I gave all my pot away because I realized it wasn't making me into who I wanted to be.

So anyway, I now have this manager, and he wants me to be a movie actor. He wants me to change my name to Charles Overon, so I'd have a Latin name. I tried to tell him Negron *is* Latin. So Danny, Cory, and I go to my manager. He wants the band. He puts a ton of money into us, and we get ourselves a record deal with ABC Dunhill, whose big act is Steppenwolf. They are also managed by my manager. So we became Three Dog Night, and recorded our first album, and went out on the road. From our very first show until the end in around 1975, we never did a show that wasn't frantic, standing ovations, and drove the audience nuts. There was something wonderful about the seven of us that captured the hearts and souls of young America. We turned 'em loose. I remember how once in Japan the promoter told us, "The audience will love you, but you won't feel it like in America, because they are very polite." We took it as a challenge, and we got them crazy, and they were frantic. There was something momentous about being able to excite people in that way with our music. It was something I had never experienced. I was a shy guy, a New Yorker whose concept of "cool" was very laid back, very subtle, so it was foreign for me to be the way I was on stage.

The drug element was always there, but when we went on stage, we were pretty together because the drugs hadn't consumed my life yet. Then, all of a sudden, we crossed this line where cocaine took over. I broke my nose in Germany. I hit a glass extension in the dressing room and shattered my nose. You could actually see my sinuses. It was very bad. So anyway, cocaine was introduced to us, lots of cocaine. Everyone in the band used cocaine except Cory. Cory was a different kind of guy. He had a family:

two daughters. We were all bachelors. So I exclude Cory when it comes to drug talk, because he really didn't participate.

So we were out there, getting a reputation of "don't follow this band." We go to the Miami Pop Festival and the Denver Pop Festival. Jim Hendrix headlining. Joe Cocker. Everyone who was anyone was there. All of a sudden we're getting bumped to go on later and later, and we found out that the other acts didn't want to go on after us. Of course Hendrix didn't care! Then we had our first hit record, "One," and it all started to change.

Money came into the picture. Mercedes-Benzes and big homes. The other guys had these things long before I did. I was busy working in the studio, and I still played basketball with my buddies. I had a full life. So one day our photographer showed up in a Mercedes to take some group pictures. He bought it with all the money he was making off of us. He said, "You ought to drive this, Chuck." And I did and said, "Oh, man." I was still driving a Volkswagen. So anyway, I went and bought three Mercedes.

The reason I bought three was that the salesman was rude to me. I found out years later from the same guy that "The reason I didn't help you was because you pulled up in an old beat-up Volkswagen, and you parked in the *bus stop*. You were in a bus stop, Chuck, and you got out of your car wearing cutoffs and a tank top, and you looked like you couldn't see. I wasn't being rude to you; I was afraid of you!" So I showed them; I bought three!

The drugs hadn't really hurt me yet except in my relationships. After seeing each other for a while, Paula and I got married in 1970 and had a baby, but she just couldn't take it anymore. On our honeymoon, I was stoned and fell asleep. Paula spent her honeymoon abandoned in a Palm Springs hotel suite. When I woke up, I got high and cheated on her. Then she thought I was going to kill myself or hurt the baby. And I'm totally oblivious to this. She ended up having an affair with one of our road managers, and she leaves me.

My next wife, Julia, and I started our marriage with a heroin honeymoon in 1976. We turned into recluses and had all our food delivered from Greenblatt's Delicatessen on Sunset Boulevard. Our day consisted of scoring heroin from dealers, going to the bank for more cash, and snorting until it knocked us out. It took me years to understand that if you're going to be with someone, it's give-and-take, a two-way street. I was being a young rock star and not being faithful. That marriage ended. Secretly I was scared. I felt alone and beyond help.

Drugs led to all kinds of problems. Some dealers once shot through the walls of my house in Los Angeles when I was inside. They wanted me to pay my drug debts. I remember terrible fights—one with Janis Joplin where I called her an ugly slut. She was a nice, sweet person and was one of many musicians I knew who died defeated, tortured deaths.

I don't know why I stayed alive. I used dirty needles. Four people were beaten to death with baseball bats at an upscale heroin shooting gallery in Laurel Canyon. Centering on porn-film legend John Holmes it became known as the Wonderland Murders. The carnage happened in the very place I was spending most of my evenings at the time—except that murderous one. Once I almost drove my whole family into the canyon as we headed down Mulholland Drive in our little red Volkswagen. I had popped some downers before we left home and blacked out. At the last minute, Julia slammed on the brakes. I almost bled to death after demolishing my car on a Sunset Boulevard streetlamp. I cracked my head open, collapsed a lung, and mangled my body. The firefighters had to cut me out from that automobile.

With musicians I knew toppling like ten pins, death was very close up, and I thought about suicide and attempted it as well. Once I hung myself with a belt in the closet of a shabby motel room, only a rusty overhead pipe collapsed and saved me. Another time I walked directly in front of a moving bus on purpose. Compared to facing my probation officer with another dirty drug test, it seemed like a good alternative. I overdosed routinely. Other druggies had to beat me back to life after one overdose, subsequent to which my body was black-and-blue from the neck down.

One time I remember I went to see my business manager, who had connections with some doctors. When I walked in, I didn't even realize it, but I weighed 142 pounds—and I'm well over six feet tall. He took me directly to this therapist, this high-end guy in Beverly Hills, who said, "Hey, we're putting him in the hospital, a lockdown nut ward." I was falling apart!

The wear and tear of the drugs and the emotional give-and-take was getting to me. I was feeling all the feelings, but I wasn't caring. Kind of a drug-induced depression. I felt my feelings but my response was "I don't give a shit."

When I started seeing the people that were in the hospital with me, that really had problems—young people my age, old people who had real mental problems—I had a moment of clarity and said, "This isn't the way to live, Chuck. Straighten yourself out." My father came to pick me up and said, "I want you to live with me," which I did. Paula had taken all the cars, so I went and bought another Mercedes.

Now I started going out every night. I really wasn't a club guy, but I became one. The Rainbow, the Roxy—I became one of those guys. I found that I drank more than normal guys, so I was drunk every night. I started getting arrested. The police were actually quite nice to me. I became the town drunk, but the town was Los Angeles! They'd see me pull out of the Rainbow and they'd have a cop right there. The cop would say, "Chuck"—he'd know my name—"don't turn left, go right." And I'd turn left, and they'd take me in.

Eventually I lost everything and ended up living in a cardboard box near skid row in L.A., shunned and a goner. When I was forty-nine, I was cornered by circumstance. I needed a way to be sprung from jail, and all the rehabs refused me. My only option was another detox. Dr. Michael Myers, who had detoxed me many times, devised a new plan. "Forget detoxing," he said. He said I needed long-term care, and he got me into a last-chance drug rehab facility called Cri-Help in North Hollywood. I didn't believe I could quit. The desire to die and end it ate away at my soul.

I needed a supportive friend and found one in Mike Finnigan, who had been a professional musician his entire life, having done studio work with Jimi Hendrix, Rod Stewart, and many others. He toured with Crosby, Stills & Nash for twenty years. A recovering alcoholic himself, Mike came to visit me often at Cri-Help. I told him I couldn't take my life anymore and asked him what I should do.

His advice was simple: "Chuck, I've never seen anyone but God help a junkie like you. Maybe you should try prayer."

A few days after he said that, I got down on my knees in my room. What I prayed was for God to either let me die or to give me one minute of peace from the obsession and sickness that was tearing me apart body and soul. That's when the agony broke inside me. I was able to get a good night's sleep for the first time after weeks of sheer misery, and when I woke up, I knew I had been given a gift. I had a chance, some window had opened, because I felt willing to go through that day before me. I surrendered my soul. I remember the clear thought I had: "If I am so willing to die, why not be willing to live?"

Once I surrendered, I was so drained I couldn't lift myself off the bed. Yet I felt free from all the fear, anger, and rage that had beset me. I saw that the demons chasing me were nothing compared to the heroin hell I had chosen for more than twenty years. I went from feeling weak, desperate, and dying to saved. That's the only way I can explain the beginning of what was for me a miracle. I got a fresh start on life. It was an epiphany, and it was set in motion by the act of prayer.

I try to help others overcome their habits today. After receiving the gift of sobriety, I want to share it with others. I wanted to share it with Mark, who had lived with me in an abandoned building. I helped get him cleaned up and found him a billeting at a recovery center in L.A. He lasted five months before he went back to jail on a heroin possession charge. I know that even a few years clean and sober at the end would be better than a die-hard junkie could imagine. It can be that way for Mark and others like him. I think of Mark as me. I cannot give up on any addict, because I know you can make it if you are willing to go the distance. It may sound simple-minded, but if you are willing to change everything, everything changes. That reality has penetrated my soul.

Now I spend much of my time working with recovery programs. I also perform at ten benefits a year to raise money for recovery and sober-living houses. Sometimes a rock-and-roll manager offers to pay me to go out on the road and watch over a druggie singer. Most of the time I try to help but don't want to be paid. Helping others who suffer from this terrible disease is my favorite work. I'm not a Holy Roller or selling anything. I'm on a spiritual quest to be the best person I can be, knowing that peace in this life will come to me as I strive towards that goal.

As someone who had a lifetime of abuse, I can only see my success with my struggle today as a long, long process. Considering how long I used drugs, you could say I am a recovery baby. I've taken ugly shortcuts and wrong paths so much in my life that it's a fight to keep the proper focus. I still need treatment on a daily basis.

To be in recovery is to participate in a living miracle. Rarely does anyone address the fact that addicts really pay the consequences of their actions. We are often dismissed for having made a choice to do something bad. And we are not asking you to forget what we did or for a break. We change our whole lives—from top to bottom—more than most people do or even consider. I think addicts are taking more abuse than anyone could wreak on them for their mistakes—I'm thinking of people who claim that alcoholics get off easy in the moral dilemma by crying, *"Mea culpa."* I would like to silence these people and get them to see the facts, because the alcoholic or drug addict does pay a huge price.

It was one of those midsummer Sundays when everyone sits around saying, "I drank too much last night." You might have heard it whispered by the parishioners leaving church . . . heard it from the golf links and the tennis courts, heard it from the wildlife preserve where the leader of the Audubon group was suffering from a terrible hangover. "I drank too much," said Donald Westerhazy. "We all drank too much," said Lucinda Merrill. "It must have been the wine," said Helen Westerhazy. "I drank too much of that claret."

—John Cheever, "The Swimmer"

Mariette Hartley
(actor)

ABOVE ALL, I ADMIRE Mariette Hartley for her bracing, forthright honesty. This fine actress has had the courage to face in her life the anguish of an unhappy background. Mariette has spoken out so eloquently in her writing, to recovery groups, and in prisons. She talks about how she went from dark to light. How she overcame the tyranny of outward appearances that whipped a girl into shape, requiring of her impassiveness, restraint, and "the stiff upper lip."

She has told and shown others who have been abused that when the child and creative self are crimped and crippled by an environment, it is possible as an adult to widen one's circumference and regenerate fully. Mariette is known to many for helping reclaim individuals who are abused as well as addicted—reclaim them from placidity and despair.

Although I interviewed Mariette in Los Angeles where she lives, this lovely woman's formation was in New England, where harsh winters and lush summers epitomize the life cycle. An old regional term is "to hive away," meaning to close the shutters on the outside world and to recede into self. The feminist literary critic Tillie Olsen wrote about the silences, harmful, anguished ones to which creative women have been especially prone: "The unnatural thwarting of what struggles to come into being but cannot."

Mariette has struggled with the silence of extreme denial, and is!

I come from a highly creative community: Westport/Weston, Connecticut, before it was gentrified and made fancy. Before Banana Republic . . . B.B.R.! I grew up in the forties. It was a very artistic, hard-drinking, alcoholic community. I didn't know of many families that didn't drink, and those that didn't were boring, so I never wanted to go over to their houses. Drinking was a desirable life-style that books, movies, and advertising romanticized. Getting blotto on the 5:31 [commuter train] was the source of myriad *New Yorker* cartoons.

I was kind of a typical kid living in the waters of extraordinary dysfunction without being aware of it until much later on. It's like being a fish and being used to where you're living. Until you jump out of the tank, you don't really get to look at how muddy the water is. I have a brother, a wonderful brother, Tony, fifteen months younger than me, and I had two parents who fell down a lot. Martinis were the thing, and my father was caught in the morass of that. Absolutely stuck.

In those days, that's what everybody did. They drank their lunches, and you'd sober up if you could in the club car coming back home. Dad's drinking began a slow but steady escalation when he began the Westport–New York commute around 1946. As I look back on it, I guess Dad was pretty high every time he came home from the city. Advertising men were not only famed for their martini lunch, they were also notorious for infiltrating the bar on the 5:31, the commuter special, the traveling cocktail lounge. And we would come and meet my father singing "here come my Daddy now" in our little Dr. Dentons, in the old Buick. It was like missing two people, because Mother by this time would have started drinking. She was a buddy drinker. And of course, we weren't aware of any of this. It was just not part of our vocabulary.

My brother and I used to sit at the top of the stairs in this wonderful farmhouse we used to live in, and people would arrive at the famous

Hartley parties. My dad made the best martinis in town, and I'd watch people gradually fall over as the night wore on. It was a daily occurrence. Not necessarily with my parents, but with guests that would come. I remember watching a woman just fall over completely backwards once. Watching my father fall off . . . slide off of a sofa as we were watching television. He had delirium tremens and was foaming at the mouth. It became a devastating rescue a great deal of the time. And again, I didn't understand what it was, which is why education is so important for me now.

It wasn't until much, much later when I started working in the mental health community that I realized that both of my parents were mentally ill, and that alcohol was their way of handling that. My father was a manic-depressive who was painting horrible manic-depressive paintings before he died. My mother was either the same as my dad or clinically depressed—I was never quite sure. When you are the child of two alcoholics who are also mentally ill, you're defending against their defense. It's a quagmire. So much of my recovery has been posing the question "What is the reality and what is the fantasy?"

Breakfasts were odd for me because it was always as if nothing had happened the night before, so I hadn't seen my mother curled up in the forsythia bushes the night before. I hadn't carried her home or helped her into the house. I hadn't seen what I had seen: the rages, the fights. I didn't know what a blackout was. I just knew you didn't talk. In the unconscious, it was a blackout. And I grew up believing their mythology, which was a mythology of silence: "Don't tell." Blackouts were big in my family, particularly with my mother. Nothing was ever discussed. The family started disintegrating even more when I was in high school.

I started drinking when I was fourteen because my boyfriend drank. He was also an alcoholic, or alcohol dependent—I can't really call him an alcoholic unless he calls himself that. Because I had so much shame and guilt, which I felt on some level I was born with. I had sexual feelings at an early age. I describe myself as a ripe peach in a family of dried up bananas. There was this feeling I was the juicy one, and an outsider. I had these feelings and didn't know where to put them, and my mother greeted me with this extraordinary silence. In that silence, there is this sense of extraordinary shame. Not only do I have these feelings, but I'm leading little boys down the block into hell! . . . "I'll show you mine if you'll show me yours." I think what my mother ultimately tried to do—and she said this—this is a very Waspy thing, I think, because they drank: She was drinking with me one night, heavily, and she said, "You know, the only way I thought I could control you was through guilt." What does that leave a little child with but that "my feelings and needs are too big, I'm too tall, I'm too everything." If I was going to be sexual during high school, which was something I was kind of being pushed into, the only way I could do it was to drink. You see, I couldn't deal with the shame. Also, it kind of loosened me up and I had less resistance. I was incredibly resistant.

An example of my denying my physical body and my internal wounds was when I was nineteen and involved in an abusive relationship, and had jumped from the frying pan to the fire. I was a married teenager, doing the play *St. Joan*. I'd just come back from the library where I'd written down her whole trial for witchcraft and heresy. I'd copied it word-for-word. It had taken days. We had written the piece for CBS. My husband and I were driving in the car and he started to hit me, and I could see his hand coming at me. In order to avoid the hit—and this is how my brain was and how it had been trained—I jumped out of the car. We were going thirty miles an hour! My whole right side hit the curb, yet it never occurred to me to get help or see a doctor. It wasn't talked about. This seems an astonishing reflex to me now.

When I tested pregnant, it was Christmas Eve, and again I was working. I was on tour here in Los Angeles. My mother said to me, "Well, you're going for an abortion, aren't you?" And I wanted that child. I was devastated. It may have turned out for the best, whoever knows? But all I said was, "Well, I hadn't planned on that."

Christmas Eve I was still performing. We went down to Mexico, had the abortion on a kitchen table, came back, and had Christmas dinner with my aunt and uncle in Pasadena, and it was never mentioned. And I went on stage that night! You can see how thoroughly I learned not to tell family secrets, not to reveal. I'm working on a one-woman show, and it's like "How can I say these things without blame? But it's not to blame, it's like painting." In my father's terms, we painted ourselves with guardedness. Even the wonderful things in my growing up had an edge of negativity of judgment. And the big voice in my head wasn't my dad's. He was mushy and adored me—there was that whole wonderful, unspoken feeling that he and I got each other creatively. It was my mother's, without understanding. So often those people who don't give us what we need, it's from their limitation rather than ours. But when you're the fish in this tank asking for food or whatever growing up, you don't know that.

We children know not to ask for things, not to tell people directly what we wanted or needed because someone, usually my mother, would have a terrible reaction. My brother would come home from a fair or the park, and he would have ice cream all over his mouth. She would get physically ill. There was a sense of physical messiness being sin.

I work with young women who have been brutally abused. Some come from cults whose families would threaten to kill them if they didn't do what they were told. "Don't talk. Don't talk." The young women say, "I can't talk about that." They are used to a kind of abuse where they don't see and verbalize it. I was taught that nothing I did counted. You get sober—you've got to because this mythology you received isn't working anymore. You burst out and show your candle, not keep it under a barrel, really show it. And you know the only way you can do that is to stop anesthetizing any of that stuff and look at it, as terrifying as it may be. How do you walk away from this kind of family mythology, when that's what you know? Instead, you begin to abuse yourself and do shameful things because you can't win. It's taken me years to uncover these scars.

It's funny, I hear so many people say they loved drinking, they just loved it. I never loved drinking. I always knew that I was betraying some promise that I wouldn't drink, which is what ultimately got me into recovery. I was never a falling-down drunk, although when I drank by myself after my dad's death, I was in a vortex towards hell that I wouldn't wish on anybody. It was never fun for me. It was a necessity on some level, but unconsciously I knew that I was somehow obeying a family myth again. That was the way to anesthetize pain. I watched it happen in my family ever since I was born, so I chose to swim in that sea.

Not happily though, never happily. I was never one of those "rah, rah, yea, yea, let's go out and get drunk" people because I had too much shame about it. I was more of a closet drinker. I never went to bars; it was not my style. To be alone was the only way for me.

I was involved in a hideously brutal marriage, which to this day I've never totally understood. It was like going from the frying pan into the fire, in the sense that I had lived in an extremely permissive household, and what this man promised me was that I would gain morality. My boyfriend in high school didn't marry me, and this man said he would. He picked me up, and presto, in three weeks we were married. I was nineteen years old. It was a marriage full of domestic violence and excruciating brutality. I was drinking as much as I could to get away from the pain.

I was working all during this time. I came out to Hollywood and did Sam Peckinpah's first film, *Guns in the Afternoon*, in 1962. That was the beginning of a realization that I had to get a divorce. I was so terrified of my first husband because he was such a frightening man. Finally my parents came out to be with me, and we three lived together in a little apartment in Brentwood.

It was a house full of guns. We had guns everyplace in the house, we always did. My dad was a hunter. He was a farm boy from Missouri. My mother's father was a very famous behavioral psychologist, a man named John B. Watson, who believed that children should not be touched or held. They should be kissed lightly on the forehead before saying good night, if anything. My grandfather thought boys were basically raised to be homosexuals and girls were basically raised, because of pajama parties and things, to be lesbians. There was an extraordinary kind of sexualizing in my family. My mother, how can I say this, she was deeply in love with her father. She doted on him. It was very much like the father of the professor's wife in *Who's Afraid of Virginia Woolf?* Her father represented everything that my father wasn't, and his presence was in the eaves of our family house. My grandfather was a huge cloud to whom my father was compared constantly. I was too when I wanted to nurse my children, which was revolting to my mother. And a lot of that was because my grandfather kept saying, "It's going to destroy your breasts, Polly. I won't let it happen." He lived right around the corner from us too, so we were constantly visiting him. He was a pretty terrific grandfather until he French-kissed me one night when I was twelve. Needless to say, it was a very confusing family.

So my dad brought whatever guns he could in the car. He must have shipped some out to Los Angeles, but he was going deeper and deeper into his depression, until he became catatonic and I would get down on my knees and beg him to seek help.

I was working with Mary Astor at the time, who was in recovery, and she said, "Try to get him drunk and get him into a rehab." Well, we all got drunk and tried to get my father into rehab, and that didn't work. The very next day, Mom and I were having breakfast when we heard the gunshot. We went to his room and Dad had shot himself. The next six or seven hours were just life-changing. Absolutely life-changing. I didn't know how life-changing until months later. The last I saw of him was in a brown paper bag, in bloody pajamas. I remember going through one of his pockets, and he had left us a $5,000 life-insurance policy.

I think the real horror to me was that in the ashes of my father, I was eventually brought back to life. Did I need that kind of drama? Did it take that kind of explosion to burst through to me? I'm not proud of it. I didn't know I needed that. I'd been kind of suicidal until then, and when I saw my dad wheeled out, I thought, "Oh my God, this really works!"

I don't mean I got well, because I lived in a death house. My drinking got much *worse*. My mother was perpetually committing suicide; my father finally completed it. When she attempted it again, I saved her life. Same hospital, same L.A. emergency, and it went on and on. There was a part of me stuck in that morass. I was living by myself then, which made the drinking worse. I had nobody to drink with or at. I found myself living in my little apartment on Wilshire Boulevard, and I had no bounds.

I went back to school, studying psychology and philosophy, and having attention deficit disorder, I was terrified of the tests. I would drink a case of beer on the weekend by myself, and eat. An eater and a drinker. Then I was bulimic, so I could eat and drink some more. I gained thirty pounds and was like my dad: a mushy, falling asleep drunk. My mother had the violent rages.

I'd fall on the floor dancing, and be carried home, and wake up in a pool of the evening's remains. I would wake up with this extraordinary headache. My hangovers were hideous, which helped push me to stop. As people say, it's a progressive disease. For me, that means I would drink less and wake up with worse hangovers. My body became so allergic to it. The last, the second time I stopped, all it took was four beers after a show—Foster's, so that's more than four—and I'd wake and could hardly move.

Then I got into therapy and was able to make the emotional break from my mother, which was extraordinarily difficult because there was total enmeshment. Now they call it codependency. It was a very difficult relationship to pull myself away from. I finally said, "This is ridiculous. What's the point?" Even though the alcohol had kind of freed me and released me. That's what happens to women alcoholics. We lose our sense of self, and we end up places where we may be in danger of rape and so on, and have absolutely no idea how we got there.

I went into recovery in 1966, and went into it full force. I knew that my agent's wife was in a recovery program, and I always knew that there were other people, maybe, not drinking. I couldn't do it alone. Just couldn't. You know, I'd start at eight o'clock in the morning with the idea "Today I'm not going to drink. Today I'm not going to drink. Tonight I'm not going to drink. Oh, but there's that party tonight. Yeah, but that's okay, I'll very easily say, 'I'm not drinking today. I'm on the wagon.'" What is "on the wagon" anyway? "Do not fall off the wagon." That's what we used to hear from our parents. Or "I'm on the wagon." This conversation would go on every ten or fifteen minutes in my head. You know, "I'm a pretty smart person. I can think of other things," but I couldn't when I was in the middle of the obsession with drinking. Once it hit me, there was just no way that I could not do it.

I would go up and knock on the door. The hostess would open the door and say, "Hi, Mariette! Gee you look great! What would you like to drink?" And I'd say with no hesitation, "I'd like a very cold, very dry martini." As if none of those thoughts of stopping had happened!

Anyway, so I knew that Beverly, my agent's wife, was sober, and she took me to a meeting, and it was awful. It was wall-to-wall smiles. Yet I saw something behind their eyes. They had what I wanted, and I knew I was willing to go to any lengths to get it. . . . I thought . . .

About six years later, I had not been able to work out any of the stuff, any of the trauma with my father. My shame and rage were intact. I still felt the young startlet and an outsider. Sobriety wasn't working for me. I had piled the recovery on top of my problems. I was the good daughter again in the support group, giving myself away and not filling myself up with what I needed. It's interesting because I work with survivors now. This has been the great gift of his death. I'm deeply involved with the survivor movement. I co-founded an organization called the American Foundation for Suicide Prevention in the eighties, and it's been an amazing journey.

If I could have written my life, as I sat in the Fine Arts Theater in Westport, Connecticut, all I wanted to be was Ingrid Bergman or Norma Shearer. I'm sure they didn't want to be themselves either! My vision of what my life should have become is so limited compared to what it has become, and everything that it has become has been a result of tragedy. Of having tragedy transmute itself into a gift.

When the Vietnam veterans came back, many of them had post-traumatic stress disorder, as my father had it from his ships being sunk in World War II. The servicemen had doubts about our presence there. They saw atrocities you wouldn't wish on anyone. It's such an odd thing to describe to those who haven't experienced that kind of violence—what it's like to see a body blown apart and then to clean it up afterwards, which is what I did at the age of twenty-three. It's an experience that is almost indescribable. To come back from the UCLA Medical Center with a paper bag in my hand, and my mother and I then saw what was on the walls and on the rug, and we had to clean up my father's brains. That's what happened.

What do you do with those pictures? What do you do with that moment in your life? What do you make of it? Where do you take it? In those days, I didn't even know if there were any survivor groups. There was only one in Los Angeles: the Los Angeles Family Group I started in 1963, which is when my dad died. I learned how hard it is to survive a suicide of someone close. Harder than any other bereavement, without making it sound like "we're so different and aren't we great?" It has nothing to do with that. It has to do with the stigma and the shame and the blame—society's view of it. Religion's vision of it. For hundreds and hundreds of years, we're left with the idea of sin. Sin washes over you even if you're not religious, so not only can you not grieve, you are constantly defending yourself.

That was completely true with the Vietnam veterans. They fought that war they wanted not to fight. Saw those atrocities, came home, tried to talk about it, and nobody wanted to hear them. Many ended up in mental institutions and on the streets. So what post-traumatic stress work did was begin to rehabilitate them by changing the workings of the brain. The actual trauma began to be exposed and reversed. I finally surrendered to my need to do that in 1988, because I had started drinking again.

My family was wonderful. I had my two beautiful children, and I don't know why I started again. Everybody will say, "It's 'cause you wanted to." People are very tough on that. Probably somewhere in my brain, I saw myself as a normal drinker, but I don't know any normal drinker that goes out to prove they can drink like a normal drinker. Clearly the disease had taken over on some level, because I'll tell you that I was in an emotional blackout. It's inexplicable. I got caught in that place where it's said "Suddenly you have no defense." I was so full of shame that I might as well be killed for a sheep as for a lamb, and I couldn't find my way into the rooms of recovery. Just couldn't. I had married a man who didn't think I had a problem. He was French and loved champagne and wine, and what the hell difference did it make? And I was functioning, totally functioning. When I did the *CBS Morning Program*, I had stopped drinking but started drinking near-beer. I could drink three or four of those, and look so forward to that at the end of the day. That interlude I could look forward to.

But when I was in Jamaica doing a movie in 1988, I realized that my drinking could escalate back to where it was. I called it *Fuck Me in Paradise* because I always rename my movies. I did another about Jackie Cochran that was so hideous, about Charlie's Angels gone World War II, which I called *Chopper Pussies*. Anyway, the real name of this one was *Passion and Paradise*, and it was a Harry Oakes story with a good cast. But I started drinking with the crew and cast and by myself. I lived on Red Stripe, and

I could barely make it back to the house before I'd pass out or black out. By now my marriage wasn't working. I had the feeling I was going to be alone again, and then I knew I would be in trouble. So I started in recovery in Jamaica, which was extraordinarily anonymous. That was just what I needed.

When I came back from Jamaica, I began to see a wonderful therapist. He was the first person ever to take me into that room with my dad, and scream the scream and sob the sobs that needed to be sobbed, fully and deeply and primally. Without the journey back, I was going to stay stuck there. It was around this time that a group of people came to me and asked if I would be part of this suicide-prevention organization, and I said "Wow!" Up until this point, I had been sworn to secrecy about my dad's death. My mother had absolutely forbidden me to talk, and I was a good daughter, you know, I would have died with my secret. I had finally met other survivors, people who had lost loved ones but were in the movement, and they begged me because of my visibility at that point.

I was very visible because of the Polaroid commercials and some marvelous movies-of-the-week I'd been doing on television. Movies like *Mothers Against Drunk Drivers* and *Silence of the Heart*. I was the movie-of-the-week queen. When people urged me please, please to come out about it, I said, "Over my dead body!" I really believed that's what would have happened had I spoken out. As anyone in such a situation knows, the exact opposite happens. As I shared my story, I began to heal.

It was very difficult for my mother, however. She found my act indulgent, shameful, and reprehensible—totally unnecessary. These were her words. I couldn't communicate with her much until she lay dying, but by then, our relationship had healed. She ultimately died in my arms in 1990, just after my book, *Breaking the Silence*, came out.

Sobriety has been sixteen years of an extraordinary life. I've lived through my mother's death. I've lived through a terrible, terrible divorce where I was walking a battlefield, picking up body parts, and trying to put them on my daughter, my son, and myself—and not having much anatomy left.

But thank God for people in recovery! I recall a moment when I was in New York, and I was sobbing. I had lost control. I didn't realize how powerful a force this family that I'd created was. How much it meant to me. My daughter is gorgeous. My son is equally gorgeous. And they are wonderful souls and terrific human beings. And they talk! They've talked since they were babies! And I nursed them until they were three and four years old. I joke that it wasn't that I tried to overcompensate for my grandfather's theories, but I think Shawn was sixteen and got his driver's license when I said, "Okay, kid, I think it's time for you to be weaned!" For me and my children, it's been a long, nurturing relationship on both sides. The moments I would rock in that rocking chair and nurse those kids—oh my God! That's when I learned about meditation.

So when the family cracked, I begged my husband, "I don't care what you and I have done. Can we work on this relationship? These kids are my life. This unit is what we've created." He said, "I don't want to do any more work." And if I'd been really bitchy, I would have said, "I don't remember your ever doing any." But I didn't! I had supported this man for eighteen years, and he was French and he loved his wine and champagne. Call it an ideal relationship. He didn't believe I was an alcoholic, and when I stopped drinking, things completely changed. He was threatened. He scoffed because he believed in moderation, and I said, "Can't do it. Don't know how."

I remember speaking to a group once and crying so hard I kept saying, "I'm trying to find the light at the end of the tunnel, and not have it be the train." And this wonderful woman, I don't know who she was, one of those angels that often appear, said, "You know, we always look for the light at the end of the tunnel. Look around you. Every single person in this room holds a candle." That thought has stayed with me. The wisdom of angels in recovery, these messengers. Sobriety has been a powerful, very eclectic journey for me.

We recognize the whole emotional life of an alcoholic or someone who depends on alcohol, but there is an absolute physical, genetic allergy too. Once I started drinking, once the weakening and opening to it began, the preoccupation with it would take over—what we call the obsession or compulsion. And we can use anything to lose ourselves in. With the familial arms around me, I'd kind of pushed through my dependency the first time I got sober. Then when I found myself completely alone, that was when I began realizing my huge, profound biochemical disorder. I see this constantly: underneath how many people were depressed since they were kids, though they didn't look like it, and drink to balance their extremes, whether shopping until you go crazy or becoming hypersexual, and then dropping into suicidal depression. I remember when I was doing a comedy, *Sylvia*, at the Manhattan Theater Club in 1994, standing . . . sober . . . on the top of the Zeckendorf Towers. And I looked down and said, "Wow, what an interesting drop." And then I saw my kids' faces in front of me and thought, "They can't pick up the pieces as I did."

So there was sanity but a realization that I needed others' help. As we say, often when we go into those depths is when we hit the walls of old defenses that don't work anymore, old ways of dealing with our problems. I think that's the power of recovery when you hit those invisible walls and suddenly say, "What is that?" And you're able to talk to people or write it out, or perhaps go to a doctor and say, "What is this?" And you get an answer, because we are born now. We can get the answers now. I found that most of my stuff was answered with the support of suicide survivors. I like the idea we survivors are literally soldered together by our common experience.

I think that the toughest thing in the world for those of us who are alcoholics to accept is success. It's not just the drama—we're used to that. It's learning how to say thank you and shut up. Not just in a small way— in a big way. This also concerns receiving love in relationships, and learning how to become successfully intimate. We have to learn what it's really like to be with a loving companion.

All of us are in such a process of integration, constantly, whether we want to be or not. What the opportunity of recovery or sobriety does for me is I become conscious of the integration. Even if I'm doing the same things without alcohol, I can learn from that situation now. I don't have to go back into that rat's cage again and again and again. Which is what alcohol does. It makes me forget. It's a disease that keeps saying I have no disease.

Once when I had just come out West, I was going to do a movie called *Come Fly with Me*. Dolores Hart and I were going to do it together. She was one of these young starlets under contract, and I just fell in love with her. We were going to go on this incredible trip with the wonderful actor Karl Malden when I got sick. I ended up with a crazy doctor who said I had hepatitis but I didn't, and another actress got the part. Then Dolores got smart and became a nun. My work with survivors was getting very heavy because I wasn't a trained therapist. I hadn't seen Dolores for forty-five years when I went to her as a spiritual adviser. We sat opposite each other, with this makeshift trellis between us in this tiny cloistered room, and I said, "I'm in trouble. I want so much to be of use, but I don't know how to continue doing this." I expected her to say, "Why are you going back to that place: your pain?" To the contrary, she said, "Mariette, this is your journey, your mission, probably why you were born." And I went, "Oh fuck!" Then she talked about resonance. When you drop a petal in the water and the ripples go, do they stop at the water's edge or continue? Then she said what stayed with me. "You know, I've learned in my thirty years of contemplation . . ." You know, that blew me away because if I'm quiet for fifteen minutes, I think I've died! She said, "One's deepest wounds, integrated, become one's greatest powers."

We are all traveling on this earth together, and what these unexpected visitations in your life, the angels, do is help us to shift. I've had more of a chance of recognizing angels sober. That's a glory of this experience. I can learn from my mistakes. I don't have to hide from anybody. I'm a part of the Good Host. It's the recognition, and being still and knowing. Once I finally surrendered—and this is what I wish people got—you have to be careful, because it's bright. The light is very bright. And people who hide don't necessarily want to see it. . . . Holy God, it's like learning how to live all over again!

The field of moral choice affords man's
  Feet crackling ice
  To tread, and feet are
  A sensational device.

—Marianne Moore, "Man's Feet Are a Sensational Device"

Dick Beardsley
(long-distance runner)

AFTER LOSING MY home in Malibu to a messy and painful fore-closure, I moved to the Hawaiian Island of Maui to chill out. I hadn't yet quit living wildly or using drugs, but I did start to make some important changes. I began eating with some consciousness, enjoying the fantastic array of local fruits and seafood. I even decided to reclaim my physical body, which had taken far too much abuse the past several years, and joined a six-man outrigger canoe team made up of five other guys over the age of thirty-five.

To get in shape for the difficult daily ocean paddling workouts, I decided to start running. I'd never been very fit, and my first attempts were far from pleasurable. I purchased a pair of serviceable running shoes and took daily early morning jaunts on gravel pathways paralleling the ocean. How exhilarating these workouts became. Slowly, but surely, I gained strength and endurance, and my running went from being a chore to a pleasure to a passion.

Fat began to melt away, replaced by the leanness associated with long-distance runners. I became fanatical about my running. My addictive personality was switching from negative and self-destructive drug addiction to life-affirming exercise addiction. Within six months, I was running several miles a day, pushing myself in the early morning sun to go farther, run faster.

One day, I read in the newspaper about the upcoming Honolulu

Marathon, and a new challenge was born. I would have about two months to train, and it became a full-blown obsession. I bought a book on marathon training and followed it religiously. It was extremely hard work, building my endurance for this grueling ordeal, but I loved it. Aside from my daily training runs, I continued paddling canoe. Since I wasn't working, preparation for the marathon became my life. I ate properly and got plenty of sleep. All was going exceptionally well until about two weeks before the marathon was to be held. I was in the best shape of my life, both physically and mentally, but I began to notice pain in the toes of my right foot. I tried to continue my training regimen, hoping it was only a temporary condition, but the pain got progressively worse. Finally I made an appointment with a local doctor and discovered, to his seeming amusement, that I had fractured three of my toes from the continual pounding. I was told there was no way I could run with this injury. I was more than disappointed not to participate in the Honolulu Marathon, an event for which I had worked my butt off. But I still experienced an inner joy because I had found a life force deep inside me that I never knew existed.

Two years later I was back in Los Angeles, still running with conviction, entering 10K races almost every weekend, and becoming a complete devotee to my new sport. I had begun reading all I could about running and was fascinated with what I was learning about the marathon. The idea that anyone, let alone me, could run 26.2 miles was mesmerizing.

I started to read about this runner named Alberto Salazar, who was tearing up the world of distance running with his record-shattering marathon performances. I remember being totally spellbound watching him do battle with a runner named Dick Beardsley in the 1982 Boston Marathon, while both of them broke the existing world's record. The race was referred to in *Runner's World* magazine as "the duel in the sun." They ran so close to each other that for most of the last half of the race, Beardsley, while in the lead, monitored Salazar's progress by watching his shadow on the asphalt. "Neither man broke, and neither, in any meaningful sense, lost," according to the magazine.

"Damn," I remember thinking, "this is something I got to do." In the summer of 1984, I ran and completed the inaugural running of the Los Angeles Marathon. Who would have suspected that twenty years later I'd be interviewing Dick Beardsley for my book on recovering substance abusers?

I met Dick at The Lenox on Boylston Street in Boston on April 19, 2004, twenty-two years to the day when he competed with Alberto Salazar in the most momentous Boston Marathon ever run. We went up to his room to do the interview and check out the marathon on television. I asked him if watching the elite runners line up at the starting line didn't make him itchy to run with them. A huge smile burst from his face and he chuckled. He told me that to ensure against this happening, he had gone for a leisurely twenty-mile run the day before. No way could he compete in a marathon today. Especially in heat that was approaching eighty degrees.

If you met Dick, you'd guess he is a runner. Rail thin, high-waisted, with a powerful chest, bones in his face that stretch the skin taut, and legs that are extra long. A person who shucks off running three marathons in two weeks, winning one of them, as "no sweat."

Dick tells his story with great enthusiasm, eager to share his experience with those who might be helped by it.

To account for my addiction, I go back to my childhood. My mom and dad drank a lot. They were both alcoholics, but I didn't know that at the time. From when he got up in the morning until he went to bed, for the most part, he held an alcoholic drink in his hand. But as a young kid, you never think much of that. And my mom—you hardly ever saw her drink except if my folks had company over. But playing hide-and-seek with my two younger sisters, we'd find empty bottles under the bed or a half-emptied bottle in the utility room—some kind of booze. Every once in a while my sisters and I snuck into the back room hiding, and my mother would be there drinking out of a paper bag. We never put two and two together.

When I was in the neighborhood of eight, it started getting rough around home in the evenings. My folks had been drinking all day, and my dad had a short temper anyhow. And then when he was drinking, it just took the smallest thing to set him off. And when my mom would get to drinking, she'd get real obnoxious. If you said, "It's a beautiful day out," she'd reply, "Nah, it's terrible out." We'd get around the table for supper, and, gosh, my dad all of a sudden would blow up because there wasn't enough. We'd be eating sweet corn and there wasn't enough butter on the table. Or the saltshakers weren't completely filled up.

I remember a couple of times seeing my dad whack my mom right off the back of the chair. I thought, gosh, when I get older and have kids, that is not for me. I'm not going to be drinking and doing that kind of stuff. And my parents—I'm sure it was because of the alcohol—after about twenty-two years of marriage, they ended up divorcing.

But the good part of that whole story is my dad finally found sobriety in 1982 and had fourteen years sober before he passed away from cancer. And he became my best friend. It was amazing how when he quit drinking, we reconnected big time. My mom found sobriety a lot later in life, but she did before she passed away, unfortunately also from cancer. So I saw them drunk and realized, "Man, this isn't for me." Then as I got older and into high school, of course on the weekends—I came from a small town—kids were always partying and doing drugs. I never did any illicit type of drug in my life. But I remember coming back to school on a Monday and a bunch of my buddies said, "Oh Beard, you missed a great kegger out in so-and-so's pasture Saturday night. Man, we were all drunk and havin' a good time." And I thought, "Euh!" I could see what the drinking did to my folks. When I turned eighteen, in the state of Minnesota back then you could legally drink. So I thought, "I want to just see what it's like. I might as well try it for myself." Some buddies had a birthday party for me in some pasture. I was going to stay there all night, so I wouldn't be driving. We had a bunch of friends and a big bonfire, and I had, I don't know, fifteen, eighteen beers. I went from not drinking at all to all those pints. I mean it was coming out both ends! I had a headache for a week. And I thought, "If this is what drinking is all about, forget it!" So that initiation was a good thing. It turned me completely off of that.

Of course—I was in high school in the early to mid-seventies—all the kids were doing drugs, smoking dope, stuff like that, and it never even crossed my mind to try the stuff. I was offered it but just turned around and walked away. You got called names and teased, but I thought I'm just not interested at all. Plus this was about the time I started getting into running a little bit. I wasn't very good, but I thought, "No way." And that was against the rules anyhow. So I went from there, and my running time did start to take off when I got into college. Drunks and drinking, nope. And when things started to change was after my competitive running career. I retired from competitive racing at that high level, back in 1988 after the Olympic trials, and then we moved back to our dairy farm. About two months after we'd been back, I got into a real bad farm accident. It busted up all my ribs and punctured my lung. I broke my arm and had a piece of steel driven into my chest. My left leg was just about torn off. At that point, I was laying on the ground and my wife Mary's calling the ambulance, and we're waiting for them to get there, and you don't know if you're going to live or die and are in an incredible amount of pain. And so the ambulance finally arrives and they get into our little hospital and do all this checking out. And about a half hour later, after I go into the hospital, the nurse comes in and says, "Richard, I'm going to give you a little something. It won't take the pain completely away, but at least it will kind of take the edge off a little bit." She gave me this shot. And I had no idea what it was. And I'm telling you, about twenty minutes later, I got this warm, fuzzy feeling in my head that I had never felt before. And it was like a million bucks. The pain was still there but it was like, "Ah, big deal!" I didn't even care. I remember waking in the room. I said, "Man, what was that you gave me?" She said, "Well, it was Demerol, a narcotic painkiller." Every three or four hours, she would come in and give me another shot. Honest to goodness, at that point, if the sheriff of our county, who came out to the farm accident, would have come into my hospital room and said, "Dick, we could take you out to the farm and wrap you back up in the maw of that machine and turn the power take-off on and let you flap around a few more times and kind of re-create how the accident happened," I would have said, "That's fine, but bring that nurse with the needle."

I was already getting off on that stuff. I didn't know it yet, but I was. I'd never felt a drug high before. For a couple of days, I was in our local hospital. They got me kind of stabilized and then transferred me down to the Twin Cities [Minneapolis and Saint Paul, Minnesota], where I had two or three operations. I was in the hospital for a number of weeks. After a week of the shots, one day the nurse walks in and says, "Richard, we're going to discontinue giving you the Demerol shots." It was like they were taking away my teddy bear. And I go, "You're kidding me. Man! I just got out of surgery a couple of days ago. I have a lot of pain." "Oh no, we're not stopping it, we're giving it a new way 'cause your butt's like a pin cushion." And I said, "How're you going to do it?" And she said, "I'm putting a needle in your vein. See that plastic tube?" "Yeah." "Well, it's attached to that pouch of Demerol up there." And she handed me a little button thing. "This is set so that every three-and-a-half minutes you get a dose. And instead of having to wait twenty minutes to hit you, it'll be instantaneous."

Honest to God, I could hardly wait to push that cotton pickin' thing. Seeing me react, she laughed and I pushed the button, and right away felt a tingle go into my arm. And it was like, *wham, boom,* right to my head. The problem was that they were giving me a pretty big dose and it knocked me out. It would make me fall asleep. So I remember getting that first shock or first push and losing consciousness. I woke up thirty minutes later thinking, "My gosh, I missed eight doses!" So I wore my runner's watch. I set the alarm to go off every two-and-a-half minutes, and I set it next to my pillow. So I'd give myself a little jolt, knock myself out, and two-and-a-half minutes later I'd hear *ding, ding, ding, ding.* Whether I needed relief or not, I'd push that button again. At the time—now it's so much easier to look back and see all those signs—but at the time, you don't think anything of it. So then eventually they weaned me off of that and put me on Percocet, which is heavy-duty too. But I took it in a normal pill. I was sent home with some Percocet, and then gradually they weaned me off of that.

Most people get off the analgesic and don't have a problem with it. I, too, was fine for two-and-a-half years, until we—my wife, Mary, my small son, Andy, and I—were coming home from a couple of days away from the cows. And we were about forty miles from home, and a lady came barreling through a stop sign on a connecting road and just T-boned our car. I busted up my back and had some whiplash and a bruised spinal cord—and I was right back in the hospital. As I lay in the ambulance, I knew I was hurt but that I wasn't going to die. But, man, all of a sudden it was déjà vu: "I betcha I'm going to get some more of that Demerol." Sure enough, it was almost the exact scenario. They went from the shots over to the drip in the vein, then down to the Percocet. I got out of the hospital after a couple of weeks and was sent home with the Percocet, and was using it not as I ought. If it said one to two tablets every four to six hours, I took two every four hours. I would call for more, and because I was from a small town, with that kind of drug you're supposed to have a written prescription. Well, our pharmacy, that certainly didn't have a fax machine, said, "Listen, Doc, we'll take it over the phone, and just send it to us." So the pharmacist would fill it for me without a written prescription.

After a couple of months, I went back for my last checkup with her. As I left, she said, "Dick, this is your last. Here's a prescription for 30 more Percocet, but when this is done, it's done. You've started to feel better now and it's been long enough. Ibuprofen or aspirin should do the trick." "Okay," I said, but home again, I started having an anxiety attack. I'm thinking as I pull into the parking lot of the pharmacy, "Man!" Before I know it, I'm looking at this prescription. "This is it. Thirty and it's gone!" So there was the store next to the pharmacy, and I knew they had a copy machine in there. So—again, I had never stolen a piece of bubblegum in my life, I'd never been in any trouble—but I went in there and thought, "I'm just going to run this through and see what it looks like. And if it looks really good, maybe I'll keep an extra one or two, just in case." Well, I ran it through there, making sure no one was looking. The second I pushed the button, I felt guilty. Then I really felt stupid. When I came out and looked, you could tell it was a copy. The pharmacist would have had to be the most stupid person in the world to take it. I thought, "You'd better throw this away before somebody happens to find it. They're going to start asking me questions." So I sat out on my truck, and I'd never smoked in my life and had no idea how to operate the cigarette lighter. It took me about five minutes to figure out you have to push it in for it to heat up. Finally figured that out. It got hot and I sat out there and lit that copy on fire. Opened the door of my truck, and the sheet burned, and I watched the ashes blow away in the wind. Went in with the real prescription, got it filled. Took it as prescribed but to the max side of it. Once I go through with it, I'm fine. Back working on the farm, fine. That was late July or early August of 1992, and I was fine until January of 1993.

I'd been in Fargo, North Dakota, at an agricultural seminar. Got done with it. Was back running a little bit, not hard, but out running. It had snowed all day long, and I'd always liked running in a snowstorm. I went out for a run. I was running down this one-way street with the traffic, knowing that's not the way to go. But with the sidewalk clogged with snow, I thought I'd run on the main street until the next block and turn off on a side road. Well, I never made it. I ended up getting hit in the back by a truck. They found me lying in a snowbank and loaded me up into an ambulance, at which point I came to. As they took me to the hospital, I asked what had happened. "Oh . . . uh . . . you got hit by a car or truck when out running." "Am I going to die?" "Oh, no, but you're banged up pretty good."

Honest to goodness, I almost started high-fiving the ambulance driver. I knew I was about to get more Demerol! I had that warm fuzzy feeling again without even getting the drug—anticipating. At the hospital, almost the same scenario repeated. They checked me out and shot me with Demerol, put me in my room. Then shots for a few days, then the IV, then over to Percocet. Got home, was laid up and recovering and such.

When feeling well enough, I drove down to the Twin Cities to do a speaking engagement. And on the way home, about forty miles from home—I should not have been driving that day because of blizzard warnings, but I was eager to get home—I was driving a Ford Bronco truck, and it came out from behind a windbreak and the wind caught my truck and it slid across this icy road and hit a big, tall snowbank and rolled about a dozen times. The emergency crew tried to cut me out 'cause I was hooked upside down. It was twenty below, and they couldn't get the Jaws of Life to work, so they basically yanked me out of there the best they could, as they smelled gas.

That same week, I was scheduled for a checkup with the doctor. Instead I was hospitalized—same floor, same room, same nurse as only a few weeks before. And on the stuff again!

A few years ago, after three years of sobriety, I gave a talk at a little elementary school in a small town nearby where we live. Afterwards—you know, kids are great because they're not afraid to ask you anything—this little girl, about second grade, came up and said, "Mr. Beardsley, did you ever like purposely get into an accident so you could get the drugs?" I was dumbfounded! I never even thought about that. She set me back on my heels like I hadn't been for a long time. I sat there thinking and thinking about it and gave her an answer, and then thought about it more that night. I never purposely jumped out in front of a vehicle or drove my truck into a ditch, but without question, I put myself in situations subconsciously. Sure I didn't want to die. I loved life. But I loved the drugs and put myself into situations where there was a pretty good chance that something could go amiss—where I'd get into an accident or car wreck or whatever and get some of the drugs again. I mean, it took me three or four years of sobriety to admit that.

So I'm in the hospital for another ten days, I'm discharged, get sent home with some Percocet. I'm lying at home, been on my back a lot, taking a lot of the pills, and one afternoon Mary came home from work and we sat around downstairs. I said, "I'm going upstairs and take a nap." I wasn't feeling good. We live in an old farmhouse with narrow steps. I get to the top of the steps and either blacked out or got dizzy and slipped. Anyhow, I fell backwards down the stairs and ended up busting some ribs. It was a Friday, so Mary was home and took me to the hospital. The doctor they wanted to have me see was off for the weekend. They just had the on-call doctor, and they were giving me big doses—shots—of Demerol every three hours. My roommate told me that the doctor coming in Monday was a really good doctor but with a poor bedside manner. So Monday morning, I'm in the far bed, and the doctor walks in and pulls that old curtain as if that's going to keep out any sound of what he's ready to tell me from the roommate. He's got this clipboard, and he doesn't come up and address me, "Hey, I'm Dr. So-and-So." He just comes up to the side of the bed and opens up his chart. He says, "Beardsley, I think you're addicted to these painkillers."

And I yelled back. (Usually I'm an easygoing person.) I said, "I am not addicted to this stuff. You could cut me off of them right now." I-don't-ever-need-this-stuff, I'll-show-you kind of thing. He said, "Now, I'm not just going to cut you off. We'll wean you gradually off of them and get you back on the right track." Of course I didn't want to hear that, although he was right. Dead-on 100 percent right! So they gradually weaned me off the Percocet and put me on some methadone, which made me real sick. In fact, if I took the methadone and didn't lay down for the first forty-five minutes afterward, I would end up throwing up. So I got home and they got me off that too, and I was fine until . . .

That would have been late February, and I was doing pretty good. I wasn't using anything after that for two or three months. I was back running a little bit, and went out for a run one day, and go about 150 meters down the road, and thought, honest to God, someone had come up and stabbed me in my lower back. The pain was excruciating. I couldn't right myself. I hobbled home and got into my car and drove to the family doctor. By the time I arrived, I had these big knots in my back. "Yikes, we got to get you into some physical therapy," the doctor said. And also he wrote a prescription for some Percocet. When he asked, "Have you ever used painkillers before to help with any problems? Of course I had but didn't want to tell him that. I just said, "Yeah." He said, "Have you ever used a drug called Percocet?" I played dumb, "Maybe one time a doctor . . ." You know, I could have spelled it backwards for him! So he wrote me a prescription for 30 or 40 Percocet and then put me into physical therapy.

Three weeks later, when I wasn't a whole lot better, I went to him and he said, "Dick, you know I have to get you to a specialist for that. I can't keep giving you these painkillers 'cause they're very addictive, and we need to get this condition taken care of." So he sent me to an orthopedic back specialist, who did a bunch of stuff and planned to test some more. In the meantime, he was very liberal with his prescription pad. Now not for one moment have I blamed any doctor for the problems I had, because doctors are between a rock and a hard spot. They have compassion for people, plus I could make myself hurt a lot more than I was just to get the drugs. So the specialist wrote me a prescription for 60 Percocet, and I walked out of there. I never had 60 before, and of course, I was using them two or even three at a time now. I continued to go back and get more and more and more. Well, finally I ended up . . . that was late summer of '93 . . . by January of '94, they figured out that I had these busted-up vertebrae, and had to go in and do about eleven hours of surgery. For the twelve days in the hospital, they had me on the IV pump and then on the pills. Then I got out, and once I started getting recovered from the surgery itself, my back actually felt much better. I remember thinking, "You know, I really need to get myself to not be using these painkillers. Dick, enough is enough."

And I did get myself off of them. I'll never forget. My checkup was the first part of May. The doctor says, "Hey, Dick, how're you feeling?" I go, "Like a million bucks, Doc. I'm walking an hour and a half every day, doing the exercises you recommended. And the best part of it, I haven't used any narcotic painkillers, just a little aspirin and Advil for a month now." He goes, "Dick, that's great. I'm glad to hear you're doing so well. But the surgery we did on you, it takes twelve to eighteen months for that area to heal. I know you're a person that likes to push the envelope with your recovery. If you ever start feeling like you're overdoing it and think you need a few painkillers, let me know."

Holy cow! When he said that, it opened that door, and I shoved it open full bore. I'd just told him how great I felt, and when he opened the door that little bit, I kicked it wide open. I said, "You know, Doc, come to think of it, every once in a while my back does get quite sore. Since I'm an hour from here and you're a busy person, maybe I ought to get a prescription from you just in case." "No problem." I told him I'd get it filled if I needed it, and he said, "That's not a problem." So he wrote me out a prescription for 60 Percocet. I shook his hand, walked out of the office. The medical clinic was attached to the hospital at the other end. I walked down the long hallway. At the other end was a pharmacy. I went in there, filled the pre-scription, bought a Diet Coke, got into my truck. I snapped the bottle top off the can and took not one but three Percocet. I mean my mouth was drooling as I walked out to my truck, knowing I had these Percocets! And twenty minutes later as I drove home—'cause that's how long it would take to get into my system—damn, I got that fuzzy feeling again and was right back just like that. And continued to use and abuse, and continued to return for more and more. I could make myself hurt! I'd say, "Doc, my back really hurts. I must've overdid it. Can I come over and get another prescription?" "Yeah, come over." And so, on the way, I could do these contortions with my back where you kind of tighten it up, so by the time I drove there, I had big knots in my back that would stick right out. I'd be hobbling in there, and the doctor would look at me, and who isn't going to give the kid some painkillers? I mean, I was purposely doing that just to make sure. . . . I was so sick!

Of course, a tolerance level continues to rise, so by now, I used more and more. It was late summer of '94 when I got up one morning to go out for a walk, and honest to goodness, I got out of bed and could hardly move. The doctor said, "Get in here. I got to take some pictures." So they take me to X-ray, and then I'm back in the doctor's office. The doctor comes in. I could tell by the look on his face something was wrong. He says, "Dick, this is unbelievable, but it happens in less than 2 percent of the patients. That big bone that we took out of your hip to fuse your lower spine, your body has reabsorbed it into your system. Your lower spine is down there hanging like it was before you even had surgery." He said, "The only thing that can be done: We need to operate again and fuse it onto the back side. We'll be opening you up on the front side and use some rods and pins and screws." He said, "The back side I have no problem doing. The front side, though, is a very delicate operation. You're talking a lot of nerves down there. You might become impotent." He said, "I don't feel comfortable doing it, so I'm going to see if I can get you into the spinal clinic down in the Twin Cities where they do that quite often." So he made a phone call, came back. "Listen," he said, "I made you an appointment to see the doc-tor. They'll schedule you for surgery. And as of today, I'll give you another prescription for your painkillers. But after today, those doctors will have to take care of your pain management."

He wrote me out a prescription and shook my hand and said, "Good luck. Keep in touch. Let me know how you're doing." As I'm walking out of his office, down towards the pharmacy to get this filled, I happened to open it up and looked at the prescription. He'd written it for 300 Percocet! As bad as I was hurtin', I almost felt like doin' cartwheels! Honest to God, I walked in that pharmacy and had a big smile on my face. I felt like Jed Clampett on the *Beverly Hillbillies* when he shoots that rabbit and strikes that oil and becomes a rich man. I walked out of there with two big canisters of pills, 150 each. Why, I felt there were a couple of mortar shells underneath my armpits. And I'm thinking to myself, "These are going to last me for the rest of my life." And less than a month later, they were gone: 300 Percocet! In the meantime, the surgery was scheduled for October, and it was still six weeks away, so I called down there and he says, "Dick, I'm sorry, but I cannot call in a Class 2." So I said, "A pharmacist will probably take it over the phone." He said, "Naw." He just wouldn't do it. He said, "I'd have to send it up there, and it would take a couple of days. I can call in some Tylenol 3 with codeine in it."

I'm terribly allergic to codeine. I break out in hives and get itchy and stuff. But I thought, "What the heck, it's a narcotic. Maybe my body has changed since I last used it." So he called in a bunch, 30 or so. I knew they weren't nearly as powerful as Percocet, so when I got home from the pharmacy with them, I took like 10 or 12. A half hour later, I was itching so bad and was broken out in hives. I called back down there. I said, "Doc, man I broke out in hives and I'm itching." He says, "Dick, listen. What you need to do is go to your family doctor. Let your family doctor take care of your pain management until you get down here."

So I hopped into the car. I hadn't seen the family doctor for over a year. Well, I get up there and he'd moved to some other place. But there was a new doctor that had just came in, and they gave me him. And I walked in there and showed him the knots in my back. 'Cause I had 'em but I made 'em even worse, you know. And I get in there and he says, "My gosh!" And he looked at his nurse. "Nurse, bring in a 120 milligram shot of Demerol."

'Cause I was in pain, but in worse pain than I actually was. And I said, "You can give me a Demerol shot here in your clinic? I don't have to go to the hospital?" "Oh, yeah," he said. "Listen, Dick, if you get like this again, you come in here. We'll give you a shot anytime." So I'm thinking, "Ooooh," 'cause that to me was the ultimate, to get the Demerol shot. Pills were good but . . . So he gave me a prescription for Percocet and said, "Gosh, if your back gets this bad again, we'll give you a shot anytime."

About once a week, I went in and made it hurt real bad, worse than it was, to get a shot of Demerol and a new prescription of Percocet. I did that every week and got the load of drugs right up until the time to go down for surgery. Had the surgery, was in the hospital a week, and was sent home with Percocet, that was all. The doctor down there wasn't real big on the painkillers. He aimed for you to get by on as little as possible. So I got home and, after a few days, was just about out of pills. It was a Friday. And I was in a lot of pain—the front scar. Again, it was painful, but part of the pain was from knowing I was just about out of pills. And that psychological-rebounding kind of a deal occurred. So I remember telling Mary, "Mary, I can't handle the pain anymore." And they took me into our little hospital into the emergency room, and the doctor on-call there—our family doctor was gone for the weekend—gave me a 150 milligram shot of Demerol right away. Then he put me into my own room, and instead of giving me shots, they hooked me up to an automatic drip. And they must have had that bugger cranked up but good! Basically, for two-and-a-half days, it comatosed me. Seriously, every once in a while I'd wake up, but mostly I was in the ozone layer. When the bells and whistles of the machine went off because it was empty, I'd sense the nurse come in and put another bag up there, reset it, and close the door.

Monday morning, Mary is in visiting with me, and she has the chair by the bed and is talking to me. Pretty soon there's a knock on the door. The door was actually kind of half open, and the doctor knocks on it and pokes his head in. A lot of doctors are so busy they'll knock on the door, push their head in, "Dick, how're you doin'?" "Okay." You know, "We'll see you tomorrow," and they charge you a hundred bucks or whatever. Well, he knocks on the door. Mary says, "Oh, come in." He walks in and closes the door. Right away I'm thinkin', "Uh-oh, that's not a good sign." Then he goes over to the corner and grabs a chair and brings it over to the bed. I'm thinkin', "This is really not a good sign" because I knew what was coming. He had the charts. And the last thing I wanted to hear was what he was about to say. But even worse than that, the last person in the world I wanted to hear what he was about to say was Mary. I didn't want an official, a doctor, to say with her listening that "I think Dick has a problem." 'Cause if I would have been there alone, I never would have come home and said, "Hey, Mary, the doc thinks maybe I have a problem with the painkillers." She knew I was banged up. She didn't know how many pills I was taking 'cause she worked during the day. For more pills, I called the doctor and would go and get 'em. For all Mary knew, I'd been home all day long. I didn't talk to her about my mental state at all. I kept it well hidden to keep her from asking questions, as I feared she might. Mary's the kind of person who might pick up the phone and call the doctor then and there: "Hey, I think this guy's gettin' hooked on this stuff." So I really played it cool around her.

So the doctor says, "Dick, my God, the amount of Demerol that you took over the weekend—it could have killed a herd of elephants. I really think that you're becoming addicted to it." Well, I started bawlin' 'cause I didn't want to hear that, and as I said, especially didn't want Mary to hear it. "Listen," he says, "we're not going to cut you right off. We'll work you through this." He says, "We'll reduce it little by little. You'll be fine." And that's what they did. They cut the shots down gradually over a few days. They weaned me off. And the day I was going to get discharged from the hospital, the nurse comes in and says, "Dick, here's a prescription, and the doctor says to just take the medication as prescribed and you'll be fine. The doctor would like to have you go across the road to the mental health clinic to get evaluated. Make sure everything's okay." But there was not talk of treatment for any abuse. And I looked at this prescription, and it was for 75 pills of 100 milligram tablets of Demerol. I go, "They make Demerol in a pill form?" She goes, "Oh, yeah." I'm thinking, "This is unbelievable!"

I get discharged, go over and get my mental health checked out—no problem. So I'm using this Demerol, which is to me better than the Percocet even. And I was taking it way more than I should have been, and finally was getting down toward the end of my supply. Obviously the doctor wasn't going to be giving me more drugs. I had one last checkup with my back surgeon. Well, by the time that came around, I was down to one 100 milligram pill of Demerol. And Mary drove me down to the Twin Cities. It's a little over a four-hour drive from where we live, so I took that pill before we left and was fine on the ride down. But he checks me out, and I start having anxiety attacks. I'm out of the pills and have a long way home. I said, "Doc, do you think I could get a prescription?" And he said, "Absolutely not!" He was even mad to be asked. I went on, "Doc, I've got a long way to go. I own a pickup truck, it's not like driving a car." And I begged. And begged. And he's goin', "Nope," and I kept begging. I would not leave the office! (Mary wasn't with me, she was out in the waiting room.) Finally, just to get rid of me, he wrote me out a prescription for one tablet, one 100 milligram tablet. There was a pharmacy right down below. The pharmacist looked at it three times! You know, I came that close to takin' a pen and adding a zero. But if the doctor called downstairs, I'd be in big trouble. Well, one was better than none. So the pharmacist filled the one, and the ride home I was fine. But by the time I got home, the drug was wearing off. Then I really started having anxiety problems. I broke out in sweat. My muscles twitched. My whole body was wretched. I drew a hot water bath and sat in the tub, hoping that would relax me. "What," I thought sitting there, "am I going to do?" A few months before, I'd read in a magazine about people who go to detox. The first couple of days, they put you on some kind of drug to help you come off of it. I thought, "Man, I bet that's the way to go!" So I called Mary, who came into the bathroom, and told her, "I need to go into a treatment center and get help. I'm flipping out here!"

Mary and I packed my bags and we get to the local hospital where there was a treatment center on the top floor. You have to sign up for a minimum of seventy-two hours. You're locked up and can't leave. I filled out this form, and gave Mary and Andy a kiss, and they walked out the door. They took me to my room, the nurse came in, and I asked, "When do I get some Percocet and Demerol?" She starts laughing. I said, "What's wrong?" and she goes, "What makes you think you're going to get some drugs?" And I go, "I read somewhere that when you come to places like this, they do that so you don't . . . they ease you down off the stuff." "Well," she goes, "they might do that at some places, but we don't do that here." And I'm looking at the one and only window in my room, small with steel bars on it, and I'm thinking, "Oh my God!" I start bawling. "Why, I gotta have some of that stuff!" She goes, "Well, I'll give you some Valium." I'd had Valium, and it kind of relaxes you a little bit. So I'm sobbin', and she comes in later with this paper pill cup and hands it to me with a glass of water. And I look in it and say, "Man, you forgot to put the pill in there." She goes, "No, it's in there." Valium is so small anyhow, and it was like a quarter of a Valium. I go, "This isn't going to do any good." I'm bawling. She says it will take the edge off, so I take it. I didn't use the water. Then after I swallowed it, I took my tongue and licked out that paper pill cup for any residue in there. About forty-five minutes later, I could feel the effect of the pill. It kicked in, sort of relaxing me, but I remember thinking I had to talk to the doctor, knowing I could convince the doctor to give me some drugs. I just knew I could!

Well, it was three days before I could see the doctor. I go in there and the lights are turned down, and he's looking at somebody's X-ray on that lighted board. And I said, "Doc, if you just give me one shot of Demerol, I promise I won't ask anymore." He didn't say anything. He just kept looking. I asked him again. He still didn't say anything. Honest to goodness, I get down on my knees, I start tugging on his pant leg. I said, "Doc, one shot of Demerol and I won't ask you again." He looked down at me slowly. "Stand up, Dick," he said. "You've been over three days now without anything. I'm not going to give you anything, so don't even ask again." And he sent me back to my room, sobbing and crying. You get so emotional during that time. For me, withdrawal and hitting the wall in a race are both very much alike! It's like the last few miles of a marathon where your whole body aches, especially your bones. Even though they are much alike, the marathon aches pale compared to the withdrawal aches!

I was there for nine days, and on the ninth, a doctor, a couple of nurses, a counselor, and my wife, Mary, came in. They go, "Dick, your body has pretty much rid itself now of all the toxins of all those painkillers, but now we have to teach you how not to abuse these drugs anymore. What we'd like to do is have you stay here for thirty days for in-patient treatment." She didn't get the word "treatment" out of her mouth. I said, "Treatment! I don't need treatment." I said, "Don't you know who I am? I'm Dick Beardsley, the marathon runner. I've got willpower! And now that you've got me off this stuff, thank you very much, I appreciate what you've done, but now that you've got me off of it, I promise you this, I'll never use that stuff again, because I've got willpower like nobody else."

They go, "Dick, willpower doesn't really have anything to do with maintaining your sobriety." I said, "It has all to do with me. You could come in here right now, take a chainsaw and cut off both my legs and both my arms, and I guarantee I wouldn't ask for an aspirin." "Dick, that's really not the way it works." I said, "Well, that's the way it works for me. Nope, I'm not going to treatment, whatever you call it."

The next day, they came back and repeated the same thing. I said, "No way. I'm out of here." At that point, they had to let me go. So they let me go home, though Mary and everybody . . . they just tried to talk me into it with me saying "No way, no way." And for about two-and-a-half months, I was fine, until . . . I'd been a fishing guide since age fourteen, and it was getting towards spring, and I was getting my boat ready and was working on that. And I reached down to pick up a big battery for my boat: the starter on the motor. And when I reached down, I must have grabbed it wrong because I felt the muscles in my lower back just go *rip*. And I'm telling you, I set that battery down. I waddled out to my truck, went up to the family doctor. He didn't give me Percocet but another drug almost as powerful, and it was even more powerful because I would just take an extra pill. And I was right back on the stuff!

Then I ended up having to go in for more surgery on my leg from the farm accident. They had to realign my bones. Of course I didn't tell the doctor there I'd been on all these drugs, so he gave me Vicodin, which is an awful darned good drug. But he kept saying, "Gol darn it, Dick," he says, "your metabolism . . ." I do have a high metabolism, but he says, "Boy, you really need a lot of pain medication to get your pain level under control."

I said, "Yeah." "I can't figure it out." Well, because my tolerance level was so high. So now I was on some drugs from him, the Vicodin, but of course I didn't tell him about the doctor back home I was getting some pills from. And at that time, my dad calls me. By now, in my thirties, my dad and I had become best friends, and he's sober and calls me. He'd moved away to Michigan where he and my stepmother had bought a place on Lake Huron, 'cause my dad loved perch fishing. We would talk a couple of times a week. When he phoned, I could tell something was wrong. He'd been having some stomach pains, and he went into the doctor's, and they found a big tumor. They suspected pancreatic cancer, and that's what it was. So my dad said, "Gosh, I'd sure like you to be here when I have surgery." So I drove up there, and by this time, my family doctor . . . I wasn't getting any more pills from him . . . but the surgeon who did the operation on my leg was giving me the Vicodin. So I had some Vicodin and went down and out to my dad's, and he had about thirteen hours of surgery. I was starting to get low on Vicodin, so one night about one o'clock in the morning, I'm thinking, "Well, my dad's in the hospital." You know, we get so selfish we don't think about anyone but ourselves, so I thought, "My gosh, my dad, if he needs pain medications, they have these in the hospital. They'll give it to him there." Of course I didn't think, "What happens to him when he gets home and needs the medicine?"

So I snuck out of bed that night. Their bathroom was a separate entity. It wasn't in their bedroom. I thought, "My dad's had stomach pains for a couple of months now. I bet he has some painkillers." I opened up that honkin' drawer of that medicine cabinet, and there was the unopened bottle of a hundred Vicodin—even stronger than what I was on. I thought they wouldn't miss a few pills. By the time I left a few days later, you could see the bottom of the pill bottle.

God, I get back home and am just really using, abusing Vicodin now. I went to another doctor that I kind of knew from fishing, had him on a guide trip, and said, "Gosh, it must be compensating for my knee 'cause now my back's starting to bother me." And it was a little bit. It wasn't bothering me that bad, but it was bothering me. So now he started giving me some Percocet. Of course I didn't tell him about the other doctor. Pretty soon the Vicodin doctor says, "You've had plenty now." But I still had this other supply. After a week he said, "Gosh, I need to send you to a back specialist, 'cause, you know." So he sent me to this doctor. I didn't tell him I was on the Percocet, knew how to play it from day one. The doctor said, "Dick, I'm going to put you on a drug called Percocet, but you'll be on it for at the most fifteen days. It's very addictive. The last thing I want to happen is you become addicted to the stuff." "Aw yeah, I don't want that to happen." I was so addicted to the stuff! "And we need to get to the bottom of your problem." And so I was back, getting the pills from him. And then my dad . . . they thought they got the cancer, but by May of 1996, my dad called and said, "It's back and it's all over now, and they've given me a couple of months to live." At this point now we're insecure financially. The business we had wasn't doing real well. Our son, Andrew, whom we adopted from Honduras, was having a lot of issues, mental problems. Instead of dealing with things in a positive way as I always had, I was starting to take pills to forget about the problems I was having at home. It started getting real bad. Then in early July of '96, my sister called and said, "Dick, the hospice people say Dad's only seventy-two hours to live. You need to get out here right away."

It was a Thursday afternoon. The only doctor giving me drugs now was this back doctor, and I was just about out. I jumped into my vehicle and drove to Fargo, North Dakota, where his office was, and got there late in the afternoon, and said to the gal up front, "Gosh, I have to get a prescription for Percocet from Dr. Thomas 'cause I'm going to my dad's. He's dying and I need to get there." She said, "I'm sorry but he's out until next Tuesday." I said, "What about his assistant?" "Well, he's at a conference, I'm sorry." I walked out of there not knowing where to turn. It was clear no other doctor around was going to give me anything. Then all of a sudden I recalled a week before, he had given me a referral to a pain management doctor. What he did when I was in his office was he tore off one of his prescriptions and turned it over and wrote the name in pencil on the back with a phone number. I had that in my wallet. I took it out and opened it up, stared at the front, here it all was, his name on there, his DEA [Drug Enforcement Administration] address. And I went to a copy store in town, and to the furthest away copier, and ran this through there, and it came out just like the real thing.

I ran about twenty more copies through, and bought a ruler and sharp little cutting knife, and got into my truck and took that ruler and copied it with a pencil, lined them up, cut them out perfect. When I had them side-by-side, you couldn't tell the real one from the one that I'd copied. And I drove to the K-Mart store in that town where I was at, where I'd gotten real prescriptions filled, and sat out in my truck, and because I'd had so many prescriptions for so long, I knew how they write. The doctors write different from how you and I do. I sat out there and wrote a prescription. I was shaking so bad, knew that what I was doing was totally wrong, was against all what I was taught growing up, signed my doctor's name, walked in there knowing I was going to get caught, shaking when I handed it over. I went and hid behind an aisle where the pharmacist couldn't see me, because it seemed for sure he would push some little button and some police were going to break the doors down.

The phone never rang. No police ever came in. Pretty soon I saw the bottle of pills sitting out there. I went and paid for them, walked out of there with 60 Percocet. Jumped into my car, drove across the parking lot, across the other road to the other parking lot where there was a Wal-Mart where I'd gotten real prescriptions filled too, pulled the same thing, handed the paper to the pharmacy, and pretty soon there were 60 more I'd paid for. Now I had 120. I pulled out onto the highway to return an hour to my home in Twin Lakes and I see a Target store—"I bet they have a pharmacy in there!" Now I'm cocky, thinking this is easy. Pulled in, wrote another prescription, walked in there, nervous but not as nervous, and handed it to him. He filled it. Now I had 180. I get back into my home in Twin Lakes, pull into our family pharmacy, and before I did, I ordered a prescription. Honest to goodness, I walked in and handed the pharmacist that paper! In my mind, it was like I had come right from the doctor! And I sat there and BS'd with the pharmacist, and he filled it all and I walked out. Now I had 240 Percocet, and it was like A-OK because I made a deal with God. I said, "God, if you just let me get through this until my dad dies and we get him buried, I promise you I'll get help." And once I made that deal with God, in my mind it *was* A-OK.

The next day, a Friday morning, I left for Michigan. I arrived that night. My dad died on Tuesday. We buried my dad on Saturday. When I left the church to go back home, 240 Percocet were gone. In eight days they were gone. And I lied to my stepmother. I said, "I think my pills are at your house." 'Cause my dad got buried in his hometown, and where they lived was a hundred miles distant, and I had to go through that town to get back home to Minnesota. I said, "Could I stop and get that?" She said, "Oh yeah, but the doors are locked. Ask the neighbor for the key."

My dad had been in so much pain. He had morphine going down his mouth and morphine patches. There were bound to be all kinds of narcotics. I went and ransacked my folks' house. Opening drawers and going through everything, but I could not find anything. And my two younger sisters who knew something was going on with me, just knew—I don't think my dad had died five minutes and they got rid of every narcotic pain medication there was. So I jumped in my truck and came to the first town with a pharmacy and said, "Will you take a prescription from a doctor in North Dakota?" "No. Sorry, he has no license here." So I drove like a maniac to northern Wisconsin. Same thing. No. I get into Duluth, Minnesota, about eleven o'clock at night and drove all over town looking for a pharmacy, and finally found one that's open and write a prescription. The pharmacist fills it and I get back in my truck and said, "God, I know I promised you I'd get help. But jeepers, my dad just died. You knew we just buried him today. Once this bottle is gone, I promise you I'll get help." Well, what alcoholic or addict doesn't say that? One last drink or joint and I'm getting help. Of course, once that bottle was about done I said, "God, here's the deal. There is no deal." I said, "I'm bummed out about my dad. I'm bummed out about what's happening at home. I need this stuff."

Now I was in full bore. I started writing prescriptions, not just for Percocet but also for Demerol and Valium, and because I was taking so many, I knew I couldn't go to the same pharmacy often, so I kept track in a little book with my own code. These little towns along this main highway that went to Fargo were small dinky towns, most of them with a ma-and-pop pharmacy where I would stop. I had an account at every single one. And I knew when to go back 'cause I could look at my record, so they didn't get wise to it. And I was totally out of control! My whole world revolved around taking the pills and getting the pills and making sure nobody saw me. I'd hide them all up under my dash. Nobody ever questioned me 'cause I made sure. We had a bait-and-tackle shop at the time in our town, and I'd go in, open the door deliberately. I'd always be on time and extra careful to make sure nobody would say, "Gee, what's wrong with him?" When talking to customers, before I said something, I thought through each word. And I would pronounce, almost overpronounce, not to slur. Walking, too, I concentrated and told myself, "Okay, Dick, one foot in front of the other." When I drove my car down the road, I did not exceed the speed limit, put two hands on the wheel, 'cause the last thing you want is to get pulled over for something. But the people I put in harm's way in my vehicle! I was taking people on guide trips, but there, too, nobody ever said, "Jeez, what's wrong with you?" I mean I hid it really well.

Before I'd get home, I'd take my last multiple of pills. Once I sat down at night, I was knocked out. Mary was getting real perturbed, and my son, Andy, would say, "What's the matter with you, Pop?" "Aw, I'm just working a lot and I'm really tired." Finally one night Mary says, "You think you could keep your eyes open long enough to watch a couple of movies with your son and me?" So I forced myself just so as not to get caught. The next morning Mary says, "On your way into town, why don't you drive by the video store when you drop Andy off?" That afternoon she called and said, "I know you don't have a guide trip 'cause of the bad weather. That was sure fun last night. Why don't you drive by and pick up a couple more." So I went to the video store and spent about a half hour looking for a couple of videos, and grabbed two I'd heard were supposed to be pretty good. I get home and walk in the house and say, "Here are the movies." And Mary says, "What'd you get?" And I answer, "I don't know, I've heard they're supposed to be pretty good. That's what somebody was telling me." And she looked at them, and all of a sudden her face got as white as a ghost and her jawbone hit the floor. I said, "What the heck's wrong with you?" "Why Dick, we just watched these last night." I couldn't even remember!

I remember another time when I must have blacked out. I came home—before I did, I popped a bunch of pills. Mary made roast beef and mashed potatoes and gravy. I was sitting at the supper table, and I must have blacked out. My head and face fell right down into those mashed potatoes and gravy. I was snorting mashed potatoes and gravy into my lungs. If my son, Andy, had not been there and grabbed my head out, I could have seen the obituary where "Beardsley suffocated on mashed potatoes and gravy"!

By that point, late August to mid-September, I was taking a cocktail of Percocet, Valium, and Demerol—80 to 90 pills a day. It was getting so bad that my gut . . . I must have been burning a hole in it 'cause I'd have to take half a bottle of Maalox to coat my stomach since the pain was so bad. I started having incredible severe headaches from drugs. When I got the headaches, I took more pills. The pills made the headaches go away, but half an hour to an hour later, with the headaches pounding, I actually would take more pills. I knew I needed help. I knew I was sick. But I was too ashamed. I didn't know who to turn to. I really believe I was within a day or two of going to sleep one night and never waking up again, 'cause those pills I was taking, they slow down your heart rate and breathing. One night I would have gone to sleep after a handful of pills and just never woke up again.

Finally, on September 30 of 1996, I went in with three fake prescriptions to get filled up, to the pharmacy I'd gone to many, many times. I handed them to the gal and she said, "Oh, it'll be about ten minutes, Dick." I looked over at the pharmacist—his name was George—and I'm waiting for George to look up and say, "Hey, Dick, how're you doin'?" 'cause he was a real avid fisherman and I'd seen him over in our community fishing. And all of a sudden, he just stopped counting his bills, and he just stood there looking down. I knew at that point it was over. And he finally walked around the back, and he came over, and he gently took me by the arm and marched me down an aisle nobody was, and he says, "Dick, the doctor and the police know what's going on." I said, "George, I need help." Walked back into his office and called the doctor. The doctor said, "Dick, why don't you come in this afternoon?" So George shook my hand and said, "Dick, good luck."

I knew I was in a lot of trouble, but it was also like a million pounds was taken off my shoulders. And I knew the only chance of getting better was to be 100 percent honest with people and take responsibility for what

I did. I went right home, told Mary all about it. That afternoon went right in and met with the doctor. The doctor says, "Dick, you're not a bad person at all, but you're really, really sick. I will do whatever I can to help you, but there are two federal drug enforcement agents in the next room that need to talk to you." He left. They walked in. These two federal drug enforcement agents come in. They got their federal badges on their hips. They got a stack of papers, a huge briefcase full, and they sat down and they go, "Dick, in the month of August alone, you wrote prescriptions for over 3,000 pills." They go, "When we see something like that, the red flags go up, and we all think the guy must be dealing these things." Man, when they said that, honest to goodness, I had never cried so hard in my life. I was blubbering so bad I was hyperventilating. I could hardly breathe. "You guys," I said in there, "I swear to God, not one pill did I give away or sell to anybody. First off, I was too selfish. If I got 'em, I was takin' 'em."

The federal agents interrogated me for over an hour. At the end of that hour, they said, "Dick, we've been doing this for twenty-plus years. We believe what you're telling us. We have a lot more investigating to do, but we believe what you're telling us. If you are telling the truth, we will do everything we can to keep you from going to prison. But do you realize that you can go to prison for a minimum of five years and receive a $10,000 fine?" And I am out of control because I never even seen a prison, let alone been inside or had to go to one. They listened to what I had to say. They said, "We will do what we can to keep you out of prison, but this will be your one and only pony ride. Should it ever happen again, we guarantee you'll be thrown in jail." And one of the officers took me to the hospital in Fargo, and for nine days, I was in the psychiatric ward.

I was locked up. I was so sick. My head just spun. I was glad now for a chance to perhaps get better, but yet I knew it was only the beginning. My family and Mary's family and our friends didn't know any of this was going on. And it was a really hard deal. I got right out of the hospital after nine days, and into a treatment center. It was outpatient, four times a week, four hours a crack, in the evening. Intense. I was assigned to this group and counselor, and listened to somebody talk about addiction. Then we divided into our little groups. I remember sitting in a circle—I'd never been in a group like this and didn't know what to do. They went around and introduced themselves. First our counselor says, "I am Sue. I'm an addict and an alcoholic." Next, "And I am Joe. I'm an alcoholic." They get to me and I say it. "I'm Dick. I guess I'm an addict." People looked at me and didn't say anything. Boy! That night, that first time, I just sat and listened. And I thought, "Boy, these people have some problems here." But when I said that word "addict," that was the first time I ever mentioned the word. It was never in my vocabulary. I said it, but I said it because I had to say it, not because I believed it. I did not believe it for a second. I thought to myself, "I might be overusing these things a little bit, but man, an addict? I'm not an addict. Heck, I got a family and a job, and don't have track marks up and down my veins and live in a burned-out apartment building and haven't taken a shower in months." That to me was an addict.

But I sat there and went to every meeting. Once a week was a one-hour one-on-one session with just the counselor. After the third time of that, she says halfway through, "You aren't taking this seriously, are you?" I say, "Yeah, I'm taking it very seriously." "Well," she says, "you're always smiling. You seem to be in a good mood. You're just trying to pull the wool over our eyes." I say, "Wait a minute. I always look on the positive side of things." That's just how I am 'cause months later my counselor, who saved my life, apologized for that because she found out I am like that. But I remember those one-to-one meetings with her. There was barely a session I wasn't crying, 'cause she told me things I didn't want to hear. At last, after going to them for three weeks and saying, "Hi, I'm Dick. I'm an addict," one night they went around and I said, "Hi. Dick. I'm an addict" and it was as if the lightbulb went on. When I said it that night, I believed it. And from that moment on, I started getting better and contributing more to everything. And I remember having to do my First Step. Writing my First Step. And it was twenty pages long. And I sat there that night when I had to read it in front of the group. I was crying, and everybody else cried, my counselor too, 'cause I just laid it there on the line.

So I got through that and remember when Mary got to do her First Step—where we were in a circle. I was looking at Mary, and my counselor was to her side and the group around us. And the counselor said, "This is

Mary's night, and you do not say a word." Mary started out and I thought, "This is going to be a piece of cake. She's hardly saying anything bad." Then Mary started getting a little more, a little more, and I tried to defend myself. She just hopped on me! Pretty soon Mary got on a roll, just letting me have it with both barrels. Mary didn't guess I was abusing the painkillers for many years. I think the last couple of months, she had an idea that something was going on, but I did a heck of a job of keeping it from her and most everyone else. I made sure when I talked that I knew what I was going to say ahead of time so not to slur my speech. When I walked, I made sure I put one foot in front of the other so as not to stumble. I was very careful how I acted so people would not catch on. It was hard work! Mary lost and my son, Andrew, lost all trust in me! It took about three years into my sobriety before I felt like I had earned it back with both of them! She does not really talk about it a whole lot.

All in all, it was very hard on Andy! When kids heard about it on TV or the radio, of course, because it was a drug offense, they thought I was dealing and using cocaine. He wouldn't go to school for a few days. When he did, I think he tried to ignore what the kids were saying, and eventually when the whole news story was revealed, they pretty much quit bugging him.

It was good for Mary to get it off her chest, and good for me to hear it. I'm tellin' ya, I needed to hear it, 'cause you don't realize what you put your families through. On our ride home that night, I felt we started to get back closer to each other again.

But I remained on this methadone. While I was in the psychiatric hospital, one doctor had put me on methadone, had tried to convince me I was probably going to have to be on it for the rest of my life for the chronic pain, as my pain was giving me a lot of problems. My back feels good now! Once they took the hardware out of there that had caused an infection, the pain pretty much went away. Don't get me wrong, it still acts up once in a while, but nothing that a little Advil can't take care of. Hopefully it will stay that way! It does not bother me at all while running.

Welcome to my nightmare
I think you're gonna like it
I think you're gonna feel like you belong
A nocturnal vacation
Unnecessary sedation
You want to feel at home 'cause you belong

Welcome to my nightmare
Welcome to my breakdown
I hope I didn't scare you
That's just the way we are when we come down
We sweat and laugh and scream here 'cuz life is just a dream here
You know inside you feel right at home here

—"Welcome to My Nightmare"

Alice Cooper
(musician)

THE FORMAL INVITATION read "The Coming Out Party for Miss Alice Cooper," a debutante ball, to be held at L.A.'s most prestigious and oldest hotel: The Ambassador. If memory serves me right, this was around 1971, when rock and roll was rocking and rolling.

Shep Gordon, Alice's much-talked-about young manager, and some of the PR innovators at Warner Bros. Records were putting together an event the music industry would not soon forget. Shep and I had become good friends, although he would not hire my PR firm to represent Alice. I remember him telling me that we could become *great* friends, but if we worked together, it would get in the way. I wanted both, but Shep prevailed. I never represented any of the artists he managed, and our friendship has lasted for more than thirty-five years.

Great anticipation surrounded the party for Alice. The Ambassador had no idea what Shep and Warner Bros. had planned for the evening, thinking it was just another debutante affair. The huge ballroom contained many formally set tables, complete with large, exotic, white flower centerpieces and tuxedoed waiters—the whole deal.

I knew the night was going to be way different when, as I was entering the reception area, I was approached by a "cigarette girl" offering "Cigars, cigarettes, Vaseline!" Closer inspection revealed "her" to be one of San Francisco's notorious Cockettes, the fabulous performance drag queens. This was going to be fun.

The open bar was crammed with partygoers intent on slamming down as much free booze as possible to ready themselves for the festivities. I ran into Shep and congratulated him for pulling off another media masterpiece, and he winked and directed me to a private men's room located behind the ballroom stage. I knew people would be going there to get high, but I was totally unprepared for the young lovely who greeted me in front of a toilet stall. She directed me inside for a special treat. "Have you ever had an opium suppository?" she queried. I reached to unhitch my belt. "No, but I think I'm about to."

The festivities took on a surreal quality under the influence of the chemical potpourri I had ingested. The bar-mitzvah-style chicken dinner was followed by the evening's entertainment: a mixed bag of musical wannabes. The closing act was a nude three-hundred-pound blues singer named TV Mama. Her husband and bandleader introduced her by proclaiming, "She may be TV Mama to you, but to me, she's TV dinner."

This oversized beauty came to the front of the stage. Ignoring the hooting and hilarity, she leaned over, shook her enormous bare jugs, and proceeded to sing "Happy Birthday" to Evelyn, the stunned wife of Mo Ostin, the head of Warner Bros. Music. I kept looking over my shoulder, wondering if this was being filmed by Fellini.

The evening culminated with a short set by Alice and his merry band of pranksters. I recall him as the most normal performer that night, which highlights how crazy things got.

I became better acquainted with Alice in the ensuing years, thanks to my relationship with Shep. Although Alice drank, I considered him pretty straight. He and his lovely wife, Sheryl, were as nice as warm pie and never seemed as weird as you'd expect. I'd hear stories of his exploits on the golf course, his golf cart filled with Budweiser. I always thought of how peculiar an image that was: Alice, Budweiser, and golf!

It was no surprise, really, when I learned that Alice got sober. You don't continue a career as demanding as his, for as long as he has, if you are drinking to excess. What I enjoyed most about Alice's story was the explanation about the relationship between alcohol and his Alice-self. Hope you enjoy it too.

—

Well, Gary, you knew me back then. I was in a band with a bunch of guys that were on the road with a new and successful album. We were sort of pioneers out there. We lived on the road for five years, six years. We didn't really live anywhere. People would say, "I want to send you a shirt. Where do I send it?" And I'd say, "You can't. We don't live anywhere." We were basically gypsies, playing five nights a week, sold-out shows. You know, you'd get up in the morning and you're going to get on a plane, so the first thing you do is pop a beer, have a cold beer. That's a nice good-morning beer buzz.

Nobody even thought about alcoholism. That wasn't even a consideration. When I thought of alcoholism, I thought of Ray Milland in *The Lost Weekend* or Jack Lemmon in *Days of Wine and Roses*. Really out-of-control business guys. You never thought of rock-and-rollers having alcohol problems. They just drank. They just drank beer. It was never a problem.

But it wasn't medicine then. It didn't become medicine until later on. Right then it was just fun. We would go through two, three six-packs each during the day. We always thought we were lightweights 'cause everyone else was doing heroin and cocaine and acid and Quaaludes and everything, and we drank beer. We were kind of the lightweights. It was always funny to me that groups like Alice Cooper and Black Sabbath—and groups like that—were beer drinkers, and then you would find out that James Taylor and The Monkees and The Mamas and the Papas were junkies. It was just the opposite of what it should have been.

The beer never raised any flags because I never missed a show. I never slurred my words. I never missed a step. I was the most totally functioning alcoholic on this planet. Maybe more functional than Dean Martin! It became part of my image. Having a beer in my hand was always part of

Alice's image. The Budweiser. We made it into a joke.

Later on I would say, "Oh yeah, I like hard liquor, but I don't drink that until after ten o'clock at night." And then it was, "Well, nine o'clock at night." And then it was, "Well, eight o'clock is okay." Pretty soon I was drinking two or three Seagram's VOs with Coca-Cola before I'd get out of bed in the morning. And that's when it became medicine. It took about four or five years to get to that point. It was a very slow creep. It wasn't like all of a sudden there I was drinking that much. I wasn't aware it was happening, and nobody else was. Again, I didn't miss shows. I never missed an interview. I was totally functional.

That's what fooled Shep and fooled me and fooled everybody. If I would have gotten horrible hangovers and been unable to do shows, we would have said, "Uh oh, there's a problem with alcohol here." But since I was too professional, even when I was feeling bad, to let alcohol stop me, we just kept ignoring the fact that I was drinking so much. I think if Shep would have realized how much of a problem it was, he would have taken me off the road. But none of us did. None of us understood that. We said, "Hey listen, we're not into the heavy stuff. Alice is just drinking and having fun and doing his shows."

But when it became medicine ... It got to the point during the Nightmare Tour I would look at my stage clothes, and I would look at the bottle, and I would realize that I would have to drink at least a half a bottle of that whiskey to put those clothes on and get on stage. I would start to cry because I realized that putting my Superman costume on was killing me. My inner self was telling me that every time I go on stage, it's killing me. And I would think, "Yeah, but there's an audience out there, so I'm gonna go do it."

The funny thing was that when I finally did get to a hospital, the psychiatrist sitting there said, "Okay, tell me about the whole thing. How much does Alice drink?" I sat there and thought about it and I said, "You know what? I never drank on stage. The show would be two hours long, and Alice would never drink." So he said, "Let me get this straight: You're blaming Alice for the problem, yet Alice doesn't drink." And I went, "Yeah, you're right." So it really wasn't the Frankenstein monster. It was the Dr. Frankenstein that was the drinker. The other twenty-two hours during the day, I was messing up. When I was on stage, I was fine. But I couldn't stay on stage twenty-two hours a day. So it was really funny, the juxtaposition: that when I was on stage working, I didn't drink, but all the other time was when I drank.

It got to a point that when I got up in the morning, I'd sneak out of bed 'cause Sheryl was there. I'd have two or three drinks, go into the bathroom and throw up blood, and then get back into bed, have a couple of beers, and I'd be okay. I felt that having a couple of beers was going to make things better. That next drink would make it better. Which was just the opposite. You know, I had pancreatitis, gastritis, I had zero potassium in my system, I was wiped out. And I was dying of it. The doctor finally said, "A month, two months of this and you'll be dead." And that's when I was in the hospital and had to take care of it. I went to the hospital on my own, but this was the crazy thing: Shep and Sheryl took me to the hospital the first time after the Nightmare Tour and checked me in. I could barely sign my name; I had tremors so bad. Sort of like the first three days, and it's a New York law, they can keep you for observation for seventy-two hours. Well, after seventy-two hours, I was really kind of okay. I got my sea legs back and was feeling all right. I spent about three months in the hospital. When I came out, I didn't have a drink for a year.

I remember this so distinctly. We were driving to Vegas and Sheryl had a glass of white wine, and I hated wine. I said, "Let me have a sip of that." I had one sip of her wine, and by that night, I had three bottles of whiskey hidden around the house, and I was drinking again. It wasn't like I slowly started drinking again. I was right back to where I was. It wasn't gradual at all. So anyway, I went to the hospital a second time. This time I went in there with a purpose to stop. I think any alcoholic better get that idea into their head, that if you're going into a hospital, you're not going in to slow down. You're going in there to stop drinking. When I came out, as much of an alcoholic as I was—you never saw me without a drink—I came out of the hospital and went to a bar, sat down, had a Diet Coke. I knew I was going to be around alcohol, and it never dawned on me to have a drink. I never went to a recovery program, never went to a psychiatrist. I just never had another desire to drink. It was as if I never had a drink before in my life.

To this day, when I'm on tour, people around me drink beer or whiskey, and it never occurs to me to have a drink. Never in twenty-two years have I had a craving for alcohol. It's like I had cancer one day, and the next day didn't have it.

I've been married to Sheryl for twenty-eight years, and I've never cheated on her. And I quit drinking twenty-two years ago, and I never cheated on that.

I became as addicted to being straight as I was to being drunk. I can admit one thing: I love the taste of beer, cold beer. But I won't even tempt myself by having an O'Doul's nonalcoholic beer. Why would I do that? Maybe just lighting that wick that doesn't need to be lit.

Looking back at my drinking days, I don't even recognize that character. It was another lifetime ago. And I look at the character of Alice Cooper, and when I was a drinker, Alice on stage was a victim. He was a character that was always getting beat up, always getting killed. He was the brunt of every joke and the outcast. I look at my posture on stage and I was always bent over. Always the whipped dog. And that was Alice Cooper.

The very first time I went back on stage as Alice Cooper—the very first time playing Alice Cooper sober—can you imagine that? I got four platinum albums as Alice Cooper, three number-one albums, all while I was drinking. The alcohol was part of the formula. Now, I'm standing there ready to do a show in Santa Barbara, and it's the first time I'm ever going to put on the Alice makeup sober. I'm thinking, "What is going to happen? What if I walk out on that stage and Alice doesn't show up?" I'll tell you what, I wore a path in that dressing room rug. All day I walked in a circle going, "What's gonna happen tonight? What if I get up there and nothing happens, and I'm just me, and Alice doesn't show up? And I've got an audience in front of me." That was the most afraid I ever was in my life.

I got up on stage. I'm covered in leather. All of a sudden, I thought that Alice is not the whipping boy but Alice was going to go in the opposite direction. He was going to be the arrogant villain. The super villain. Which means he stood straight up. He was Captain Hook now. He was going to be the elegant, arrogant bastard. I stood up there. My spine was straight. I had a riding crop in my hand. I looked at the audience and said, "You're mine!" It was an entirely different Alice. This Alice was in total control, whereas the other Alice had no control. I created a new Alice in one night! I never saw this Alice coming at all. All of a sudden, this Alice stood there and said, "I feel great. I own this audience." And they loved it. That's how I play Alice now. Now the character wants total control. Before he didn't want any control. He gave into the alcohol and said, "Okay, I'm at the mercy of everything," whereas this Alice says, "Everything is at the mercy of me."

I really enjoy playing Alice now. I can't wait to get on stage. Off stage, I'm just the nicest guy in the world, talking about my family, talking about baseball, but the moment I go in front of that audience, the moment Alice is standing there, the spine straightens. The whole attitude is different. It's like, "Okay, you're mine." People love the character.

The transformation takes place totally because of my sobriety. Now Alice has more ego than Mick Jagger. The character looks at the audience and thinks, "You are so lucky to be here tonight." Which is just about the opposite of the way I think. Alice became completely fearless—bigger than life.

Sheryl and Shep were the two people I cared most about, and they both went through it with me. But Shep only saw the fact that everything was fine. He was never there in the morning when I was throwing up blood. I never let him see that. Sheryl was the person that picked up that I was sick: "He may not come off as being sick, but he's sick. We have to get him to a hospital." Shep was saying, "What do you mean?" and Sheryl was telling him, "You don't understand, he's throwing up blood in the morning." And of course Shep was like, "Are you kidding me? He never told me that."

Looking back now, I was probably the most gregarious drunk around. Me and Keith Moon of The Who, we were probably the nicest, funniest drunks there were. Neither one of us was destructive, except to ourselves. We were the life of the party. But you never saw Alice when he was in a dark, black mood.

And the party was continuous. Sheryl and I had been married five or six years. We went to dinner every night with Bernie Taupin, Rod Stewart, and Elton. We were living the Beverly Hills life, which entailed drinking every night. But when I got to the point that I couldn't get out of bed any-more—for three or four days at a time—Sheryl said, "That's not you. I don't know who this is." At the beginning she just thought I was sick—the flu or something. Then she realized that I hadn't eaten in about a week but that I was drinking every single night. Yeah, she went through it with me, but she believed in me the whole time. Although there was nothing to believe in for a while.

Then when I went to the hospital and came back out, I said to her, "It's over. I know it's hard for you to believe, but let me prove it to you." Now, twenty-eight years later, we have never been happier.

I find myself running in circles
Lost and half insane
And I need a cure sometimes
To knock out the pain

So I yell out for some kind of angel
To come down and rescue me
Be as soft as you can
Put a drink in my hand
I'm as scared as I ever could be

Gimme lace and whiskey
Mama's home remedy
Double indemnity
Fills me with ecstasy
La-aa-aace and whiskey

Lots of things I really want here
Lots of things I really need
There's an animal soul inside
That I've gotta feed

The hot mama living above me
Always gets a rise from me
She's so soft in my hands
I give her all she can stand

Make a full fledged man outta me
Gimme lace and whiskey
Mama's home remedy
Double indemnity
Fills me with ecstasy

La–aa–ace and whiskey
La–aa–ace and whiskey
I ain't hard assed
So babe don't make me mean
I want a hot place
To go and show you things
Gimme lace and whiskey
Mama's home remedy

Double indemnity
Fills me with ecstasy
La–aa–ace and whiskey
I'll end up a broken old hobo
With red and yellow eyes
Swear' and drunk and dyin'
But no one's surprised

That's a long long way from today babe
As far as I can see
So shake off your shoes
Go and get me my booze
Lay your love and your laces on me

Gimme lace and whiskey
Mama's home remedy
Double indemnity
Fills me with ecstasy

La-aa-ace and whiskey
La-aa-ace and whiskey
La-aa-ace and whiskey
La-aa-ace and whiskey

—"Whiskey and Lace"

For what is a man profited, if he shall gain the whole world, and lose his own soul? or what shall a man give in exchange for his soul?

—Matthew 16:26

Pat Day
(jockey)

PAT DAY LEARNED to ride bareback as a boy on his parents' small ranch in Eagle, Colorado. His father was an auto-body repairman who had been raised on a ranch in South Dakota. Pat helped his father break and train horses for neighboring ranchers. He was a natural-born rider with an uncanny ability to relate to horses. After high school, Pat managed a gas station and, on weekends, rode in rodeos. It was by riding bulls that he learned how to fall and get back up again. This is a talent that would serve him well as a jockey and as an alcoholic/drug addict.

I met Pat for our interview at his condominium in southern Florida, while he was rehabbing a shoulder injury prior to the winter racing season at Gulfstream Park. Pat was about to resume riding after a six-month layoff. He was eager to get back in the saddle, and I could feel his excitement as we spoke. Pat's story is flamboyant, but he tells it quietly. He seems to want to minimize what addiction did to him and to focus on the part of his life when he found salvation and got back on track.

Coincidentally, my sobriety date, January 2, 1983, was the date of a wild binge for this then-young jockey. I was throwing in the towel, while Pat was going the other direction. Both of us had long runs, and abused drugs and alcohol for many years, but Pat hit the wall without ever getting thrown from the saddle.

Pat found sobriety through his religious conversion, which he speaks of with great enthusiasm. After we finished the interview, Pat invited me to go to a prayer meeting with him. Looking for an opportunity to experience his world, I readily agreed, thinking that we'd either be going to someone's house or perhaps a local church. I said, "I'm Jewish, but I'm happy to come with you to this thing." He nodded. "Good."

I took my own rental car, as I planned to continue on to my hotel after the meeting. Following Pat in his new Chrysler convertible, I noticed his license plate says "JESUS." We drove for what seemed like a very long time, passing some unique attractions along the way: a sushi diner where you can get sushi for breakfast, lunch, or dinner, and an intimidating-looking roller coaster situated only a few feet from the highway. It looks like the old, wooden Cyclone at Coney Island. The hand-painted sign says "Ride All Day for $10."

Finally we arrived at an extremely large parking lot, the kind you find at a major sporting event. Pulling in behind Pat, I observed a theater-like structure with a huge marquee proclaiming the evening's prayer meeting. I thought we were going to a Bible study with a few friends, but it turned out to be a full-scale revival with more than four thousand loyal followers. The meeting was fire, brimstone, and spectacle. Standing next to Pat, watching him completely caught up in the spirit of his God, I was truly impressed by his dedication and devotion.

Pat is a terrific example of what someone living a sober life can achieve. About a year after our interview, I saw Pat on a beautiful summer Sunday afternoon at Saratoga Racetrack in New York. He is still one of the premier jockeys in the country. To be at the top of this demanding game at more than fifty years of age is quite an accomplishment. I'm sure if you asked this humble man, he'd tell you he owes it all to Jesus and sobriety.

I was raised in Eagle, Colorado, in a great environment. My mother and father weren't opposed to having a drink on occasion, but they were not drinkers. My father was home every night. He wasn't an alcoholic that we had to pull out of the bars; he was probably the most responsible man I've known. If my father told you something, you could bank on it. He was a person of integrity, and the environment in which I was raised was opposed to over-abuse of anything.

I didn't have my first drink till I was a junior in high school. I started drinking a little bit of beer with kids on the weekends and didn't foresee it being a problem. After I graduated, it slowly became a problem, an every-night thing.

Two years after I graduated high school, I got introduced to the racing profession. In Arizona I went through the trenches, so to speak, and in July of 1973, I began riding races. I started doing very good almost immediately. My life-style at the time was going to the bar as soon as the races were over, partying until all hours of the night, and then getting up and going to work in the morning, going to the races in the afternoon, and starting right over again. It didn't seem to have a real negative effect in that I was able to do what I was doing and do it with tremendous success.

After I'd been riding for about a year, drugs started becoming readily available. I went from drinking daily to messing with drugs. I began smoking dope and using little speed pills known as "white crosses" or "bennies." The next winter I was riding down in New Orleans, which is a pretty wild town, and the partying continued. In the spring of 1975, in Chicago, I had drug paraphernalia and some drugs in my car. I was searched and they were found. I was suspended for fifteen days and put on probation for six months. You'd have thought that would have been a wake-up call of some kind, but it wasn't. Success, especially in the sporting arena, can lead you to believe you're above the law. You can get out of a lot of jackpots, which just perpetuates the problem.

By the grace of God, I was able to regroup after that. I got my business back together and started doing good again. Then cocaine became my drug of choice. As time wore on and I continued to do well, the thrill of victory on the racetrack and the success I was having didn't seem to satisfy me. That gave me a good excuse for drinking and doing drugs. I told myself, "I'm in a high-stress environment, and I need this to unwind." When you want to do something bad enough, you can make some pretty good excuses why you could or should do that. That's what I was doing at the time.

Doing coke made me feel I was bigger and better. I remember going into the jocks' room with coke on me, but determined I wasn't going to use that day. I would go out and ride two or three races and wouldn't do good. So then I would succumb to the temptation. I'd do some coke, and it seemed like the next horse would win. Which further convinced me that "Yeah, that's my go-to medication. That's what I need." There again it's a lie right out of the pits of hell because it takes you down the road to destruction.

I've ridden considerably better without the drugs than with them, but while I did cocaine and rode, I had myself believing I was much superior when I indulged. It was a false sense of bravado. Eventually I phased out the drugs, but I was drinking every night. I was a blackout drinker.

I failed to tell you that I was raised in a Christian home. I was con-firmed in the Lutheran faith. We went to church. I wasn't living a Christ-ian life-style yet considered myself a believer—there was never any doubt on my part of that. In 1982 I was the leading rider in the country, but as time wore on, that success didn't hold the meaning or feeling that I thought it would. That sent me searching for answers and asking some serious ques-tions: "Exactly what am I here for?" "What is life all about?" "What is my purpose in all of this?" I remember vividly going out at night and looking up at the sky, at the immense heavens, and saying, "Where do I fit into this picture? There's got to be more to life than what I'm doing."

I think probably in large part due to the fact that I'd been raised in a Christian home, taking that upbringing for granted, ultimately that would be the last place I would look. I thought I was a Christian, and that didn't seem to be the answer I was looking for. Sort of like in that old country western song—"looking for love in all the wrong places"—only I was doing that for the meaning of life. I was looking behind every bush and under every rock, figuratively speaking. Yet I think God had been working on me ever since I'd gone to church, that I was raised the right way, but during the early years when I made a name for myself in racing, I kept pat-ting myself on the back. The fame and the abuse had developed a horribly destructive mind-set. My ego had got more and more out of hand, and I was not listening.

Where cocaine gave me a false sense of superiority, I never drank and rode. I've come to realize that drugs of any kind are mind-altering merely in that they send you in the direction you're already going. People think if you drink it will lift your spirits. I believe it plays as a catalyst. For exam-ple, if you are down and depressed, alcohol drives you farther down. Now if you go out for an evening and are having a great time and have a couple of drinks to loosen up, it could enhance your evening. But I wouldn't rec-ommend that, you see; I'd recommend instead you just go natural and enjoy it, just have fun and try to live each moment to the fullest.

There was a cartoon some years ago captioned "The Power of the Martini." The first frame depicted a bar with a man at one end and a woman at the other, both not very handsome or attractive, not blessed in the area of looks. And it shows one martini and they've changed and are looking better. Two, and they look a lot better. Then three. By the fourth martini, they're glamorous—you'd think it was some god and goddess sit-ting there. The power of the martini to change your perceptions: I've thought about it often, how drugs and alcohol mess with our perception of people, places, and situations.

In 1983 I was the leading rider again, but by now I knew that it was going to be a short-term satisfaction for a long-term problem. It was not going to be the joy, peace, and contentment that I was seeking. But we got the title, and then in late January while vacationing with my family in Colorado, my brother and his wife and my wife and I all tied one on. We continued to mix it up pretty good, drinking beer, wine, and I don't know what all. In the aftermath I got quite sick, so I didn't drink anything. On January 27 I flew from Colorado to Miami, where I was scheduled to ride in a race on the twenty-eighth at Hialeah Race Track. I arrived in late evening. I was traveling by myself and checked into the hotel near the Miami International Airport.

When I got into the room, I turned on the TV set, as is a habit of mine, oftentimes just for company or noise, and went about getting ready for bed. I went about hanging up my clothes, when I noticed that I had tuned into a televised crusade of Jimmy Swaggart, the evangelist. Because I felt that I was a Christian, I didn't think what he had to offer was what I was looking for. I certainly wasn't going to sit and listen to some Bible-thumper preacher. Really at that point in time, I thought that to be vocal about your faith was for women, children, and wimps! It was a sign of weakness in my opinion. You had to "be a man," to have a go-it-alone kind of attitude.

So I flipped through the channels and nothing got my attention. I turned the TV set off and went to bed, and when my head hit the pillow, I went sound asleep. This was highly unusual—without several drinks as a sedative, it would ordinarily have been a difficult chore—because that evening I was probably as sober as I'd been in a long time. It was an incredibly deep sleep, and when I awoke, I felt I'd been sleeping all night. I woke to the distinct feeling that I wasn't by myself in that hotel room, which initially was reason for concern. I sat up in bed and looked around. I couldn't see anything, but I felt a definite presence there with me.

I don't know if the Lord at that point prompted me to get up and turn the TV on, or if I did it on my own to rid myself of these feelings. But I got up and turned it on and realized, as the picture came on the screen, that I hadn't slept long at all, because Jimmy Swaggart was still on, and he had just delivered the message of salvation and was having an altar call—where he invited people to come forward and invite Christ into their hearts. I realized in that instant that the presence in that room with me was the spirit of the Living God. I was being given the opportunity to bend my knee and invite Christ into my life.

Now, they say that when you die, your whole life passes through your eyes, and in a sense, my whole life passed before my eyes that night. I could see the number of times in the previous thirty years that, given the drinking and drugs and the kind of life-style that I was living, I was headed for destruction. I would be one step away from self-destructing, and this hand would materialize. It would gently nudge me back from the edge. At that moment, I intuitively knew that what I'd been longing for and what I needed was a relationship with God. I knew that the void in my life was a

God-shaped void, and only God could fill it. I fell on my knees and wept and cried and invited Jesus Christ into my life.

I don't know how long I was on the floor. I finally got up and went back to bed. I do know that when I got up the next morning and went outside that it was a decidedly different world. The world hadn't changed, but I had. The Bible says that when you accept Christ into your life, you become a new creature. The old things pass away, and all things become new again, and I was a new creature in Christ.

Now, I couldn't have verbalized that and told you at the time. I've since come to learn and realize that what happened was I became born again through the spirit of the Living God. I went on about my business that day, and it was incredible. The grass seemed greener, the sky bluer. All of a sudden, my senses were so in tune with everything around me. Whereas I was so dulled with the drugs and alcohol and the life-style I'd been living, now everything has taken on a new brilliance.

So I went about my way that day and finished up the races and got on a plane to fly back to Colorado. After we got into the air, a stewardess came by and asked if I wanted a drink. When I was sober, I was really a pretty polite individual, yet I snapped at her. I said, "No!" She said, "Okay, fine." I can picture the look on her, the astonished and shocked look on her face that I would snap at her like that. Then I sat back in my chair and said, "Now where did that come from?" I started looking inside. I realized that not only did I not find alcohol appealing, but I found it repulsive. And I truly believe that at the moment I accepted Christ into my life, He broke the chains of bondage to drugs and alcohol.

I have never gone to rehab or had a relapse. I've been in the company of people doing drugs and alcohol, and it's not like I have to fight the urge. What I do is try to talk to people who are doing it into not doing it: "That's not the way to go. That's not what you need to be doing. This isn't the answer to your problems. Here, I have the answer, let me share it with you." The people that I was trying to witness to and minister to were the same ones that I had partied with. They were like, "Git owda here!" That caused me to have to find a new circle of friends. Whether you are reaching the pinnacle of success or falling on your back, until you want help, God

Himself won't separate you from the habit or addiction that you don't want to get rid of.

A lot of people thought that the change that had taken place in my life was a momentary thing, and that I would come out of it, but Christianity to me is not a way of life, it is life. It is a continual, ongoing, ever-growing, intimate walk with the Lord. He is faithful. They now recognize that what happened to me was for real, that it wasn't a passing fancy. I recovered the day I accepted Christ. I was set free. When I sat down on the plane that night and snapped at the lady (and I apologized), the change had already taken place. As I said, when you accept Christ into your life you become a new creature.

I truly believe that if someone with an addiction of any kind has a heart's desire, a heart's cry, to be rid of that addiction, God will give that person the power to overcome. In my case, He instantaneously delivered me from the bondage of drugs and alcohol. Now, there's other areas of my life that the Lord and I together work on daily. I've always been competitive, but I wasn't a very good loser, and I was known to throw a temper tantrum if I got beat a nose in a race or if something didn't go my way. I had a vicious temper. But with the Lord's help, today I've got that in check.

And I realized right away that I was going to have a hard time witnessing for the Lord and living for the Lord if I used the kind of vulgarity that is second language—sometimes primary language!—in a locker-room environment. I was clear on that: Stay away from coarse talking. So the Lord has helped me and is continuing to help me to monitor my words and be careful about what I say and how I say it.

It's all a process, and God is continuing to work in and through me. God is faithful even when I'm faithless. So I'm not in recovery or recovering, I'm going in the spirit of the Lord and in the grace and knowledge of Jesus. As far as drugs and alcohol, I was set free from the moment I accepted Him. The Bible says that if you know the truth, then the truth will set you free. Elsewhere it says Jesus Christ is the Way and the Truth and the Life, and nobody comes to the Father except through Him. He is the Truth, and if you know the Truth, then the Truth will set you free. If you invite Christ into your life, you experience the power of God working in your heart and in your life. You experience the forgiveness of your sins, you are reconciled to God, and you have the power of God to tap into. It's not by might or by power, but by my spirit, sayeth the Lord. And it's the spirit of God working in and through me that allows me to be the person that I am and to be where I am today.

My life is better than it's ever been, and getting better by the day. I'd be lying if I said it was all just smooth sailing! I have good days and bad days—everybody does. That's part of being human. But my life is so incredibly better than it was twenty years ago.

I joke that I was like one of those life-sized cartoon characters, Popeye and all, air-filled but weighted at the bottom. That weight will finally bring them upright. For me, God was the weight at the bottom. My mother and father laid the foundation by raising me the right way, and I just waffled back and forth, back and forth, until on January 27, 1984, when I accepted Christ and finally came upright. By the grace of God, I have stayed that way for the most part.

My mother is still living; my father passed away in '86. Both parents saw me sober and straight. They had seen me at my worst, and it wasn't something they were proud of, yet at the same time, I think they recognized that they had raised me right—they had laid the groundwork. When the rubber meets the road, ultimately the choice has to be made. Needless to say, both my mother and father were ecstatic when the change occurred in my life. I wish my father was alive today to see the continuing change that has taken place, the success that the Lord blessed me with, and the positive influence that I trust I'm making on people I come into contact with in racing.

My daughter was born in 1986, so she never saw me under the influence of drugs and alcohol and never saw me in bad shape, but we have talked about the dangers of such. I've shared harrowing stories with her—near misses and close calls—and tried to impress upon her that I'm not proud of that. I only share with her for the reason I share with you, that she might learn from my mistakes.

I often share my testimony and tell people that if they're out there today and have a problem, know that there's help. I don't share to glamorize alcohol or drugs or make it look like what I did was all right—not by any stretch of the imagination! I despise what I did to myself, my family, and my friends—and what I very nearly did to the God-given talent and ability to communicate with horses and ride races that the Lord has blessed me with. To treat His love, grace, and mercy with disregard is disheartening to look back on, but I share in hopes that if there's someone on the verge of getting involved that they'd recognize it's the wrong way to go. That if they are involved, there's hope and help, and that they can turn away from that life.

> yes, it's true—I'm mellowing
> in the old days
> to cross my room you'd have to
> step around and between
> discarded trash and empty
> bottles but
> now the trash is
> packed neatly into
> sturdy garbage cans;
> also I'm a good citizen, I save
> my bottles for the city of Los
> Angeles to
> recycle
> and I haven't been in a drunk
> tank for a good ten
> years.
> boring, isn't it?
> but not for me as I now
> stay in at night,
> listen to
> Mahler and watch the walls
> dance;
> as newly mellow recluse that's good enough
> for me.

so I'm turning the streets back over
to you,
tough guy.

    —Charles Bukowski, "Poems for the Young and Tough"

When you turn the corner
And you run into yourself
Then you know that you have turned
All the corners that are left.

—Langston Hughes, "Final Curve"

Richard Lewis
(comedian)

As OFTEN HAPPENED with this book, a friend of mine recommended an interview—in this case, the ubiquitous and uproarious comedian Richard Lewis. Richard's publicist, Michelle, happens to be an old acquaintance of mine. I called her, and she told me she would contact Richard with my request. Within what seemed like minutes, I got an e-mail from her telling me that Richard would love to do my book. After a few more e-mail exchanges trying to set a time and place, Michelle gave me Richard's phone number at the hotel where he was staying in New York and suggested I call and make my own arrangements. I called, Richard was out, so I left a message. What follows is the phone message, verbatim, that I received from Richard that afternoon.

Gary, it's Richard Lewis. I'm in Manhattan, uh, but I'm not here a lot. The best thing to do ... First of all, I got your nice e-mail. I read your lovely note to Michelle. I guess you guys go back a long time too. Listen, here's a couple of options. She had mentioned the twenty-fourth. I fly the twenty-third, but those last few days in August, I have to finish up a *Play-boy* article for ... You know, that's my deadline, those few days. And you said a half hour. I usually go a little over. We could plan on forty-five minutes to an hour tops. Plus I wrote a

219

book, *The Other Great Depression,* which would fill in a lot of blanks, as I literally did write my story in that book. I think it's like ten dollars on Amazon now. I'll have to buy you a muffin if I ever see you.

But look, I have a show tonight. You e-mail me at [————]. Here are some options. I mean, today I have to prepare for my show, but tomorrow in the morning, I have to meet someone at noon, but I get up pretty early. You know, if we did it like nine o'clock, nine-thirty, or ten. And then I'm done with lunch at . . . After two-thirty, as close to two-thirty as possible, that's a possibility tomorrow. Like between . . . anytime between nine-thirty and eleven is good tomorrow. Tuesday, uh, I'm sorry. Yeah. No, no, wait, what am I saying? Jesus Christ, I'm so jet-lagged! Tomorrow, fuck me! Let's see. Mmm. Uh. Mmm. Mmm!

Sunday, huh, huh, okay. I'm going to get beeped off here, damn it! Monday I have a . . . I'm out of here from eight-thirty to around, uh, eleven, okay? Then I have lunch from twelve to two. So like after two-thirty on Monday is good. Okay? On Tuesday, uh, shit, I'm sorry . . . Tuesday I'm cool in the morning after nine-thirty. I have a lunch from twelve to two on Tuesday. And then I'm free after two-thirty, okay? Monday I'm free almost all day, the earlier the better. I have a dinner on Monday. Tonight, today's no good, okay? But, uh, Sunday, uh, I have a dinner, uh, but that's it. So Sunday is good. [cut off by answering machine]

Voice mail, twelve seconds later:

Gary, it's best you leave me some options for your . . . I forgot today was Friday. I have a concert tonight. So today's no good. Tomorrow I could find forty-five minutes on the phone with you. You know, I'm up after nine o'clock, nine-thirty. The earlier the better for me. You just e-mail me and tell me if I can call you. If you even work on weekends. You had mentioned the twenty-fourth, or Michelle did, but I come home the twenty-third. Then I have three or four days to finish a big piece for *Esq* . . . *Playboy* in four days. So I could do it, but I just . . . I'm in New York and I have some spare time, so . . .

So tomorrow I could find the forty-five minutes to an hour, say. That's more than a half hour, but that's fine. I also wrote a book, *The Other Great Depression*, which is easily gotten off Amazon in a day for like ten bucks. So that will fill in the blanks, should you even care to look at it. I mean that. I'm . . . you know . . . but you're . . . I'll . . . the interview will be good.

Sunday I have a dinner, so I'll be working Sunday. I have a . . . so Sunday I could do it too, from my hotel, if you wanted to spend forty-five minutes on the phone. Okay? Monday morning I'm out of here from eight-thirty to around eleven. Okay? And, uh, so that takes care of the morning on Monday. And Monday night . . . But Monday after eleven-thirty I'm good. Tuesday I can't do it. I can do it in the morning, but I can't do it from twelve to two. And then I have the evenings fucked up . . . But, you know, we wouldn't do it in the evening anyway. And, uh . . . so that's that. Those are good windows, right? And then Wednesday and Thursday I'm going to be pretty much here writing a few essays to try to sell another book. And I have to prepare for a big concert Friday night, so I'll be mainly in my hotel Wednesday and Thursday. I easily could find the time to do it with you Wednesday or Thursday. So that's like almost four or five days. It would really be a pleasure to get it over with, only in that it would help you to help me, rather than wait till I get back after the twenty-third, because it's going to get a little jammed from the twenty-third to the end of the month. I could do it, but I can find the time here, I mean.

Uh, so those are the windows. Play the message back and then e-mail me and let me know. Give me a couple of options, and I'll e-mail you back or call you and then hopefully we can do it while I'm here.

All right. And then, good luck with the book. It sounds fabulous.

———

This morning I was writing somebody I've been trying to help, giving him a panorama of New York. Telling him that while I was here performing, I was just walking around, seeing the Chrysler Building and thinking that John Ritter is dead, and Zevon's dead, and Farley's dead—not just alcoholics. The guy I was addressing is very well-known in show business, and I said, "It's your choice. It's a beautiful day here in New York. I'm sitting in my hotel room writing. I got my headphones on listening to Jimi Hendrix, and who knows for how long?" I said to him, "If a safe doesn't fall on your head, you got to be out of your fuckin' mind to go back to using again."

I know anything can happen. I'm a Friar and I went to the Friars Club yesterday. There's a lot of elderly people there, and I found out that two friends had passed away. I knew they were getting up in age and were ill, but I was really shaken by it, so I walked around New York City all day yesterday and went to all my old haunts. I visited all my old bartenders. They all know I'm sober now. These are guys I love. It was such a great feeling, to see them and greet them. Have a Diet Coke, tip them in a little grandiose fashion, but it was okay. I just wanted to say, "Hey, I'm alive." These guys took care of me. None of them would let me get carried out of their restaurants. Now it was just fun to go to a bar and not drink. To be sober at a bar.

It's hard to know exactly when I became an alcoholic. What I do know is that growing up I felt misunderstood, not appreciated, and needing validation. I didn't feel I was getting it from important people in my life. They had their problems, their own concerns. I felt sort of invisible. The way I handled that was by leaving. By going to college, which was great. People were listening to me. They were younger of course—it was college—but I got validation for my point of view. Then I found out that I was funny, and I realized that this was like a natural high. I could make people laugh. So when I got out of college, I became a comedy writer.

My father died before I ever went on stage. He was a great caterer and a powerful figure in my life. I put him on a pedestal. I would have become a comedian eventually, but when he died, when I was twenty-three, it had such an impact on my family, on my mother and my siblings. It was such a shock. He was a giant to us, such a Babe Ruthian figure. I had a hole in my soul when my father died. I had already begun to write jokes, but that wasn't filling me up. So I went on stage, but I was thrown into a business where I was judged every time I went on stage. Whatever psychological problems I had—and I had my share from growing up—were accentuated being in an environment with so much booze. Slowly but surely drinking became my way to relax, to celebrate. It was a way to numb the pain of bombing. It was a way of dealing with things I didn't want to deal with. Drinking made me feel not as miserable. It was a great Band-Aid.

It progressed, but it didn't stop me in my career. I've done well, and I was an alcoholic at the height of my career, when I really hit. When alcohol really got me by the throat, I quit stand-up comedy. Acting was easier. Easier to stay sober most of the time, do my work, and know I'm off for three days. Then I'd drink as much as I wanted 'cause I didn't have to show up anywhere. I did most of my drinking alone, but I certainly did a lot of drinking while dating. The women weren't enabling me . . . well, maybe a few did, offering me drugs toward the end. Not all of them knew I was an alcoholic. I hid it well early on. I remember one woman said, "You're so much nicer when you don't drink." Like everyone else, I have these tremendous horror stories, and my life by my early forties was totally controlled by my need to drink.

One very economical visual would be . . . On the road, I had finished my concert the night before in Albuquerque, New Mexico. A lot of these cities have different rules for alcohol. It was Sunday and it was in the afternoon, but there was this cage over the bar. It was closed, but I felt like a wild animal wanting to break into the bar. All sources of alcohol were closed. Apparently they didn't sell alcohol in Albuquerque on Sunday. I wanted to pry open the metal cage.

There were tip-offs, even way early. I remember getting some sort of sexually transmitted disease that was going to last for a week. I had to take certain antibiotics, and I remember the doctor very nonchalantly saying, "Oh, by the way, you can't drink for five days." I was going to New York to appear on the Letterman show, and all I thought about was, "Oh my God, there I am in first class, five-and-a-half hours in an airplane, without booze. There I am in New York with my friends and no booze. I can't even have a couple of glasses of wine in my hotel room to relax before the show." That's all I thought about. I wasn't thinking of my career. I wasn't thinking about anything but "I can't believe I can't drink." It was horrifying. And that was thirteen years before I bottomed. I tell a lot of people now, in sobriety—like I told someone today who had almost two years and he slipped—I said, "You know you really put a lot of sober time in the bank. You have to know that that time you spent sober is not lost. I've heard you and seen you inspire others when you were sober, including me, man, so believe me, not only was your life better off, but so was ours and it's time not lost."

I left rehab because I was ashamed. People recognized me and that made me ashamed. Plus, I guess I hadn't bottomed out yet. I knew I had to stop drinking. It was murder to do, but I had to stop. I knew I was going to lose everything: my career, my friends, my house, my work. I could go crazy. Anything could have happened.

A friend of mine who is a psychologist said I would never survive rehab because of my shame, and he was right. I felt that I was there not just as an alcoholic like everybody else needing help, but I also felt like "the celebrity" and it made me feel singled out and even more ashamed of myself. So I left, but I knew I was in trouble. So I went to this self-help group back in Los Angeles, and I've been going ever since. I've had two slips. One slip, and then I had a really bad slip, and that was my bottom. These were brought on by God knows why.

It got to the point where I was in my early forties. I was very depressed and in my house. Then the epiphany happened. I flashed back to wandering the streets of New York. Broke. Then I thought, "You know, I bought this house in the Hollywood Hills by telling jokes. It's a dream come true." I was hallucinating. I was emaciated. Holed up doing coke for six nights. I was just isolating and using, and I said, "This is a nightmare, what I'm doing." I felt like I was sinning against myself and whatever God I believed in. I was ashamed to waste my life, given all the blessings I had. That I would throw away my life needlessly. To have a disease that I could stop giving myself, if I surrendered, finally.

Then I called some friends and said, "I've had it." And that night, I did surrender. I quit. *No más.* They took me to an ER where the doctor recognized me and the nurses were pointing at me, and it was similar to the experience I had before in my brief rehab stint, but this time I felt no shame. I was just so thankful. A nurse came over and I was sweating, and she rubbed my brow. Then the doctor looked down at me—he was a thirty-something guy who probably grew up watching me on Letterman— and he said, "Richard, what are you doing?" I said, "I'm killing myself, but no more. I quit. I can't beat this disease." And that was it. August 4, 1994, and I'm just glad my bottom was there and not in the ground.

It was like what I told this guy today, "You didn't waste a damn minute sober. That time is in the bank. Go back to your sobriety bank, and remember how you were last month. You know how it feels to be healthy."

When I was in the treatment center and ready to leave, some of the staff walked me around for hours telling me it was going to be all over for me if I left. They were really firm about it, but I was still in denial, so I had to get away. I felt scared bolting, but I was too fucked up to surrender, although if it hadn't been for the embarrassment, I would probably have left anyway. I would have said the beds were uncomfortable or something. My disease was cunning. Now, of course, I look back and wish that I had stayed and left with a better understanding of what had got me there in the first place. Yet even though I bolted, I'm fairly certain I wouldn't be sober today without spending that one night and morning, a hopeless drunk, feeling humiliated and out of control in an actual rehabilitation facility. I realized I was not superhuman, that I was teetering on a demise and had to acknowledge my alcoholism. The real reason I left rehab was I wasn't done trying to die. It was three months later I hit my real bottom.

Again though, the therapists told me in no uncertain terms that if I left, I was flirting with death, doom and destruction, insanity, and all the rest. They were right. I've been to enough funerals in the last decade of people who I'd once held by their lapels, begging them to stay the course yet never ever seeing the light of belief illuminate their eyes. It was clear to me, even in very early recovery, that the only people who ultimately saved themselves and seriously entered recovery were those who not "just maybe" knew that they needed it, but also wanted it. I've discovered that those who tried to get sober for anyone other than themselves usually had a tough go at it or failed completely. It takes a lot of courage—and faith. I had that darkness of denial and disbelief in my own eyes up through that night when I looked in the mirror at my house and didn't even recognize myself. I had no idea who I was looking at. When I looked in my mirror in my bedroom, when I hit rock bottom and saw how I looked, I realized I was throwing my life away. That's when I totally surrendered to the disease. You know, everyone has a story, but for me, I felt pitiful. "Pitiful" is a good word to describe how I felt. I felt it was a sin to die of this disease if I didn't have to.

Right now I'm in an almost-seven-year relationship, a relationship I could never have been in if I was still drinking. It's funny. This woman saw me in a sitcom back in the late eighties, but she said, "Oh, he's too neurotic." Believe me, the neuroses wouldn't have done us in; the booze would have. This is a woman who has never seen me have a drink. She's known me seven of my ten sober years. If something comes up and we have a little argument, I fall into the trap of saying to myself, "You have no idea how bad this argument would be if the Drambuie was hidden behind the cornflakes, man! You have no idea what an asshole I'd be."

In fact, many times, especially early in recovery, I felt that I deserved recognition simply for acting saner and more principled. Of course, I felt this way, in particular, with people and in relationships with those who never saw me loaded. Almost as if I expected to feel, from time to time, like there ought to be a ticker-tape parade in my honor, with yours truly the grand marshal, sitting atop a float waving to the cheering throng and saying, "Hey, look at me, I'm sober! Thank you, thank you very much!" But, of course, there's no parade. It took me quite awhile on my sober path to feel grateful just for not drinking. For any alcoholic, it's true what I heard a fellow addict once share: that for us, even if we do nothing else in a day other than not drink or use, that alone is huge.

For sure, when the feelings hit home, sometimes they hit harder when you're not high. You feel them full force. I sometimes get a little irritated when things aren't going my way, because I'm feeling the feelings too strongly. But at least I'm able to feel them and be relatively clear. This was never the case before, when I was high and the disease made clarity virtually impossible. It's a pleasure in recovery not just to see things the way they really are, but to know that your side of the street is clean and finally be able to trust your own feelings.

I wish I had more sober time with my mother. My mom died in 1999, and I regret to say she had a horrible last couple of years. She really didn't even know who she was. My mom had a great sense of humor but a lot of problems. My father was a workaholic and a great caterer—sort of a big star in New Jersey and New York. When you needed a caterer, he was the best. After so many years of struggling, when I became successful and well known, it seems to me that I became a threat to my mother. It wasn't like she was mean spirited. I think my father was a real big shot. Not that he flaunted it, but he was. My mother gradually slipped into the shadows. I really don't understand it. I have an older brother and sister, and I don't think even they know. I do know that my mother had a tough time and really didn't enjoy her life. Consequently, I inherited a lot of her traits. I didn't enjoy a lot of my life either.

I would say to my mother—and it's very humorous now—I'd say, "I'm on *The Tonight Show*," and she'd say, "Who else is on?" You know, it was the opposite of a nurturing mother. Now, at fifty-seven, I can look back and see that maybe behind my back she'd tell people that her son is on *The Tonight Show*. But to me, she was very hard.

A mother is a mother, and if you're not nurtured in a way that is loving early on, there's like a dark hole that can stay with you through decades of psychotherapy. A lot of that is filled with the need for accolades, applause, and affection from women. I ultimately needed alcohol and drugs, for which my mother is not to blame, but she had problems. My father was never home, my sister moved away when I was eight, and my brother had his own stuff to deal with. Left to my own devices, I became an alcoholic. My mother was also a hypochondriac and had all these dysfunctions, which I think she left me in her will. We weren't an odd couple; we were basically two peas in a pod.

It was important for me to get affection from women, but I was also scared shitless. You know, in sobriety I've made amends to every woman I had a serious relationship with. They all told me that they cared about me, loved me, and I'm still friends with some of them. Some are alcoholics, and I've tried to help them. I might have hurt them or hurt their feelings at the time, but I gave them enough love, affection, and caring when I wasn't high that they knew I had a disease. After the fact. I'm proud I didn't burn almost any bridge. I didn't burn my career, wind up insane, or go to jail. I didn't kill anyone while drunk. I made amends to everyone I thought I hurt. All my relatives and everyone said they loved me and they are proud I'm overcoming this disease.

I can't say that for a lot of people. A lot of people I know have blown up their lives and sometimes can't get a lot of it back. I remember an older guy I met who would always say, "Hi, I'm so-and-so, and I'm a grateful recovering alcoholic." He'd been in recovery for thirty years. I just thought it was his hook, you know, like every comic has a hook. An alcoholic with a punch line. But now I totally get it. Sometimes I even say it. I've stolen his hook! I mean, "I am sooo grateful for two main reasons: I didn't kill anybody, and every amends I made was taken with love and respect and best wishes for me."

Back to my mother, who was unfortunately the type of woman who felt guilty about everything. She had a very interesting personality. She was incredibly narcissistic and unbelievably filled with low self-esteem. I'm certain I inherited part of that. I'm not as narcissistic as I used to be. You have to have some to be in show business, or you'll get trampled to death. And self-effacing? I'm even less that. The more grateful I got, the less self-effacing I became.

I remember one day, I was about two or three years sober, my mom had this wonderful man, Jack, who is still alive, whom she met a year or two after my dad died. They became boyfriend and girlfriend for twenty-five years. Jack used to work in sports as a soundman. He'd work at Yankee Stadium, wherever. He's a great guy. He's getting up there. Jack was great to my mom. And when I'd be in New York, it was almost like a religious thing: the Friars Club in New York has maybe the greatest brunch in the world, and almost every Saturday, I'd take Jack and my mom. So this Saturday we were at brunch, and I told my mother I was an alcoholic. "No you're not!" she said flat out. And I blew it. I lost it. I took her into the other room in a frenzy, to talk privately, and said, "Don't you ever say that again. I am an alcoholic, and I'm in recovery. I'm a drunk, alcoholic, drug addict, and I'm fixing myself." And she couldn't accept it, because she felt responsible. At the time, I was angry because I was in early recovery. A lot of people would have said, "Hey, good for you, you've surrendered." I understand my mother's reaction now, but then it made me so, so angry. I got sober in '94. My mom started getting sick in the middle of '97 and died a year and a half later. I had moved to California so I didn't see her often. When I saw her the last time, she had lost her marbles. It was very hard to see her that way. I'm not sure she knew who she was or not. I told my older sister, who was in the trenches with my mother on a daily basis, "I want to be alone with Mom." She really was pretty gone by that point. And I held her hand, and I didn't talk about alcoholism, but I said, "Look, you did the best you could given who you were, with warts and all. I did the best I could too. I love you and I know you love me. And if you know what I'm saying, can you squeeze my hand?" And she squeezed it really hard. That was the last time I saw her.

I was born into the Jewish religion. I'm not a huge organized religion person, and I'd feel a lot better if I could see some proof. On the other hand, I'm convinced the big bang wasn't Hugh Hefner's first party at the mansion. I think maybe there was also some kind of spiritual thing going on: "All right, there's going to be a big bang, and then we're going to have some apes, and the apes are going to evolve." I think something came first, and that's where I'm at. I'm very spiritual in a lot of ways. Like Spinoza said,

"God is everywhere." I have personal ideas of what a deity is, and it saved me. Initially I had problems getting sober because I felt, being an agnostic, I was being forced into being more spiritual. I hated it. I remember in college when a new band came out, like Led Zeppelin or something, as great as they are, I waited months to buy their record. I hated to follow the line around the record store. I disliked following. I felt like people were forcing me to believe in something I didn't believe in. It took me some time, but I found something other than Richard Lewis, because Richard Lewis was going to kill me. So that was a good thing.

I guess with women, though, I was an affection junkie. I don't think I was so much a sex addict as I was an affection junkie. I really needed women. Laughs were great and accolades for my art were good, but women . . .

I guess it had a lot to do with my mom, in that I felt rejected by her so much of the time. She had no choice but to reject me, because a myriad of reasons stemming from her own complexes made it so that she just couldn't accept me. She would've had such a nicer time if she could have. I would always hear, "Oh, your mother's so proud of you," but in reality, she had a hard time being proud of me. I think I searched out as many women as I possibly could. Being well known, it was easy to meet women, but it was empty.

This past year I ran into a lovely woman whom I recognized, and we're friends now, again, but this is how bad it got towards the end. She came over and introduced herself. I had forgotten her name. I had gone out with her about three years before I bottomed, so I was really on a bad roll. Apparently, she told me, we had gone out for four months, and I had no recollection of making love with her, kissing her, seeing her. I totally blocked out the whole relationship. I remembered her. I remembered who introduced me to her. And then she started telling me specific events of parties that I recalled. She knew my license plate! She's a producer and married now and has a beautiful child. This episode scared the shit out of me. A four-month relationship! If you can't remember dating a woman for four months! Now that we've become really great friends, she has shared something interesting with me. She only went out with alcoholics. She had a problem with commitment back then. Finally though, she met her husband-to-be, and I was the last drunk that she went out with. Thank God! She said, "You know, when they carried you out of the restaurant on New Year's Eve, I thought to myself, 'You know, it's time maybe to find another kind of guy.'"

So things got really bad. As my therapist told me, I needed to get as much affection as possible from women to prove to myself that I was worthy of a woman's love. Writing and performing was a natural high, a way to express myself. I was scared when I started, like everyone else. I struggled. I was poor, but I didn't care. I had this tremendous passion for comedy, and it took me ten, fifteen years to make anything close to a decent living, but I couldn't care less. I felt like a million bucks, I really did. I felt like I was living in a castle. I was going on stage in the early days in New York for free. Getting laughs, talking about my feelings, and that's all that mattered. I really needed that. Unfortunately, alcohol came into my life. Although at the beginning I knew how to manipulate the booze while perfecting my craft, in the end I finally couldn't.

At the height of some of the greatest things in my career, I quit. I could have made a fortune at stand-up and put so much away, but I knew in the back of my mind that I would have blown it. Drinking was affecting my performance, so I just coasted.

I remember once in Hollywood during this time, I went to a screening of Penny Marshall's movie *A League of Their Own*, a baseball movie. I drank most days, unless I thought I had the flu. If I wasn't working, I would often binge, but I wasn't stumbling around like a Robert Louis Stevenson pirate all the time. You know, I'd had horrible days, and normal drinking days, and some days nothing at all. On this day, I had a little dinner and a couple glasses of red wine. The premiere was at a huge theater in Hollywood, with everybody there, every high roller in town. I was in a relatively successful sitcom at the time, with Jamie Lee Curtis. Everybody knew me. So I went and sat in the front row, and as soon as the curtain opened, I fell asleep. Literally fell asleep. I don't know if I snored. I could have walked in my sleep. I could have gone shopping for pajamas next door. I have no idea what I did, but as soon as I heard applause, it woke me up. I don't recall my exact feeling, but I knew that I had to fake something really major, 'cause

I didn't see the movie. Forget about being rude—falling asleep! I wish someone would have tapped me on the shoulder . . . "Wake up, jerk!" Instead they let me snooze for two hours.

So I walk up out of the theater and hear, "Hey Richard, Richard, over here!" The cameras—*Entertainment Tonight, Access Hollywood*—all those shows are there. "What did you think, Richard?" . . . "Unbelievable! Tom Hanks. Is he ever bad?" I was going way over the top. It was a good film, I eventually saw it, but I was so nervous that I hadn't seen it that I was making it like *Citizen Kane*.

So I got home and said, "Wow, I dodged a bullet." I thought, "Great, who knew?" About three in the morning, I got a call from a friend who knew I had a drinking problem. He said, "Let me tell you one thing, Richard. If you think nobody in Hollywood thinks you're alcoholic, I got news for you. Everybody knows." Then he hung up. And I still had three years left in my run.

I just had lunch with a friend of mine who was very responsible for my intervention. She and another friend set up the intervention in 1994 to get me to this great doctor in New York. I was in a hotel, and I was out of it. They barged in the door, all of them, including my sister. That did it. When my sister came up from Maryland along with my friends, that connection with my family just brought me down. I would have gone to their doctor but not with the same kind of import, if my sister hadn't shown up there.

I ended up going into rehab. I didn't do the twenty-eight days. I wish I had. I would have learned more about my disease had I stayed. But I worked my ass off. I couldn't believe I had ended up such a mess. Like I said, I left the facility because I felt ashamed when other people recognized me. So I flew home, but the next day, I went to a support group and I haven't left since.

When I think back now, had I bottomed by the time I got to rehab, I would have stayed. I wasn't ready. I used the fact that people pointed and said, "That's Richard Lewis," and that shame caused me to bolt. But the truth is I wasn't ready. I wanted to see if I could still do it.

There's a guy, a very famous songwriter and a real recluse, who lived a mile away from me. I'll never forget this. I was in my house. I had been doing cocaine for about six days, and I looked like hell. I knew this guy had done coke, but that he didn't do it anymore. I was scared, so I reached out to this guy. I knew he wouldn't throw me into a rehab again but was somebody who understood the disease. He flew down to my house and sat there with me. He's one of the most brilliant songwriters in the world, a rock-and-roll guy.

In my house, an old house in Hollywood, I have a lot of photographs of dead people who OD'd. Lenny, Joplin, so many. And this guy sat there, and he looked around. He told me about Miles Davis and Tim Hardin, an old folkie that I loved, and he said to me, "Look, Richard, these guys checked out way before they had to." He said, "You don't have to check out now. You're going to check out, but you don't have to." I started crying. I was scared. I thought it was over.

He left, but he started faxing me. Faxing me these beautiful letters of support. Then I called somebody, a very prominent sober person in one of my support groups, and he zoomed right over, like my songwriter pal. He said, "Okay, here's what you're gonna do." Whatever the guy said, I was going to do. If the guy said, "Don't eat mustard," I wouldn't have eaten mustard. And you know, it worked. I listened. I'm a decent actor. I know how to listen, but for a long time, I wouldn't listen about alcohol. I changed when I started to take direction.

I've also learned how to help friends. I never knew when to stop trying to help, and it took a few years to learn that they have to want it. It was really hard for me to let go. To say, "I'm here. You know where to reach me. Get sober and we'll get help." For years I would go to friends' houses. They were high; it was insane. It almost brought me down. I was told by people with long-term sobriety: "They're high, you say no. You want to get sober, call me, and I'll help you." I couldn't understand that. Now I get it. I have to watch out for my own sobriety.

One reason I love being sober is that I thought about this guy I saw before coming to New York, who slipped last week, who I spoke to this morning. I wouldn't have got up at six in the morning and written him this long e-mail. I wouldn't have been able to do that if I was drinking. I couldn't have helped this guy. To think if I walked over to the refrigerator in this hotel room and had a Scotch, not only would I let myself down but I couldn't help anyone else. It's one of the greatest things of the rest of my life. If I'm going to leave any kind of legacy, making people laugh is fine, but to help somebody get the darkness from out of their eyes and to turn their life around, it's the most important aspect to my life.

It felt like hours I was fighting with this demon.
He rips my clothes and laughs at me.
It felt like hours I was fighting with this demon.
He rips my clothes and laughs at me.
He throws his staff at me as if it was a spear.
He was surprised that I caught it.
He grins at me and says,
"What are you going to do with that?"
With a smile that a dog would make.
I said back to him furiously with my chest
Scratched
"I'm going to break it so you can fight
Me as a real man!"

—Tone One, "My Battle with Life"

Steve Earle
(musician)

STEVE EARLE REMINDS me a little bit of me. When I started getting
high on a regular basis, as a very young man in the early sixties, I was
drawn into a newly forming culture for divergent reasons. Drugs took
me to wonderfully imaginary places in my head, and using them with
abandon said a big "fuck you" to authority. Making them available to
women I knew also helped me get laid once in a while.

While my alcoholism and drug addiction led me to an inevitable
downfall and a thankful recovery, my attitude toward authority never
really changed much. Sure, I've mellowed with age, experience, and
perhaps some wisdom. But my heart still warms when I see street
protests challenging the establishment in the form of big brother, big
business, or any other "big" that wields power over the little.

So when the name of Steve Earle was mentioned as a possible
candidate for this book, my first thought was a big "Hell, yeah." I got
hold of his newest CD, *The Revolution Starts Now*, and I was immediately drawn back to my "street-fighting man" days. This is one con-
tentious hombre.

After a few calls tracking him down, I was offered the chance to
interview him at the offices of Artemis Records in New York, while
he was there for one full day of interviews promoting the new record.
I was given the 3:00–3:30 slot, which, as you can imagine, didn't give
me much time to settle into the conversational pace I'd grown used

to while doing these interviews. But Steve is professional and jumped right in. I came out of it feeling grateful for the chance to include this extraordinary artist in the book.

I identify with what Michael Moore said: "Steve pulls no punches and gives me much hope. . . . If I were a rock star, I would be Steve Earle."

———

I used from the time I was really young, smoking marijuana before I started drinking, started when I was eleven or twelve. I drank because everybody drank. It was the late sixties, early seventies, and there were a lot of drugs out there. There was a lot of rampant recreational drug use. Psychedelics were a very big deal. Probably the very first thing I had a problem with was LSD. I got so fascinated with it that I took it as often as I could. Heroin came along pretty early. The first time I shot dope, I didn't get sick. Everybody else I knew threw up. That should have told me that I was in trouble. Heroin completely, totally agreed with my system. Almost everyone else I ever saw shoot up for the first time immediately vomited. I had an uncle who was five years older than me that turned me on to the first drugs that I used. His father was an alcoholic and had gotten sober in New York right after World War II. He knew Bill W. and Dr. Bob. AA [Alcoholics Anonymous] was still a relatively small program in those days. The program really kind of started in New York. So I grew up with the Serenity Prayer and the Twelve Steps on the wall. It didn't save me, but I'm not one of those people that had to find out that the program existed.

For many years, I used what people referred to as "successfully." Being very, very driven by art and what I do, and not concentrating on any one drug for any particular length of time. I sort of settled into drinking way, way, way, way, way too much by the time I was in my late teens, and alcohol became the core rather than heroin. I was physically addicted to heroin at several points when I was in high school and after I dropped out of high school, but I could always lay down and kick. I moved to Tennessee when

I was nineteen, and heroin was almost nonexistent there. There were a lot of Dilaudids on the street, but they were really expensive and I couldn't afford them, so I concentrated on alcohol and smoked a lot of pot. I began having anxiety attacks when I smoked marijuana; I started getting paranoid and having full-on anxiety attacks, so I stopped smoking pot. About every nine months or a year, I would try it because it had been in my repertoire from the beginning, but I'd end up hiding my head under a pillow or going to the emergency room.

I did cocaine when I was younger, and sometimes mixed it with heroin when I was bored, but by the time I got to Nashville in the mid-seventies, the whole world was trying to have cocaine declared a vegetable. I sort of knew it wasn't. I sort of knew that this was a really addictive, dangerous drug, but I kind of conveniently forgot. I'd use it but I never really liked it. Everybody I knew was doing it. I really couldn't afford it. By that time I was a songwriter. I wasn't making a lot of money. I watched as it became the drug of choice in the music industry. Drugs sort of ruined the street-level democracy in Nashville because it created a caste system. Suddenly people were hiding in bathrooms and being paranoid that people were only hanging out with them because they had drugs. All these strange things happened around that drug.

I was living with my second wife. The demise of my first marriage was because of my drug use and my attraction to the woman who turned out to be my second wife. My attraction to my second wife was totally about our mutual interest in drugs. I had found a woman that could keep up with me. I thought that would keep me from having arguments at home. We almost killed each other during the three years we were together. It was ridiculous, but it was mostly about drugs. I was probably one of the first people that freebased cocaine in Nashville. I had a brief experience free-basing one night, and I thought I was going to die, thought I was having a heart attack. It was just another anxiety attack, but it scared me bad enough that I stopped taking cocaine. So suddenly I was faced with the fact that if I wanted to hang out with my wife, I had to watch a lot of other people taking cocaine when I wasn't taking it, which was ridiculous. It eventually led to the demise of that marriage. I stopped taking drugs altogether because none of them were working for me. I stopped and I stayed stopped.

Cynthia and I split up, and I didn't use for a while until I met the woman who became my third wife. She worked in a bar, so I started drinking beer. I also discovered and started taking prescription opiates, when I could get them. I had some problems with my teeth by that time, probably brought about by my drug use, so I got a few prescriptions from dentists and I remembered how much I liked opiates.

In the eighties, when I first started making records, I wasn't having much success. I was writing for different publishing companies and sometimes working a day job. You know, I would take anything with an opiate in it. That's what I liked. Later on I would take just about anything. I bought some of it on the street and got some of it by prescription. Tussenex cough syrup was one of my favorites. There were a couple of doctors that would give me prescriptions for it. There were also crooked pharmacists.

Then I made my first record, *Guitar Town*, and I was not getting strung out. I didn't smoke pot. I drank some, and when I drank, I tended to get very drunk. I was never much of a keep-a-six-pack-in-the-refrigerator drinker. I was a binge drinker. I drank hard liquor when I drank. Sometimes red wine with dinner because I was starting to make a little bit of money after my record came out, and I liked a little bit of that wine. If I drank wine with dinner and nobody else was drinking, I'd drink the whole bottle of wine. I could drink a half bottle or I could drink the whole thing. I was discerning as I started to make some money. I wouldn't drink Jack Daniel's because anybody who knows anything about sour-mash bourbon knows it's not very good whiskey. I didn't drink beer except in Ireland or England or a few other places where I genuinely liked the beer. I wouldn't drink American beer.

Around that time I started traveling, which brought me to places where there was good, cheap heroin. Suddenly I was going to New York, and I was going to L.A., and Amsterdam. I didn't use needles during this period. I smoked heroin when I was in England. That was how almost everyone did it. If it was highly refined white heroin, I would snort it. I had a pretty steady habit going. I could lay down, however, if I was going someplace where there wasn't any drugs. And usually before tours I would kick. I would usually come back off a tour strung out, depending on where we played. If there was plenty of heroin, and it was easy to get, then I'd come back strung out. That went on for . . . My first major-label album came out in 1986. I toured pretty much nonstop in '86, '87. By 1988, when *Copperhead Road* came out, even making that record. I made it in Memphis. I'd stay up for days and days, drinking Tussenex. I really liked it. Before I started using needles, I probably liked Tussenex best. It's OxyContin in timed-release form.

By the time I was halfway through the Copperhead tour, I was strung out on cough syrup. I finally ended up kicking by the end of the tour. I got strung out a couple of times as we traveled into more heroin-friendly areas. The second summer of that tour, we were asked to go out with Bob Dylan. It was a tour that never ended. I thought, "This will be my last shot to ever do this." Dylan hadn't toured in years and who knows if he'll ever go out again, so we did it, but I was pretty strung out. For the first time, I was unable to lay down and kick. I could not do it! I don't know why. I was probably just unwilling to do it. I was drinking two or three ounces of Tussenex a day, which is a lot. Most people would be flat on their ass for twenty-four hours taking that much.

I ended up in a methadone program. The one I was in was run by people who really thought they were helping people. They did encourage people to go to meetings, but they weren't addicts, they were doctors. They didn't understand how little good it does. Around Twelve Step programs everybody's welcome, but it doesn't start to work for you until you abstain. You can go, and I encourage people to go, but until you get clean, you're not actually going to get anywhere and you'll probably use again.

When you are on methadone, you *are* using. It's the most powerful narcotic ever invented. The same circle of chemists synthesized methadone and benzine. The most addictive narcotic known to mankind and the most toxic nonradioactive substance known to mankind. The Germans were kicked out of northern Africa relatively early in World War II. It's the first place they had to abandon. Mainly because of the two fronts opening up in Europe, which cut them off from their main supplies of petroleum and morphine, and you need both of those things to fight a war. So they put their guys on it, and they came up with these two substances to replace them. It was kind of a bad karma situation in Nazi Germany. The evil that pervaded may have had something to do with these guys coming up with these two horrible substances.

By the time I made the next record, at the end of the Dylan tour, I tried to kick using methadone. I got completely clean for the first time in two years. I lasted about four days, and then I started using heroin again. Shortly after that I got married again. My wife didn't use, but she was a pretty efficient codependent. She didn't mean to be, but she was. We never mean to be. I had a house in L.A. because my wife was in the music business, and a house in Nashville. Around that time, she became concerned enough about my substance abuse that she and a friend of mine put together an intervention. I slipped the net on it. I kind of ran away from home. The intervention made me so angry that I left the love of my life. But we ended up getting back together.

Around this time, I made another record in really bad shape. It's a pretty good record but kind of dark and scary. The next tour, though, was a nightmare. I played a lot of shows really sick, and I was having to take drugs before I went on stage for the first time. I had never sunk to that before. I waited until after the show. I had a habit, but I started getting sick at ten o'clock at night. We were playing mostly theaters and arenas by that time, so the shows were earlier. By ten o'clock, my body wanted to know where the dope was.

A lot of other stuff happened along the way. I got arrested for assaulting a police officer, which was one of the times I was absolutely innocent. I was trying to get a drunken crew member of mine into a cab after a New Year's Eve gig in Dallas, and this cop decided we were doing something we shouldn't be doing. He came up behind me with his nightstick and choked me unconscious, and realizing he had fucked up, he charged me with assaulting him. It cost me $100,000 and a jury trial, but finally, cooler heads prevailed and I pleaded no contest to resisting arrest, or something, and that was the end of it.

I was very open about my drug use. My denial was subtle. Opiates allowed people like me to stare into the darkness without blinking.

In L.A., my cottons were famous. [Drugs are drawn through cotton before injecting.] People wanted my cottons because I did such big, huge shots, and I started speedballing. A friend of mine walked in one morning and he had a little bag of coke. It was like Green Stamps. The dealer was giving away twenty dollars worth of coke if you bought a hundred dollars worth of dope. The dealer knew what he was doing. My friend put about a match head of coke in my spoon after I cooked up my shot. It lit me up like a pinball machine. And then I got into this speedballing thing, which increased the number of injections I did instantly. I also smoked crack a couple of times. I didn't really like cocaine, but the combination of cocaine and heroin I loved.

I was trying to preserve my marriage, but once I started to shoot dope, Theresa really freaked out. So I tried to quit a couple of times. I went on methadone again. Then while I was out in L.A., I started smoking crack again. So things really got bad, really fast. Theresa wanted to leave me. She had just lost her job in L.A., so she loaded me up in her car and drove me back to Texas. I had no will of my own at all. I didn't want to leave L.A., but I couldn't not leave. I had to go wherever she went. I really wasn't working anymore. I was trying to write music. I had taken an advance from the record company, but I wasn't getting anywhere with it.

I had a film soundtrack that I was supposed to write but never wrote a note. I was becoming unable to work. All the shit that happened to all those other junkies was happening to me. Theresa took me back to Nashville and then she left me, because I was going into south Nashville and buying crack. I hung out there in the daytime 'cause I wasn't working, and she got sick of it and left.

During this time, I wrecked a couple of cars, one of which didn't belong to me. A lot of bad stuff happened. A rumor went around that there was some heroin in Nashville, which there almost never was. This is an area known for cocaine. I wanted to check it out, so I went down to south Nashville and bought some from a guy. I didn't even go home to try it. I got pulled over and the cops searched my car. They found a syringe so they kept looking, and then they found the dope. The cop wrote me a ticket and didn't even take me downtown. Simple possession—first offense. He knew who I was and he was kind of a fan so he wrote me a ticket, which rarely happens in Tennessee but they can do it.

To show you where I was at, I kind of conveniently forgot my sentencing hearing and didn't show up. I woke up one day and read on the front page of the newspaper that I had been sentenced to eleven months and twenty-nine days. By this time I was married again to a woman I'd been married to before: Theresa. I was married a lot!

Finally I decided, after a whole series of events, to turn myself in. I drove to a neighborhood where I had been buying crack the last few years, 'cause I wanted to get me one more rock. I saw this kid I had known since he was eight or nine. Now he was fourteen or fifteen. His mother was an addict and lived in that neighborhood. I pulled up and he was standing on the street selling. Or at least I thought he was selling, but what he was doing was robbing. He threw a pistol up in my face, so I rolled his arms up in the power window of my car, and I drug him up about a half a block, and then hit the window button and dropped him. Then I went around the corner and bought another rock from another kid. I went and smoked it in the parking lot of my lawyer's office. Then we went across the street and turned me in. Great idea! "Let's smoke this rock, get paranoid, and go to jail!" So I started to serve my sentence.

The only thing that got me out of there for a while was that they decided to let me get into treatment. They sent me to a place called Buffalo Valley, a bare-bones Twelve Step treatment center. They had no medical facility, so I did my detox in the county hospital, which I paid for myself. Which was a plus because it wasn't costing the state any of their money for the program.

I didn't go to treatment to get clean. I went to get out of an orange suit. And I thought the food was better there, but it wasn't. But something happened while I was in that treatment center. I remember the guy that drove me to the treatment center from jail. His name was Chuck. That's what he did at Buffalo Valley. He'd been in jail, so they sent him down to pick people up. We stopped to eat at the Waffle House. I could barely eat. I was still pretty sick.

I thought, "Okay, I'm through the medical part. I'll go through this treatment, but I'm going to use as soon as I get out of here." But around two weeks later, I ran into Chuck and he said, "How you doing?" And I said, "Well, I'm not in jail." And he said, "You know what? You don't have to be, ever again." I realized that I never wanted to be in jail again, and for some reason, I took full responsibility for why I was in jail. I wasn't a victim anymore. I started listening to people. They had all the people in the treatment center together this one time, and I looked around the room. I knew all the counselors by then, and I knew how much clean time they had. I counted 135 years of clean time that I knew of. It occurred to me that maybe I should listen to them.

After I finished my twenty-eight days of treatment, I had to go back to jail. You know there's dope in jail, so I was faced with it in my unit three days after I returned. I just pretended that there wasn't any dope in jail, 'cause there's not supposed to be. I went to meetings—whatever meetings were available to me. Then I got out. They released me at midnight with the smelly clothes I went to jail in, four-and-a-half months later. My clothes had been marinating in there, and I reached in my jeans and there was forty dollars in my pocket, and I was in downtown Nashville. All I had to do was walk four blocks. Instead I made a phone call and didn't even leave the lobby of the Criminal Justice Center. And now I go to meetings every day when I'm in Nashville, and to meetings on the road.

They breathe truth that breathe their words in pain.

—William Shakespeare, *King Richard II*

Malcolm McDowell
(actor)

SPARKS FLY OFF OF Malcolm McDowell when he performs—a sur-real glittery sense of danger and complexity beneath his British good manners. Directors, from Stanley Kubrick to Robert Altman, have cast him in some of their most challenging roles. Like Peter O'Toole in *Lawrence of Arabia*, Warren Beatty in *Bonnie and Clyde*, and Albert Finney in *Tom Jones*, McDowell projects daring and unpredictability.

So many landmark films in the sixties and seventies were about breaking free of conventions and finding life's meaning. The stars were often iconic. Seeing them, we wondered where our intoxication with youth would lead us. Partly because we only saw a film once, or, if we admired it a great deal, twice, our suspension of disbelief was greater than that of today's viewers.

Malcolm is a natively gifted actor whose own problems with drugs came some years after he made it in the movies. In his first two great roles, *A Clockwork Orange* and *O Lucky Man!*, he came across as one scary mother. Searing as a sociopathic kid of the working class, he probably weighed on us the hardest of all. His angry and psychotic gang go to a futuristic "milk bar" for a chemical cocktail before head-ing out to cruel, violent rape and rampage.

Jane and I asked a friend of ours for an opinion of Malcolm's work in *A Clockwork Orange*. She told us that she was "bowled over" by it and has not yet recovered. "The graphic, gratuitous, joyful violence, so well depicted in the film, made a serious and lasting impression on me. Once I told my husband that a piazza, which I crossed in the late evening when leaving my work, was strikingly empty. He told me I shouldn't be there alone in the dark. I said that was ridiculous. He said, 'You don't understand. They'll cut you up for the fun of it. Just think of *Clockwork Orange*.' From that time forth, I never again walked to my car alone at night in New Haven."

—

I suppose I was a successful actor with too much *per diem*. That's basically what my Hollywood experience was like. I was invited out to do the film *Look Back in Anger* after the big success I had with the play in New York in 1980. I had been doing a bit of cocaine. Not when I was working on the play—that was too difficult. You know, a little recreationally here and there, and when I stopped doing the play and moved to Hollywood to do the film, it started to spiral out of control.

I was brought up in a pub, a bar, and I hated the smell of booze and I hated what it did to people. My father was an alcoholic, so I never really drank much. I kept away from it, but I didn't realize that cocaine was really the same thing. Alcohol eventually started getting a little out of control, but in the form of "fine wine." That was my excuse. The truth is, if you buy an expensive bottle of wine at dinner and drink every single bit of it—I would never leave a drop—that should tell you that there is a problem, shouldn't it? Even if I opened one at lunch, I would drink it all and then go sleep it off. But I didn't see this as a problem. I would say that we do this every day in Europe—it's how we are. You Americans are too uptight about drinking wine; it's like water in Italy and France. That was my excuse. So I didn't consider wine a problem, but cocaine was a problem, and that got out of hand quite fast. It had a very bad effect on my marriage. The lies and deceit and everything that goes with addiction.

I went from snorting it occasionally to now smoking it, doing freebase.

Doing as much as I could. Finish a batch at four in the morning. Driving around the San Fernando Valley looking for more of it. Driving while completely stoned, of course. How I was never in an accident, I just don't know. I had a Porsche, and one night I was so paranoid that I actually stopped on the freeway, pulled the car over to the side, because I was convinced there was somebody in the back. Now, you know, the back of a Porsche is an engine, but I had convinced myself that they had moved the engine to the front. I was in such a grip of paranoia. I was obviously totally fucked up!

It was when my second child, my son, was born that I knew I had to get sober. My wife, Mary, put it to me that if I didn't clean up, I'd never see my son. This brought it home to me. But I know that when you are in the throes of addiction, you'll do or say anything to keep it going. Anyway, that was kind of it for me. That was 1981. A friend of mine drove me down to the desert, and I checked into a large rehab.

As a rule, when I was working, I didn't use. Only once I was caught at doing that. It was on the film *Cat People*. I was told, "Great, you are finished for the day." At that I rushed to my trailer, having already called the dealer and left him a drive-on pass to come on onto the lot, and as I walked in he handed me the pipe. I threw the costume off. I felt pleased with myself: I'd done good work, was very happy, time for a little celebration. I took a big hit, was sittin' there in a daze, and a bang sounded on the door, and of course the director needed me to do the take again.

I had to get dressed again. It was unbelievable! I went down to the set and couldn't do the short scene for love or money. Could not! And I had to take the director aside and say, "I do apologize. I thought we'd finished and I took a hit of coke, and now I'm stoned." And so he talked to the cameraman and probably went, "Okay, we'll use what he did before." But it was embarrassing. It was pathetic. I did have a handle on that. If I was working, the getting high didn't mix. I managed to keep the drugs separate from the work. But it's different for an actor than a musician or someone else, say, because often I just wouldn't do the film. Did the drugs affect the work? Yes! It affected the work in that I had to say no, I didn't want to do a film. My agent supposed it was for art reasons, whereas I just wanted to stay high. . . . . I'd be on a run. The run would last a few days. If anything came up during that time, I wouldn't even answer the phone. They could never even get ahold of me.

The paranoia that went with it was a very big part for me. I sort of enjoyed it, weirdly enough—had a very masochistic view of it. In reality it's not enjoyable, but during my addiction when I stayed up nights, I used to get into hallucination. I loved that. That was really fabulous! Just embraced it. Where I used to live up in the Hollywood Hills, it was like the houses were floating like moons. Often I was alone. Once, though, I had a friend of mine there and I tormented him, saying, "There's somebody up that tree, I know it! Ghosts in that tree!" Scared the poor guy. And all that—crazy!

I was a naughty boy. Such a loser with my wife. I didn't care. In fact, I'm surprised Mary put up with me as long as she did. For a year or two, and into my recovery. But once the love had gone, it had gone; it was too late. Often you'll find with addicted people: They hold their marriages together, yet when sober, they split up. It's the strain that tells. Also, when you're in this situation of one addicted person in a couple, there is this other side of it. From the other point of view, somebody may have to play the enabler, or whatever position they take. Somehow that's also a comforting part of the dynamic of the relationship. So when that dynamic is removed 'cause that other person is on the road to recovery, and the dynamic changes completely—it didn't work for us. We tried and went on for another three years after I got clean.

The using ended because I went down to the Betty Ford Center. The friends who took me down there put me in a hotel, and I had one last binge before I had to check in the next morning at nine o'clock. I smoked everything that I had, and at the end of it, I threw the pipe in this ornamental lake. It was like the ceremonial sinking of a ship. Down it went, and in my mind, it was the end of that period of my life. Thank God. Thank God!

I didn't thank God at the time, however. I felt I'd lost a great friend or mistress, that I'd lost the one thing that I could totally trust—all that bullshit! It wasn't until I started to work on myself at Betty Ford, which is a wonderful place as is anyplace that gets you sober. Treatment for cocaine addiction was quite new in those days. I don't think they'd had any freebasers in there, or very few. Had mostly alcoholics and a few heroin addicts. It was a twenty-eight-day program, and they keep you longer if they don't think you're gonna make it. That was twenty-two years ago. I had an incredible experience.

When I went there, I was put with a cocaine dealer. We bunked together. The first few weeks, we were planning a big scam. He was a huge dealer who had a couple of kilos stashed in a place by a lake where he used to go and party. We planned—O Lord!—we were going to have the greatest boat ride on this lake. (He was in treatment because a court required it.) I remember thinking, "Two kilos, that's more than I ever imagined" as he told me his exploits, and how his father drove the cocaine across state lines. After two weeks of our plotting to do this, I came back from a group session, just looked at him and said, "You know, Gary, I'm going to give sobriety a try. Your plan sounds great, beautiful, but I'm going to give this a try." He goes, "Are you serious? You're crazy!" I went, "You know what? I'm just going to hang in here with these people and give it a try."

Then the big issue was the wine. I told them, "I've an excellent wine cellar in my house." (Ten thousand dollars worth of wine, which is like a hundred grand's worth today.) And there was a girl in our group of five, who was a checkout clerk in a supermarket, who looked at me. When I said, "What am I supposed to do with this wine collection?" there was a little *hrummph* and she looked at me and said, "Why don't you just stick it up your ass?" I went, "I get it. Okay, right. What the fuck am I wincing on about? You're so right. I'll just get rid of it."

After all that, I remained unconvinced about the drinking though. I thought it was a load of bollocks. I thought I could drink and keep it under control once I had stopped using the coke. But two days before I was to leave, it was arranged for me to meet with a chaplain. I wasn't particularly religious, but I went to have my hour's meeting with him. He was very easy for me to talk to. I was relating this problem to him: "I don't get it. Why should I not have a glass of wine? It's part of my culture." Blah blah blah— the excuses came. He looked at me and he goes, "Malcolm, why take the chance? Do you want to do all this work and then have a glass of wine? For what? It may, just may, lead you back to cocaine. Why take the chance? It's just more sensible not to do it." And a penny dropped for some reason. I guessed he was right. I thought, "Why? Is it really worth the risk? It's no big deal." So I never did it again.

What the chaplain observed made a profound impression on me. It really made me feel good about my decision, helped me see that I could come to a decision and that was that. There is really no point, at the end of the day, to deceiving yourself. You can make excuses for this, that, and the other. But there is no point deceiving yourself. They wouldn't have let me go had I *not* changed my thinking. I was genuinely looking for a way to reconcile that portion of my old life-style in my mind and saw it's no good paying lip service. You have to dig under every emotion, feeling, everything. It's no good leaving anything there. And I think that was one of the last issues of the addiction troubling to me.

The joke on me is that in the first month after I came out, that guy, who had offered me a world of drugs, looked me up. My cocaine dealer friend who'd gone through the clinic with me came by to visit, and of course brought a big envelope of white powder. I just went, "Wow!" Then I broke it to him: "I definitely am not going to join you on this. I'm really determined to make my sobriety work."

That wasn't too bad. I passed that test quite well. The next test was more lingering. For years driving around the freeway system of Los Angeles, I remembered every turnoff for a dealer. That was weird. The car wanted to turn off and go score! But, slowly, all that subsided. Through the help of my peers and all that, it slowly but surely receded. Eventually, after a year or two or more, the craving gets less and less, and at last you don't even have to think about it at all in terms of "Do I want to do it?"

My resolve when I came out of treatment was firm. Once I made that decision two weeks into treatment not to plan that run with Gary, I let that go. It had been fun talking about the pipe and the whole deal, but somewhere in the recess of my brain, my intelligence took over. It wasn't anything spiritual, except in the sense of discovering something about my own humanity. But having said that, it must have been the Higher Power looking out for me. Not a great shining light, more mundane, more earthbound: "What the fuck am I doing? Am I insane? Let's not talk about this escapade anymore because it's not helpful. I'm not going to be doing it. It was fun, but I'm here to do serious work." And, of course, it's hard work, recovery. Less and less hard as the years have gone by, but you know, the way we live our lives is all recovery in one sense or another. We go through a shattering experience like that, and everything we do in life from then on is in a way influenced by what we've been through. It has to be. Otherwise you wouldn't have any sensitivity at all, and we only learn by experiences, good or bad. I believe that there's a code, sort of a Twelve Step program that we all try. We don't succeed, but try to live by it. I'm not just talking about not taking a drink or a substance, but just the acts of living, the day-to-day being a good human being.

After treatment I retained some of my old thinking, yes, but I had help: people like my friend Rift. Rift was a great influence on me because he had been there and done it way more than me. Made me look like a beginner as we compared stories. Wow, thank God I never used with him! Rift was a protector, but it's all up to the individual how you can keep your sobriety intact.

Touch wood, thank God, I've never had a slip. My son Charlie is twenty, so it's been twenty years. My son has never seen me take a drop either of drugs or alcohol. By the same token, I've never seen him drink a beer or use anything because he knows what happened to me.

I've told him, and my ex-wife has told him too. And I'll be telling my new son, Beckett, when he is old enough to understand. I will tell him and warn him because it is obviously in the genes. But I'm very proud of my older son, how he's resisted the peer pressure. He is a surfer and filmmaker. It's very hard when everybody's doing something.

I've always been open with him about my problem, and I know that's influenced him. Charlie has never told me, but his girlfriend told my wife that that was the reason. My son wouldn't say it to me, but she told my wife, who told me. When I heard that, it was a wonderful moment. All I went through, the whole fucking thing, was worthwhile for that, to hear that. It may have saved him, and I hope the knowledge will save my small one, because I'll tell him too. At first you don't want to tell your child because you're ashamed, but it's wonderful! A very freeing and relieving thing to do.

And of course, it's brilliant for them to hear. Also means you're a real person, not an actor in a family play. I've always been, oh my God, the bundle of energy "let's have fun with" kind of dad that we see on weekends. Papa-pa-pa, pa-pa-pa-pa, like, Mr. Energy. But it's good for them to know the dark side too.

But of course the other side of it is we are what we are because of what we've done—the experiences—and in a strange way, I would never change anything. Even though it destroyed elements in my life, I felt it was meant to be. I have a feeling I'm a much better person today than I would be had I not learnt about recovery and gone through those hard lessons. On appearance, that's not a great message for young people, yet I know it to be true.

It's easier to get a rope
through the eye of a needle than
the drunk son of a drunk

into stopping
into waking—oh no, not
this guy, he's intent on

finding out and finding out
exactly
what the poor old fucker felt like

and hell,
all he has asked
is one good cold responsible

look at the corpse
when it meets him, living,
at the door— . . .

—Franz Wright, "The Dead Dads"

Franz Wright
(poet)

> My name is Franz, and I'm a recovering asshole.
> I'm a ghost
> that everyone can see;
> one of the rats
> who act
> like they own the place.
>
> —Franz Wright, "Empty Stage"

MANY OF THE WESTERN world's most well-known poets have had a sorry life trajectory. Their lives or talents are almost without fail cut off in early bloom by one means or another. What if, instead of ending up insane, defeated by addiction or venereal disease, freezing in garrets, or languishing in asylums where their helpless relatives stashed them, they had conquered their problems and reined their sensibilities, led healthy, fulfilling lives and kept working? If, instead of spiraling down from being celebrated to being bitter pariahs, they reached the *gute Endung* of a Grimm's fairy tale, the elusive happily-ever-after?

Picture a great poet like Robert Lowell without giving in to his cups. Or John Clare, the farmer-poet, when he walked forty miles home from the lunatic asylum across the moors, staying there rather than being locked up again. What if, instead of being wrenched from his family, his farm, and the inspiration for his nature poems, he had found a sane life there: returned to the plow, been reborn, and once more enjoyed his craft? The mere concept rewrites the whole of Western literature!

While the themes of a metaphysical poet cannot be pigeonholed, it is fascinating how the search into the meaning of recovery pervades Franz Wright's poems. We see that this Pulitzer Prize–winning poet wears a mantle no previous great poet ever donned, as a poet of recovery. In a spare, understandable style, his work has been lauded as confessional in the grandest sense. It has been remarked that his poems will burn themselves onto the backs of your eyeballs. Charles Simic once said of Wright that he dares to write an epic on the inside of a matchbook cover. These are poems that set fire when you strike them.

In the realm of letters, Franz Wright is an aristocrat, a poet whose father, James Wright, won a Pulitzer Prize for poetry too. He lives in a working-class near-suburb of Boston that's like a location for the movie *Mystic River*. Down the block from Franz and Beth Wright's, at Heidi's, a popular coffee shop that seems to have been there forever, none of the friendly staff on a Sunday morning has heard of Franz Wright. None of Franz's poems are posted either, nor the news when he, an alternative sort of poet with a cult following, won the coveted Pulitzer against tough establishment competition.

Franz's life has been poetry, and poetry is shoved in all the nooks and crannies of his home. Candles burn, flowers are artfully placed in vases, everything seems like sensible accessories to a discreetly bohemian domestic life. The cats, old and frisky, cuddle right up as we start with conversation and green tea—"our luxury," Franz says. The living room has three prominent typewriters too—an Underhill, a Remington, and a Hermes that Franz has painted vermilion red—all decades vintage. He spills his mug of tea on one and liquidates a poem on the curling paper in the Underhill. "Happens every day," he says, sopping up half the spill. "Doesn't matter. I know it by heart."

Franz is slender, of middle height, with finely wrought features, deep-set gray eyes, and an unusual, otherworldly timber to his voice. His speech is like rungs on a crystal staircase, where he tests each word to see whether it will hold as he climbs to the state of mind or idea he aims to express.

Though the son of a famous man, his battles with his father are a recurring theme of the poems. Franz wasn't crippled by the association; it was a rich legacy. Both his father and stepfather were terrible figures for him, one absent and the other abusive, but he was also surrounded by the most eminent poets of mid-century America as a boy. He cut his teeth on poetry. For his whole sentient life, he has been untwisting the intoxication of truth and beauty in language from the delusion of chemical highs, as he sizes it up in this excerpt from "Nothingsville, MN":

> the smell
> of beer, urine, and the infinite
> sadness you dread
> and need so much of
> for some reason

I work in a place called the Center for Grieving Children and Teenagers and watch the recovery process with seven- or eight-year-old children who have recently gone through the death of a parent. We watch the process by which they return. This happens much more rapidly with children, and it's amazing to watch. Sometimes they come in and they're really regressed. Then sometimes by the end of the first day, they'll be running around playing with all the other children, because it dawns on them, just as it does on somebody in active recovery, that they're in the one place in the world where everyone else knows what they're going through.

It's the same model as for me. You leave the company of others in recovery and you enter a world where people don't care, or if they care, they don't understand, which is equally bad. Centers like this are springing up all over the country. This is the only one for the large area of New England and is getting more and more families. We have some 9/11 families now. It's the most astounding experience. Engaging with children who are going through this kind of crisis is the most incredible thing I've done in my life. I had to go through a long period of training in bereavement issues that I knew nothing about except for my own experience. Then I realized I was doing it because my father left us when I was about that age. That hadn't really occurred to me. After I was at the center for a while, I was seeing myself as an eight-year-old. I had an opportunity—never having had children of my own—to see just how fragile and delicate and easily crushed an eight-year-old boy can be. It was terrifying for me. I was quitting every week.

Making a commitment to relate to these children was completely the result of my enthusiasm for being in recovery myself. Every single thing that's happened in the last four years, including your being here, the Pulitzer Prize, my wife's being with me, every single thing is a result of getting sober. And it's been an amazing thing to watch in others. People come back from that long underworld experience, which can go on and on. Some people go there and they just stay there forever. I mean, I spent enough time in that state, clinically. I've been hospitalized five, six times for depression. The last time was in McLean Hospital and Mass General in '97, '98. I was in a psychotic depression, and the prognosis was that I was never going to get better. It was drug- and alcohol-induced partly, but I've also been diagnosed manic-depressive, suffer from post-traumatic stress, and so forth. So I have the combination. And I was in it for two years—that was the longest I've spent. Never believed I would come out of it. I was incapable of getting out of bed for sixteen hours a day. I didn't leave my apartment for three months at a time. I attempted suicide. The hospitals didn't work. That's where drinking and drugs led me finally, and it went on for long enough it seemed it would never end. I mean, I was a dead person. I wasn't a functioning person anymore. And it didn't help to go to the hospital anymore.

Until I was seven or eight years old, I believed that most adults were crazy. I was born in Vienna in 1953, where my parents lived during my father's Fulbright fellowship. We returned to Seattle, where my father did a doctorate at the University of Washington, studying under Theodore Roethke. Our next home was Minneapolis, where he taught at the University of Minnesota, along with John Berryman. There was a lot of trouble between my parents when I was young, leading to their divorce in 1961 when I was eight. There was no way my father could stay there, my parents' relationship having deteriorated to the point where one of them was someday going to murder the other. I witnessed a lot of violence from earliest childhood. My parents didn't turn it on me as much as themselves. My mother took me and my younger brother to San Francisco. She remarried when I was eleven: a Hungarian refugee. He was more violent than my father. My stepfather had fought on the side of the Nazis. He'd been put in Siberia, in a slave-labor mine somewhere, by the Soviets. Then he got free and ended up in San Francisco where we were. And unerringly, my mother, who never had much luck with men, found her way to him. He turned out to be insane. He beat us, my brother and me. After about a year, he became very violent. Right on schedule, every six weeks, he would beat the shit out of us. We almost knew when it was coming. The rest of the time he was utterly silent and hostile. This was from when I was eleven to eighteen. We grew up feeling very isolated and afraid of the world. It wasn't being beaten. That didn't bother me so much as feeling constantly fearful and humiliated. So, later, I got the diagnosis in the eighties of manic depression and post-traumatic stress, along with the bipolar disorder I may have been born with. And I think that contributed a lot, although alcoholism runs in my family. I'm one of those people who has a dual diagnosis. I've led groups in mental health clinics with people who have that problem: who are mentally ill and addicts both. A more devastating form of affliction is hard to imagine. But if you drink, forget it, because you're utterly lost! Drinking and drugs actually work for a long time, years, to cover your terror of life and to enable you to function socially.

My father also remarried and moved to New York. We remained close despite . . . I loved and do love my father. We corresponded from the time he left until I was in my twenties. When I was fourteen, I began to write poetry. One morning I got up and wrote a poem. I was so elated I sent it to my father, who replied with a very brief letter. He wrote, "I'll be damned. You're a poet. Welcome to hell." I have the letter today.

When I discovered drinking as a teenager and in college, I was happy for the first time in my life. I loved it. Now I see I was an alcoholic. I never even drank socially. Right from the start, I used it as a drug, and people right away would look at me and say, "You know, Franz, you're going to get drunk," and I'd say, "No shit. Like, why do you drink?" It never occurred to me you would drink for any other reason. It was a door out of the world— my world—which I perceived as a hostile, nightmarish place, where I couldn't function very well. From the moment I had a drink . . . which maybe means I was born with it, but it hardly matters, it's an addictive substance and I used it addictively, so I became an addict or was born one. And for five years, it worked. I was able to talk to people, write. I excelled at school. One of the most sinister things about addiction is that it actually enables you to function for a while. If it made you horribly sick from the start, who would do it? The reason you do it is it literally improves your life for a number of years, and then you reach a point where it slowly dawns on you that you cannot function without it. So then you're fucked! But up until then, it works. In some ways, it was the happiest time in my life.

In the late sixties and through the seventies, it was very difficult to tell if you had a problem with compulsive and addictive substance use because everyone was using drugs socially. I went to high school in northern California, the mecca for all of this in the years 1967 to 1971. How would I not have been exposed to drugs and drinking! In high school, I was having these euphoric flights. I was on an exchange program in Europe for a year, but my immaturity and instability cut that short. I worked at a gas station in Berkeley for a while, then got accepted in the middle of the year at Oberlin College, which saved my life. This was the early seventies. Oberlin was a great, rigorous school, filled with fantastic scholars and artists of all kinds. It was also a sheltered environment where it was perfectly normal to use LSD. Everyone else is doing it around you. Then your friends all get to the point like, they're thirty and "Okay, I've got to stop," and they stop. And you're like just getting started! And that was me.

I will do any substance that alters my mind and mood, and have done them all. There is no drug I have not used and abused. They don't exist. I've used everything from opiates (all of them) to cocaine to amphetamines to benzodiazepines to marijuana. And drank with it. They always went together for me; I didn't do one without the other. That was my way of life for twenty-five years until I got sober. It made me sick periodically, and I would lose jobs. Then I would feel better and start doing it again. I often did my writing during these in-between periods. This went right on until my final illness in 1997, when I became so ill that I literally was too terrified to leave my house to walk to a liquor store. I wasn't even drinking. I was in bed for sixteen hours a day. I was trying to commit suicide. I was trying to jump off the Tobin Bridge. I tried to electrocute myself in the bathtub. I tried to hang myself. I tried to overdose with opiates and alcohol. I bought that book about how to kill yourself, put the garbage bag around my head and all that. But for some reason I did not—it was not for lack of trying. There was some reason for that not to work. . . .

My problem was I genuinely believed from the time I was a teenager until going on five years ago that I couldn't write without drinking and without drugs. I was really fortunate. Some people come out of that and they really can't write. I have friends who got sober and they couldn't write for a year. Then they did. Poets I was around as a young child—Anne Sexton, Theodore Roethke, Robert Lowell, et cetera—were big unregenerate drinkers, a very bad example. But right away, as soon as I got serious about the fellowship of the recovery program, not only did I start to write again but I wrote ten times more than I'd ever written, and it was better. It resulted in the last five years in *The Beforelife, Walking to Martha's Vineyard,* and my new book. So in five years I wrote three books and they're my best. I would have written something without sobriety, but it would have been the old stuff. Or I wouldn't be alive. Or I'd be permanently deranged. None of this progress toward a more human and light-seeking poetry would have happened. I'm a person who can definitely say that I would have nothing of worth. It's not like I have to go to meetings of my program. I love going. It took four years to make these bonds with people here, who are now closer to me than anyone in my family ever was, yet often I don't even know them personally. It really does work, and I consider myself an example of someone for whom it does work.

I now understand that whatever gift I may possess does not have any-thing to do with drugs—that it is here in me already, and only needs health and a sense of well-being in order to flourish.

Those poets who drank still continued to function but then they died earlier than they might have, and often their writing became progressively an illustration of a sick mind at work. You can do it. Robert Lowell is the perfect example: a manic-depressive who was an alcoholic. The biographies make a big deal about his madness without mention of his drinking. I know he was a serious classic alcoholic. I know people who've been to parties with him who would watch him when he was manic, self-medicating. He would be drinking what appeared to be tall glasses of water one after the other. Then they would get close to him and see these were tall twelve- or sixteen-ounce glasses of vodka or gin, which he was drinking as if he were a thirsty person drinking a glass of water on a hot day, one after the other, with no apparent effect on him. Enough alcohol to kill a normal person quickly. He would be so manic that it would medicate him, very temporar-ily, against the more florid symptoms of mania, then—like gasoline thrown on fire—make them even worse, until he started expounding on Hitler's virtues and so forth. And I saw my father do it. He would drink and drink and drink, and he would become more lucid. And *then* he would become psychotic, hallucinate, and cry.

But up to the point you can learn how to function. There are many high-functioning alcoholics and drug addicts. But you are never yourself if you are drunk or high, and these men were never themselves. Many writ-ers drink quite heavily at times but aren't alcoholics. I don't believe Theodore Roethke was an alcoholic, for example, despite his bravado on the subject. Drinking contributed to his premature death, but he was a manic-depressive. Ginsberg was not a drug addict either. He could use drugs. Then one day he went, "I don't need this anymore," and he didn't have to do it, although he still did a little. This is a totally different thing from addiction. I know people who can drink heavily who don't have a personality change, who can stop at a certain point and don't have black-outs. An alcoholic has a personality change, blacks out, and does awful things he would never do as his real self. Somebody like Lowell never got to be his real self. Although he produced a beautiful, incredible body of work, we can only imagine what it would have been like had he received the benefit of recovery. Same thing with Faulkner, Hemingway, Sinclair Lewis, John Steinbeck, any number of prominent American writers. They wrote these magnificent bodies of work, but what might they have done if they had got into recovery? They might have become Shakespeare. They had genius to be as great as anyone who ever lived, and in some ways still were, but you mourn what they might have been. Everyone insists, "Oh, they needed to drink." People don't understand if they think that. They suppose it's a Dylan Thomas drama—that the writers needed to be like that, and that this made them writers. No! It's always the case that they wrote in spite of tremendous suffering from a fatal disease. Then they died. Dylan Thomas died when he was thirty-nine, and Hemingway blew his brains out. They still produced a body of work, they functioned, but they can only have been terribly miserable.

The disease of alcoholism affects what you write, moreover. I believe John Berryman realized when he did get into recovering that his best work, *The Dream Songs*, had become like a textbook of what it's like to be an alcoholic. He didn't know it while he was composing. You're two people when you're an alcoholic, two distinct personalities, and since Berryman was always drunk, he was that personality and wrote that book. That same book, when Berryman looked at it with sober eyes, appalled him. It wasn't the work he thought he had written, and I think that contributed to his suicide. He was sober for eleven months when he committed suicide, and at the autopsy, there were no drugs and he had no alcohol in his system. He was pretty broken down, but I think he fell into a suicidal despair. My theory, which I've heard other people say who knew him, is that he realized that the greatest work he would ever do in his life was a description merely of what it's like to be insane. He might have dealt with that and thought, "Okay, this can be used in that manner. This is what it's like for a brilliant genius to express what it's like to be insane." But I think it must have depressed him so much that he wasn't able to get beyond eleven months of recovery. Berryman killed himself before getting even a year. If he'd waited three years, I think he would have gotten through, because I see people all the time who take three years to come out of withdrawal and depression. Others are like me. I tend to be a pink-cloud person. In two weeks it's like, "I'm back." My family, we just physically rebound. I don't know what we're made of, but I see people all the time it takes them two or three years to like being sober. If Berryman had been able to go through that, he would have been okay.

All those years I never wavered from being a poet. Secretly in my heart of hearts, I've not ever believed I'm a particularly gifted or brilliant person. However, I am an extremely persistent person, and from the time I wrote my first poem at fourteen, I made a completely conscious decision that I would be a poet or I would die. And it pretty much looked like I was going to die! Over all those years, I suffered tremendously when I couldn't write. The final illness involved the fact that I'd lost the ability to write for two years. That meant, if I could not write, the only alternative was suicide, and fortunately I didn't succeed. That was the point I reached, getting cut off from poetry, and for me that meant death—life was unendurable.

Even when I was drinking, there were intervals when I'd become sober, and then you start to become more yourself, feel better. Soon as you really feel better, if you're lucky like me, you want to celebrate, so you get drunk again. I had no program to stay sober, though I tried many times. I knew I was an alcoholic and would drink and use drugs, and when I would get really sick, I would stop for a couple of months and often be able to write during those sober intervals. But I would invariably return to it, didn't have a way to live without it. Something would happen and I'd go back. Anything could make me go back. Or I would simply feel better and decide I wanted to get high again. I reached a point where I was prepared to surrender to my powerlessness over drugs and face the fact that, in spite of my desire to stop, my own willpower was clearly not going to make me do that. It wasn't the maturity of years, because I'm not a mature person now! My wife, Elizabeth, is professionally mature, but I say the two of us are like Hansel and Gretel in the woods. I'm a very adolescent sort of person still. It's said you sort of remain at the age when you started drinking. In my case that's literally true. It's getting better. I'm starting to do things where I give an incredibly good impression of being an adult, like going down and teaching in Arkansas, or attending the presentation of the Pulitzer Prize. I don't think anyone could tell that I was really seventeen years old and utterly terrified.

Gradually I've been able to significantly contribute to Elizabeth's and my life. The prize opened up financial opportunities that were unimaginable to me, so we're able to move up a little bit more than where we were. Moving a couple of streets away to our house with a red door is moving way up from where we were, living in one room at the beginning of our marriage. It took until now to get for us what most people I know would consider a somewhat normal existence. But without a recovery program, none of this would have happened and I would have died by now. Hopefully. Or if I hadn't died, it would have been worse. I would still be in a psychotic depression. I lived in a terror and anxiety that was so severe that it never let up, even in the deepest sleep. It never let up even for a second, and my heart was damaged. (In prolonged anxiety states, cortisol is released which is useful over a short run because it gives you energy to either flee or deal with whatever is making you anxious. If it goes on for years without interruption, it physically harms you.) I had no hope of ever emerging from that state, which is indescribable. I would get up, look out the window, and think, "I'm insane. I always worried that I would go insane, and now I did and am forever." And I was in hell!

Addicts have a seductive and almost psychopathic ability to use other human beings when it comes to seeing that their own needs are met. In active addiction, one is not much bothered by conscience, one does what one has to do to get what one needs with disregard for the consequences to others. Most addicts are incredibly cunning and resourceful when it comes to survival. They get sick, then they get better, and sick and better. But this was it. I got sick and I couldn't come out of it.

The process of recovery is partly a gradual building up of the ability to face life difficulties with confidence, perseverance, a sense of having the right to exist. Now I find myself doing things that are so far beyond what I ever imagined I'd be able to do. Socially, and in terms of working and being in the real world. It's like being able to fly or walk on water or something—miraculous. We get to experience miracles. Sometimes people say that they are almost grateful that they're in recovery because they're alcoholics, because they get to know what it feels like to have been resurrected. I don't feel that way, yet to me the resurrection is not like a figure of speech, it's literal. A lot of times acquaintances now don't believe that I was sick. I can only tell them to ask Beth, or ask people who knew me six years ago, who go, "Oh yeah, Franz is not the same person." I was a totally terrified, broken, nonfunctional person in the mental health system. I was one of the people that I encounter when I work in mental health clinics, and which my brother still is.

My brother is five years younger. His diagnosis is more like schizophrenia, a good deal more serious than manic depression. He's deteriorating and also continuing to use crack and other drugs, and he's going to die, I think. Every day I expect to hear that he's died. This past year he made a particularly gruesome suicide attempt. I was in Arkansas and I'm calling to California where he lives, to the emergency rooms, trying to find out where he is. This is like business as usual in my family. It happens every few months. If I hadn't escaped from there, from my family, and gone to Oberlin College, where I started to get better for a while . . . if I'd stayed in California in the orbit of my family, I'd be exactly like him. I don't have the slightest doubt about it. Just one of those people so deep in affliction that you look at them and just know that, short of some real miracle, they're not going to come out. They're going to die like that.

[Franz's in-laws drop by, and Beth Wright gives her mother a bouquet of spring flowers to thank her for helping locate the new home. Franz has a photograph of it displayed on a bookshelf—a plain old place in the same working-class neighborhood of this in-lying Boston suburb. When Franz looks at the photo his eyes light up, and the poet makes me see the dream house he sees.]

Here's a picture of our new house. I always wanted to live with a red door, and it's got a red door. It's five times bigger. When we moved here, we thought that this was the Taj Mahal. We were living in one room in the South

End. It was a pretty room with a kitchen. Here, if we talk in a normal voice level, we can hear each other. But in a larger space, we'll try the same thing and it won't do. The house is in a much nicer neighborhood. It's sunny compared with here. So close that I can still walk everywhere that I go.

Here's a picture of me in Arkansas. There's my cross right behind me. I didn't realize it was there. I'm thinking of putting that on a cover of a book that they're reprinting. If it were Knopf, they could say you can't have the dark glasses, but this is, like, Carnegie Mellon University. I'll say, "Too bad, I'm going to have the dark glasses."

I feel that learning to have normal interchange has been a great accomplishment. I often find the most basic level of human intercourse to be the most baffling and difficult, though I am getting better at that. I didn't suspect initially that my poetry could function on a level that is nonliterary. Oftentimes people think of contemporary poetry as some higher mathematics that you need training to read. There is poetry like that, which can be appreciated only by people with a great deal of knowledge and sophistication in the art. I was always interested in keeping the poems where they worked on a literal and easygoing level, as well as a more sophisticated level. Sometimes I felt I wasn't writing real poetry—"This is too simpleminded!" But then sometimes I have the experience of showing work, or someone's catching me by the sleeve and saying, "This is beyond me." To me, my poetry seems like something anyone can read. At its best, a poem works at both the levels of language and meaning you can grasp.

It is said that the great T'ang Dynasty Chinese poet Li Po used to try his new poems out on the old woman who laundered his clothes, and that if she wasn't delighted by them, he would throw them out. I can understand this impulse. I like that idea, though sometimes you stray into ideas without realizing it where you're writing at a level a little beyond it. I want both things to happen—to have a connection with the subconscious where the words well up from some deeper place, but at the same time, to be expressed with precision and elegance. Writing about Wallace Stevens, my teacher David Young said, "The arbitrary posing successfully as the inevitable." Sometimes you do have to find that point where you know that this is going to be puzzling to a reader, and yet it looks and feels right. I like poetry that I find unparaphrasable, I do. My favorite of those poems I write are those that are very simple and clear, but sometimes I have to be enigmatic and not care whether anybody gets it or not, but *you* get it and feel somehow somebody else will. In Keats' phrase, this is the "negative capability": the ability not to become frustrated because you cannot give something you read a literal paraphrase. To accept the fact that poetry can rise to the condition of music. When people take poetry to the extreme of the lyrical absolute, and it's only music and doesn't have any sense. That's Mallarmé, for instance. And that is very tempting, to dwell in the sheer beauty and music of language.

When I write now, I feel like someone who came back from the dead. A person who has the same name. I also feel as though that person was already there before I started to drink. I'm now that person I was in my teens before I started drinking. I was totally straight, I was a very good student, I was an athlete. I was in track and ran long distance. I did drugs a little bit, but it still seemed social.

When I got to college, there was nothing social about it. In my teens, for three years, I practiced Zen Buddhism at a monastery in Berkeley with a South Korean Zen master. I sat and did it. It wasn't theoretical. I did the sitting and meditation. That was me and it didn't stop being me, but it got all buried over by the other stuff. And that's a wonderful gift, too, how that person never went away. Many times I thought that that person was dead and gone forever. It is not. As long as you're alive, those parts of your identity go underground. They become dormant, they atrophy, but they don't die. They cannot die! They're indestructible! But you have to make a choice to orient yourself in a certain way that allows them to manifest again, to come back to life. That's not easy. There are many, many days when you want to get high, and you want a drink. What you do instead is you call someone that you trust, you go to a meeting, you pray. You do all those things that you learned how to do and get through that period. It's like this bad dream that you had, and you're awake again.

But people relapse, sometimes after years, and they may die, or come right back, and often that less time in recovery is even stronger because of their renewed enthusiasm, the awe and wonder they have at being sane and alive and being able to be with other people. Although, the people with decades of sobriety are like gods. You look up and revere them. You have absolute respect for them and feel, "I could never do that, but maybe if I live long enough, I could, one day at a time." They feel that reverence too. If you tell them that, they go, "Yeah, that's how I felt. But I could also drink again, same as anyone else." And one day at a time they got to that point, but they didn't arrive there in a week. They arrived there in twenty years, but it only works today. And that is the principle that all spiritual life is based on: to live in the present. If you live in the present, you can be happy. You don't need to get high because you're already happy.

That's the other insight I had. From working with addicts this is what I've observed: They do not take drugs to get high, they take drugs to feel happy and to be like everybody else. It's literally physically true, because anyone who's taken drugs knows that it works for a little while. *Then* you take drugs in order to feel the way you'd feel if you weren't taking drugs, because the tolerance builds up. It takes more and more to get high, and then you overdose and die. Beth has asked me what it's like to be an addict. I said, "Well, you have a really fucking good time for about two weeks, and then all of a sudden you're using drugs to feel just the way you would feel if you weren't using drugs. That's what an addict is, you know."

When you see that and go, "Hey!" you get some experience in feeling like "I can get as high as I ever was using drugs from this sober way of life." I realize that I never even needed to do that in the first place! Some people have a harder time, where you can see they're just dying for their drug, their alcohol, whatever. They miss it, but I don't. I can honestly say that being sober is better than getting high. No question about it. And I consider myself an especially blessed person because I have all this proof of it. Having a recovery program that works is a miracle as astounding as healing the blind or crippled, or walking on water, or raising the dead. It's more miraculous to me personally because I know I was gone. That person was not going to write that book. So to me recovery is a miracle, and I have proof.

As I've said elsewhere, Elizabeth realized she could let me court her because I put my desire to meet her in a letter. She had seen me unreliable but could trust my written words. To me, even at my most disturbed and deranged, there was always something sacred about the written word. Paul Valéry said that poetry is the voice of someone happier, more profound and intelligent, *and happier* than any real person, and I always take that seriously.

I don't find myself inclining to the old manipulations with my wife that I was known for when stoned. When you do, you know you're doing it, and you know that when you do other things to get high that don't involve substance abuse—another way like sex, but there are a million ways to get high and still have the exact bad behavior as if you were using. But if you're in recovery, you immediately have a conscience about it. You know that the sense of joy that you have of being in the light when you are in real recovery is darkened immediately when you lie. The minute you use another person for your own benefit, the moment you stop seeing other people in affliction that you want to help, and see them as objects that you want to use and manipulate, the whole universe gets dark again just as if you had a hangover. Then you go, "Oh shit!" and you do something about it. Otherwise you go back to being—without using drugs, without drinking—you go back to the same state of mind you were in when you were drinking and using drugs. So it's not hard to tell. If you have any honesty at all, it happens immediately . . . the whole world gets dark again! You feel scared, paranoid, remorseful, terrified. Everything you feel when you use comes flying back, and you go, "Fuck, I have to do something about this," and then you try to do something about it. And you go back in the light, for a while. It's not spiritual perfection but spiritual progress. You make progress, fall down, get up, fall down, and get up. That's all there is, because we're not going to become saints. Most of us are not saint material. We're material to be, like, psychopathic criminals! And yet we have this chance to live a normal life.

Think about what alcoholics went through for thousands of years, being put in a cellar somewhere and have the key thrown away. Right up until the fifties and sixties, they put you in a mental hospital and threw the key away. Now people have another opportunity. This is why I say access to a recovery program has saved my life. It has enabled millions of others to be sane and lead normal lives, and therefore is of the same significance as any other medical breakthrough in the twentieth century. Somebody should get the Nobel Prize for this! I understand Bill Wilson, the founder of Alcoholics Anonymous, was actually in line to receive it but made it clear that in keeping with the principle of anonymity he turned it down! Recovery is as unbelievable and incredible as the development of antibiotics, just that it works in a mysterious, spiritual way.

Walt Whitman said somewhere to spend time with powerful, uneducated people. I always read that and thought, "What a fine idea." Having lived my whole life of addiction with a sense of entitlement, being, like, "I'm this special person who has this special gift, and I should be treated differently," I go to my recovery program here in Waltham and know I'm a regular person and always was. I'm a human being among other human beings for the first time in my life. I wasn't that special or lower than everyone else, which is the corollary of being better than everyone else. No, I was the same. That was the central big relief in my life. I go to my recovery program that is filled with working-class people, or people who do not have jobs, sometimes do not have a place to live or enough to eat. I go to meetings with people for whom recovery is a matter of life and death, and over a period of five years, it's just kicked the shit out of all sense of being different. I have come home, and I feel freer to exercise the talent that I do have. If I wrote ten poems in a year in my previous life, when I was drinking, when I got into recovery, I was able to finish ten poems in a month. And they are better poems. So I have that proof too.

That insane asshole is dead
I drowned him
and he's not coming back. Look
he has a new life
a new name
now
which no one knows except
the one who gave it.

—Franz Wright, "Baptism"

Boney's high on china white, Shorty found a punk
Don't you know there ain't no devil, there's just God when he's drunk
Well this stuff will probably kill you, let's do another line
What you say you meet me down on heartattack and vine.

—"Heartattack and Vine"

Grace Slick
(musician)

I WAS HAVING A hurried lunch at a nondescript burrito joint near
Greenwich Village in New York one day, when a poster of Grace
Slick and The Jefferson Airplane caught my eye. Amid the traditional
Mexican art prints hanging haphazardly, there was an odd sampling
of rock-and-roll psychedelia from the sixties. Shows from the leg-
endary venues of the time: the Fillmore East, the Electric Circus, the
Avalon Ballroom, and the Fillmore West. The one that stood out was
promoting a 1968 extravaganza at San Francisco's Winterland. It fea-
tured new sensations—The Jefferson Airplane and the Grateful
Dead—with the acid poster boys, Captain Beefheart and his Magic
Band. I noticed at the bottom of the poster that the ticket prices were
$5, $4, and $3. The tip to the parking-lot attendant costs you that now.

Sucking down my veggie burrito with extra hot sauce, I began a
trip down memory lane. I may indeed have been at that show. I often
flew up to San Francisco from my home in Los Angeles to attend
rock shows. Because I was a player in the rock-and-roll business, I had
backstage access to the shows I attended. Many a night was spent getting high in somebody's dressing room.

The Jefferson Airplane, whom I saw perform a few times, were
unusual in that they were fronted by one of the few female lead
singers of the time. Grace Slick gave the impression of being right in
her element among the bantam roosters of rock. She could kick ass

and get high like one of the guys. She bragged that she has done "most drugs known to men, and most men known to drugs." How could you not appreciate a woman like that?

———

There's a whole bunch of alcoholics on both sides of my family, but they function in the sense that everybody kept their jobs. There were no divorces, except for my grandmother, but she's not an alcoholic. She was just a wild child like I was. Our alcoholics all kept their jobs and stayed married.

In their generation, you just drank. Everybody's parents drank. There were no question marks anywhere about it. Some were better at it than others. As a little kid, I remember being amused by the mother of one of my friends. She kept on her chenille bathrobe all during the day, and her eyes were so puffed up that they were slits. She always wore her bathroom slippers, and she was puffy. Not that she ate too much, but puffy from too much alcohol. Her husband was skinny and away more than he was home. That mother was spooky, ripped all the time. So I knew there were varying degrees to handle drink.

My own father was an alcoholic, but he was never mean. He just sort of drank a little bit all the time. He was a peaceful kind of go-to-sleep-at-nine-o'clock drunk. I'm a periodic. I detested being drunk all the time. I didn't like being foggy. Yet I didn't see myself as sober all the time either.

My parents and everybody else's of my youth asked why we took those drugs. Didn't they notice when they were reading to us? Some of the children's classics our parents read us alluded to chemicals, but the parents didn't notice this. Before I was five, *Alice in Wonderland* was read to me, and Alice takes at least five different chemicals. A mushroom has psychedelic properties. Round things say, "Eat me." God knows what they are. Alice gets literally high and too big for the room. She has to take another drug to come down and get small. One says, "Drink me." She goes around Wonderland taking drugs.

Then there are the opium poppies in *The Wizard of Oz*. Dorothy and her companions all fall asleep in a field of poppies and wake up and see the magical Emerald City. Then you sprinkle some dust on yourself in *Peter Pan*, and you can suddenly fly and have adventures. As a child, I understood that the chemicals were going to make it so you have these magical experiences. It wasn't conscious, but when you hear these stories, you take that in. Chemicals can change you instantly! I thought maybe the parents weren't paying attention to what they were reading. So the song "White Rabbit" was actually addressed to the parents . . . "One pill makes you larger, one pill makes you small. . . . But the ones that Mother gives you don't do anything at all." I wrote the song at a red piano that was missing ten keys, and I was trying to tell my parents' generation that this wasn't open to interpretation, it didn't have to be figured out, but was right there in those books.

I had a *Leave It to Beaver* childhood. My parents didn't fight and stayed together. There wasn't any stuff that I was trying to get away from. There's no whining going on here in my adulthood about my family circumstances: "When I was little, my parents did such-and-such to me." In my case I believe the alcoholism is genetic, but also environmental in the sense that drinking too much is what everybody did. So, if you have it genetically, and you start in, boy, you're screwed!

In high school, we would go out and sneak beers or gin or whatever, pretty much like everyone else we knew. College, the same thing. I was a little racier than the others though. I'm from California, and I went to Finch College in New York City. Now the deal with Finch College was that it was a bunch of rich girls who didn't have the grades to get into Vassar, Wellesley, or the Cliffe, so they went to Finch. Finch basically teaches you which fork to use and how to get a Princeton boy, or Yale boy, or Harvard boy. It was also a suitcase school, and we would go to Princeton or Yale on the weekends.

I remember one time this friend of mine, who eventually married John Huston, the movie director, she and I went down to Princeton, as we usually did on the weekend. She was dancing around with her clothes on. She wasn't doing anything weird, but she was dancing by herself. I was singing and playing the guitar. Singing a Chaucerian folk song that had dirty lyrics.

And the guys—not the older proctors who, at thirty-five or forty were keeping an eye on the college kids, but the students—were so shocked they said they didn't want us around anymore. They said we were dirty girls from California. I thought, "Oh, this is way too snotty for me. What the hell is this? If one of their male college buddies had sung the same song, would they have said 'Leave and never come back'? No, they would have laughed it off." I thought, "There's no way I can stand this crap."

Sure enough, years and years later, I talked to this old friend of mine I had gone to high school with, and she told me she was envious of the life I had led, what with rock and roll and all of that kind of stuff. She had married one of those Princeton guys, and raised some kids, and was the perfect soccer mom. She had kept it together in the sense you do what you're supposed to have done. But once you get to be old and look back, it's not what you did that you regret, it's what you didn't do. At this point—I'll be sixty-five shortly—I'm glad that I had the life I did. The only thing I regret not doing is not screwing Jimi Hendrix and Peter O'Toole. I missed that!

I was aware that I was famous as a singer in the band, but I wasn't aware that I was in the same category that I could have "my people" call "their people" and say that I would like to meet Jimi or go out with Peter O'Toole. I didn't know I was capable of that, unfortunately! I know it now, but I didn't know then that it could have been arranged. Because I would have gone and done that real fast!

Like I said, I don't regret much of anything except hurting people. Occasionally I stepped on people along the way who objected to my behavior. My parents from time to time.

Anyway, I was going to the University of Miami in my sophomore year in college. I left Finch because on Easter vacation at Finch I went down to Nassau in the Bahamas for a vacation. And I went, "Hey, this is great!"

I never went to college because I wanted to learn anything. I went to see New York. You don't say to your parents, "I'd like to see New York. Why don't you give me $20,000 so I can go hang out for a year?" Going to college sounds better, so they give you the money. You couched it by going to an easy school. And the next year, I wanted to hang out in and be around

Nassau, so I went to the University of Miami. While there, I got a letter from a friend of mine, in conjunction with having first heard of Lenny Bruce. Lenny Bruce was unknown to me when I heard him in a record store when I was buying something else. I was mesmerized. So I got a Lenny Bruce album and laughed so hard my face hurt. I'd never encountered anything like it. Also in Miami at that time, I got this letter from my friend Darlene saying, "You got to check out what's happening in San Francisco. There is some stuff going on here." She enclosed an article by *San Francisco Chronicle* columnist Herb Caen. Herb wrote about the new Bay-area scene. Herb Caen had coined the word "hippie," and he was talking about all these bands and the action, and I thought, "Well, that sounds like a good deal." Especially since Darlene had already proved her instincts for promising scenes. So I went back to the West Coast, which was probably the most pivotal decision in my life, considering where I ultimately headed. My idea, though, was just to go around and hang out where the good times were.

So I returned home, and sure enough, Darlene and Herb Caen were right. Things were going on. Included with alcohol was now marijuana and the psychedelics, and new rock and roll. As you know, it took off from there. Now at that time, taking drugs was not something you went into rehab about. Everybody had their drug. Some guys like speed. In The Jefferson Airplane, there were a couple of guys in the band who favored speed. Paul was more of a marijuana guy. Marty and I drank. Spencer drank. Everybody had their drug of choice, but we all took pretty much all of them. Except our band was not into heroin. Heroin was not a no-no. From my point of view, it was too much trouble. You had to have somebody else that you relied on, and I don't care for that. Now, cocaine . . .

We had a guy living in our basement who was a carpenter and he taught karate or kung fu. Also he was a coke dealer, so we had our own coke dealer living in the basement. It was easy. You see how lazy I am. If a drug was easy, fine. Apparently it was easy to get nitrous oxide. We had a tank of it in the basement. What's more, the coke dealer living in the basement, Owsley, was around all the time with LSD.

There were a lot of pranks. Tricia Nixon went to Finch College ten or twelve years after I did, so she didn't know me. Finch College is so small that she could and did have a tea party for all the alumni. She got a list of everybody that went to Finch, and Grace Wing was on the list. So Grace got an invitation to a tea at the White House from Tricia.

Grace cracks up because she realizes they don't know who Grace Wing is. That was my maiden name. So Grace calls up Abbie Hoffman because the invitation said you could bring your husband or boyfriend, and I thought Abbie and I would go as husband and wife . . . and take a shitload of acid.

I know about formal teas because that's one of the really important things they teach at Finch. Abbie and I got dressed, showed up at the White House on time, had our invitation ready, and were standing in line. I wore a black fishnet top and black skirt above the knees and tall black boots up to the knees. Everybody else was dressed like straight Republican women. If I had worn a camel hair coat, the security guards might not have recognized me. We dressed Abbie so he didn't have a flag T-shirt or tie-dye. He had on a suit, but he's so dark that putting a suit on Abbie, he looked like a Mafia hit man. Both of us looked pretty strange.

We had to go through some security because the president of the United States was in there. What I was going to do was . . . At a formal tea, what happens is everybody stands and there is a long table with big tea urns at each side, and you have somebody—and this is so corny—somebody that you prize or your best friend do the honors at the tea table. I knew the setup. I figured that "Tricky" would be standing there with his teacup in his hand. I got my teacup. I also have lots of acid in one of my pockets, and a long fingernail to scoop it. All it takes is a little acid to get you to the moon. Entertainers gesture a lot, and I'll be talking to Tricky and I'd kind of gesture over his teacup and the acid would drop in there, and he'd never taste it, and in forty-five minutes, the guy would be gone. So I was standing in line, and I fully intended to do it, when one of the security guards came over to me and said, "I'm sorry, you can't go in." And I said, "But I have an invitation." And he said, "No, we know you're Grace Slick, and you're a security risk." And I thought, "They're right! Isn't that interesting? They don't know why, but they're right!" So they wouldn't let me in.

But the weird part is that Tricky Dick didn't need acid; he got himself out of office. You know they say he was so goofy he used to wander around the White House talking to the presidents' pictures on the wall. So if he took acid, nobody would have noticed. He would have been talking about the walls melting, and they would have said, "Yeah, sure, there he goes again."

But he got himself thrown out of office. That's mainly what we wanted to do. Have him behave in such a manner that they'd have to take him away.

Avoid all needle days—the only dope worth shooting is Richard Nixon.

—Abbie Hoffman, *Steal This Book*

The Airplane became famous as the original psychedelic band, but personally, I was more a drinker. Anything that was around and easy I took—marijuana was very easy to score, but alcohol was my drug of choice. That's the genetic deal going on, where I'm an addict in the sense that anything I like I'm all over. Like flies on shit! And sometimes that works out fine. Right now I'm a painter. That's how I make my living and pay the mortgage.

Once I start a painting, I work on it until my nose runs. Then I guess I better blow my nose. Until gravity hits me, I don't stop. In that sense, being an addict is okay, as long as you're directing it at something productive. Unfortunately I do it in any area, good or bad. If I like something, there I am right in the middle of it. That operates with men, the job, cars.

Once in the sixties I went into a showroom to buy a car. I never paid any attention to the James Bond movies. I went in to get a Jaguar. I had all this money in cash. I went in dressed in jeans and sandals—your typical hippie. And I saw this English car and thought, "Damn, this is neat looking! I like this better than a Jaguar." I said to the salesman, "What's that called?" And he said, "That's an Aston Martin." I asked, "Is that an automatic?" And he said, "Yeah." And I said, "Fine, I'll take it."

"Wouldn't you like to drive it first?" "No, not really. I just like the way it looks." So he said, "Well, how would you care to pay for that, ma'am?" And I said, "Cash!" I pulled out $17,000 in cash. The band thought it was great. They said, "Hey, that's the James Bond car." And I didn't even realize that it was. I just was attracted to its look. Talk about impulsive! That's what I mean. If I like something, it's "That's okay, I'm having that." The problem was that the British cars at that time had a problem with the batteries, and the thing didn't start all that reliably. It was like a fancy racehorse. You had to kind of coax it. We lived out in Bolinas, way outside of San Francisco, in the boonies. By then I had my daughter, China, and I decided, "Okay, I'm not going to have that type of car with a newborn baby." So I took the Aston Martin engine out and dumped a Chevy engine in. I thought the guys in the band were going to pass out and die! But that's neither here nor there. It's not talking about addiction. Although maybe it is! I do what I want regardless . . .

The sixties idea of sexual freedom was something I could relate to. My upbringing may have been proper, but I switched to the new life-style without a hitch. Diversification in bed also made sense to me, at least at the time, like with drugs. Night after night we sang together, and it seemed natural that we slept together too. Sometimes it felt like being married to seven different men.

If you live with anybody, I don't care what it is, it could be a turtle, eventually it's going to get gnarly, because of differences of opinion. That's why a lot of bands break up. That's why Metallica all went and got therapists, 'cause they figured that if you're in a band that is this successful, why would you want to mess it up? That would be crazy, we got to work this out. They had something they wanted to stay in, and that's great.

People ask me what it was like being a woman in a rock band. It's very different if you wanted to be a Supreme Court justice or head of a corporation, but there were always singers. My mother was a singer. I have a very loud voice, so rock is a perfect medium. My mom is a big-band singer— "I'll be with you in apple blossom time"—and I can sing like her. One of my friends requested I sing at her wedding, and I thought, "Oh Christ!" She wanted me to sing this Carpenter song which gagged me: "We've Only Just Begun." Me singing that! Holy shit! But I thought, "I can do it. I'll just sing it like my mother." Everybody in the audience who knew me were looking at me and laughing. . . . I didn't exert any power in our bands. I liked having fun. Paul liked exerting power. I don't care one way or the other.

In a band, you are so close to each other. Usually a man and wife go off to work, so you get a break from each other. You get no break with a band. You're with them 24/7. All the time. It's pressure because you have to look good, sound good, and be on time. We were lucky. We didn't have to change our outfits or have dancing girls and videos and all that. The sixties were real easy. You just had to show up. If you could play or sing, or whatever it is you do without falling down. Even that was okay. The audience was just as screwed up as we were.

Compared to now where they really have to work. But anyway, you're going to get on somebody's nerves. All six or seven of you. That's what happened to our band, and a lot of other bands. Jack and Jorma were mainly blues. They didn't like all that "let's go to the moon" that Paul liked. They weren't all that crazy about Marty's love songs, although Marty wrote some good ones. I didn't care. I thought it was great: four songwriters, so the pressure is off in the sense that we each wrote a couple. Two or three songs each per album, that's fantastic. But I'm also a girl. It's different. At that time, there was some sexual tension going, and it was a little easier for me. With the rest of them, it was all male-male ego stuff. It was more fun for me.

As far as my addiction went, the drugs at that point were all still working. That's why you use them. You don't find out you hate them from the beginning and keep using. That would be stupid. They do something for you. It's fun. To me, drugs were like food. I wanted variety. I liked steak but didn't want to eat it every night. You eat different kinds of food. Same thing with consciousness: I felt the same way about my mind as I did about food. I wanted to experience different kinds of consciousness. I liked being sober but didn't want to be sober all the time. I wanted to be sober for a while, then I wanted to have a marijuana high, or a booze high, or an acid high. The same as with food. In the line "feed your head," I was referring to partaking of this consciousness the same way you do food. In other words, "Feed your head some interesting stuff." That includes books. That includes new experiences. Knowledge feeds your head too. That's why I used the line at that time.

I didn't drink for any other reason than just to get high. My parents loved each other and stayed together until they died. I've had a great job. I've been able to screw anybody I wanted to. I have no claim to a miserable life. There was nothing to drink "over." The only time I drank over something was when my house burned down in northern California. My husband was in Hawaii, China was in L.A. I was sitting in a Howard Johnson lodge trying to forget what was happening, and all the local TV channels said, "Grace Slick's house burned down." Usually I drank "for"— "Now I'm going to get ripped." I like the idea of feeding my head with different consciousnesses, but I don't do that anymore because at some point the stuff stops working for you and starts working *on* you.

It wasn't acid that made me enemies, it was alcohol. Without alcohol, I'd be richer by the two million dollars that I paid in legal fees over my squabble with Marty Balin. I wouldn't have had an outburst that got him so mad. He wouldn't have said publicly in an interview, "Grace? Did I sleep with her? I wouldn't even let her give me head." I don't even know what offensive behavior of mine he was reacting to. Because of the alcohol, I can't remember. Without alcohol, I'd be richer by two million dollars that went to pay lawyer's fees.

So drugs were still working at that point. When they don't work and you don't realize it, or at least I didn't, you're in trouble. Marty did. When Janis died, he stopped. He went off drugs completely, but I didn't. I thought, "Well, that's them . . . Jimi, Jim,—Jimi Hendrix, Jim Morrison, and Janis Joplin. All these people close to me started dropping off and I thought, "Well, that's heroin." To an extent, it was the heroin that killed them. I believe the reason why is that heroin is so small.

Once we were on tour with The Doors. We played several cities in Europe and were performing in Amsterdam with The Doors. We used to alternate who went on first and who closed the show. This particular night they opened for us. They went onstage and we were backstage waiting to go, doing some amyl nitrate and whatever other drugs there were around. During that day, both bands, The Doors and The Jefferson Airplane, had gone into the shopping area of Amsterdam to hang out, buy stuff, and look around. The kids knew who we were so they were all giving us drugs as we walked along. Sometimes you'd say, "No thank you." Other times you'd say, "Thanks" and put it in your pocket. Jim Morrison did up whatever they handed him, on the spot. And I remember thinking, "My God, how's he going to play tonight?"

And so that night when Jim came on stage, he looked like some kind of windmill that was ready to fly apart. Arms, hands, and legs flying all over the place. It was just insane! They finally took him offstage, and someone had to take him to a hospital because he was full of so many drugs.

Even our band—and we were known as the acid freaks—went, "Wow! How can he do so many drugs and even move?" Jim used himself as a guinea pig. Lots of kids we knew would sign up in college for drug-testing programs. Clinical trials. Jim used himself to find out what can you do to the human brain, how far can you go? Jim wasn't a nihilist, although he was close. He had the point of view that you come on the planet, you see there is stuff to do, and let's take it as far as it will go. We were all about that . . . to a point. But the reason I'm alive is that I'm somewhat chicken, and con-servative as far as my body goes. If my body hurts, I pull back for a while. Being a periodic alcoholic, I'd get real sick and then decide, "I can't stand that for another month or year." I'd go all the way out though. I'd drink everything there was to drink to see how far I could go with it. I took a lot of acid and got real strange. I never flipped out, or wanted to kill myself, or saw anything that wasn't there. We were all looking for different realities, and Jim had either more stupidity or balls, because he would take it as far as you possibly could. It's amazing he lived as long as he did. It was only when lots of friends died we realized we were mortal.

With alcohol, though, it's a long slow process, unless you have a car accident or something. With heroin, it's so small that if you take just a lit-tle bit more, then you die. You have to have a microscope to measure out a little more and not die. That's the reason I disliked it. Heroin was too tricky. You have to tie off. It takes going to a dealer and getting the parapherna-lia, and then you get sick and go into a coma. Why would a person want to repeat an experience like that? Heroin can't be a social drug, and it was too spooky for me. Also, there's a slightly different psychology between heroin users and alcoholics. Alcoholics are generally a little more outgoing.

Even though they turn into shits. Like me, obnoxious, yelling at cops, pulling shotguns, and stabbing each other, because it is a very abrasive drug. What eventually got me was in the mid-seventies. I was stopped three different times—never in a car—for drunk driving.

It's really ironic that I've been arrested for three DWIs and always was outside the car. When you start doing shit like driving drunk, it's an indication it's no longer party time. A DWI is not like getting arrested at a protest march or with the rest of the band. This was all by myself being an asshole. They weren't as harsh then. Now is better, I'm glad they're harsh. When the police first said I had to go to these meetings, I said, "No, you don't understand, I can afford my dinner." And they said, "No, you don't understand!"

Let me give you one example. I had this black Chevy pickup truck, and I was way the hell out in the middle of nowhere in Marin County with a book and some wine. I was just going to sit out there and read. So I got out of the truck and sat down on the ground with my back leaned up against a tree, reading. I had some wine. I ate some food. Then a cop came by, stopped, and said, "You're not supposed to be here." So I said, "What does it look like I'm doing?" And he said, "You shouldn't be here." And I said, "Well, why not?" "Because I'm going to arrest you for being drunk in public." "Public!" I yelled. "You got fucking squirrels and deer and trees. You call this public? The only public is you, you fucking asshole." So I go directly to jail. You see?

So I was arrested repeatedly for drunk driving, when I was not driving a car. It was drunk mouth! But there is no number for that. It's not a 502, and it's not assault. So it's just plain drunk mouth.

I can't claim I was, like, being in a peace march or anything. I got arrested for being an asshole all by myself. It didn't dawn on me that it was related to my drinking. I thought it was my usual mouth—that blunt, jerk, sarcasm thing. I thought, "Hey, that's just me. That's how I am and it's amplified by alcohol." Eventually the highway patrol and their ilk told me, "Here, you got to go to these meetings." And I said, "You don't understand. I can afford my own dinner." I thought recovery meetings were something where you got a free meal and a lecture from a priest. I didn't know what they were. So, around 1976, I started going to meetings. I thought they were fabulous, because all the religions I'd been aware of had guys with funny outfits on and you had to pay them a lot of money. And one person was holier than everybody else. He was up in front. But in these recovery meetings, everybody was equal. Nobody owned anything either. I thought, "Okay, this is spiritual. The rest of that stuff was phony. This reminds me of early Christianity." So I liked the context, but that didn't mean I wanted to stop drinking. I was even a coffee maker, and I'd put a little rum into my coffee, and you got yours regular. Or I'd stay sober 'cause it was easy for me to do for a long period of time, being a periodic. I didn't realize that anybody can stop. The problem for me was definitely staying sober, but that didn't occur to me at the time. Also, I didn't realize they were talking about all mind-altering chemicals. I would not drink alcohol but would use lots of cocaine or whatever. I'd jump around from drug to drug. So I'd stay sober for a while, then I'd go out and get drunk again. Then I'd come back to the program and start over again. People would tell me, "You're gonna die," and I'd say, "No, I'm not." Oddly enough, I didn't, but that isn't because I'm so smart.

The band cleaned up individually at various times and for their own reasons. Three members of Airplane are in recovery. All during the eighties, I was sober. During the time of Starship. Then I got bored and went back out again. Then stayed sober for another couple of years, then went out again. Now, my daughter and I got sober in 1996. I have eight years sober again. I'm certainly not the image or the beacon to follow. My pattern or path has been to do what I want to do for my own reasons. I do hope I stay sober though. As I grow older, it's harder and harder to handle alcohol. It's particularly rough on your body, because if you don't die, everything rots.

My mind is still functioning, but I'm lugging around this rotting body, this rotting meat. That's not too pleasant, but apart from that, it's all good.

The friends I have today are all alcoholics who are sober. Alcoholics, I've found, have very interesting lives. That's a bizarre thing to say, and it sounds like I'm saying it to the exclusion of other people, but it's probably true. I don't want to be around people who have held back. I like being around alcoholics, thank you very much. Also, the deal that you're as good as your spiritual program is a strong one.

In 1970, when I became pregnant with China, I wasn't conscious of addiction. My life was all just sex, drugs, and rock and roll. But I'm not a moron, so I knew that what you put into your face goes into your body, and part of your body is what's living in there—the child. So I didn't do drugs when I was pregnant. And most of the time, I didn't use when she was around. The times it happened, I'm sure it made her nuts, but I wasn't self-aware about it until much later. You do a lot of stupid shit on drugs, but life goes on, you make amends, you don't live in that. When China started getting goofy, she knew what addiction was, what to look for, since she'd been going to recovery meetings with me from the age of five.

Life now is fine. My daughter is sober. China came in a couple of weeks after me. Into the same rehab. My sponsor was amused. She had never seen a mother-daughter combination in the same rehab. Because I had rehabbed before, there was none of this mother-daughter filial non-sense. I just let China do whatever she needed to do and didn't get into that.

China called me once when she was fifteen and said, "Mom, I think I'm an alcoholic 'cause tonight I was making out with my best friend's boyfriend, and I've been drinking cooking sherry." And I thought, "Wow, that would have been nothing to me." But she knew early on that things were not working right. So she's ahead of me. China's thirty-three and has seven years of sobriety.

So what stops me from drinking now is that the drugs and alcohol don't work anymore. Alcohol makes me a jerk, pot makes me paranoid, and I'm already wired to the tits, so I can't use cocaine. The idea of starting that process of being interested in drugs is a big waste of time, too boring. What I'm doing now is more interesting than sitting around thinking where a dealer might be.

I can paint or write songs drunk or sober. Some of what I create is good, some isn't. Alcohol doesn't make any difference with my art, unlike for some people. It makes a big difference, though, with relationships, because I'm a real asshole. When you're drawing, who are you going to be an asshole to? There's none of that contention going on. I'm a jerk as far as relationships go. I think that's true for a lot of alcoholics who are artists, writers, and musicians. For others, it will hammer what they're doing, but many of us seem to plow right through. Ernest Hemingway is one example of thousands. Alexander the Great conquered the known world before the age of thirty-three, and he was a practicing alcoholic. It doesn't get in the way of what you're doing, but your relationships are crazy.

I'm way nicer now. Say a friend walks into the room with a new sweater she thinks is fabulous and you think is god awful. Usually you say, "That's interesting," or nothing at all. Like Thumper's mother said, if you can't say anything nice, don't say anything at all. But when I'm drunk, I say whatever is in my mind. It doesn't make any difference who you are or when you are. But it's rude half the time what I'm thinking, and I need to censor my thoughts. I still think the same but don't say it because it's pointless to make people miserable. All the relationship stuff improves for me sober. I'm also better living alone sober, and I should not have lived with anybody—though I enjoyed it. I would have been a better mistress than wife—screw our brains out and then Monday return to work—because I only do one thing at a time. I like to pay attention to people when they're here, but I can't do that day after day. And I can't draw when others are around me. I'm very singly focused. The work takes precedent. Now I'm able to make a better time frame of being with people, and it's a whole lot easier to frame it out sober. When I was singing for a living, being high wasn't a detriment. I was far more interested in that than doing my relationships well. What I'm doing now is more interesting than being drunk. In fact, it keeps me from the realm of drink. Being drunk removes a lot of brain cells, and I need them all for what I'm doing now. I draw all day and pretty much all night. I do my laundry and will go to a movie with friends, but if I'm here in this house, I'm drawing constantly. I erase and correct, erase and correct. Then I'll put the paint on and do the backgrounds. I've just finished a drawing of Janis looking really joyful with her arms up in the air, and it makes me happy to look at it. Then again, I look at the other drawing here next to it, of Miles Davis. He has a hat on, and what's going to be in back of him is what has happened often in the jazz world: a person who's a heroin addict in the city, with an extreme amount of passion and talent. The look on Miles' face is different.

To some extent, LSD opened me to my own psychic ability. I used to get very quiet, and unconscious thoughts came up. I wrote some songs that predicted my own life. "Lawman" came true. Twenty years after I wrote it, I picked up a shotgun that had never been fired, just like in the song. A cop did a football roll into me and knocked me down. He got an award, as well he should. Nobody got shot. It was a mix-up where the cops came to my house to protect me, because my boyfriend called 911, but I thought they might be fake cops. In another song, it says something will slide down on you like brakes in bad weather, and that happened too. It scares me now to write lyrics. There's a cosmic thing, as though everything is happening at once, and it could be we're all conscious of that to varying degrees. When you're really concentrating on what you're feeling, you come out with some of that stuff. LSD tells your mind there's more than one reality, so your mind is open to appreciate various forms of spiritual life, consciousness, and intuition.

I always felt very close to the story of *Alice in Wonderland* for a real good reason. If you remember what happened to her, she came from a very straight-laced Episcopalian Republican background, and at some point between twelve and twenty-four—mine at about eighteen or so—you go down the rabbit hole. Something leads you down there. In my case, it was a combination of Lenny Bruce and the suggestion to come back to San Francisco from my girlfriend. Some rabbit comes along. Everybody's rabbit is different, but it comes along and you follow it. You know, life is short. I believe you follow that rabbit. What else can you do?

I've lost a good saddle and bridle,
My rope and some other good things,
But I'm sure glad to be here to tell yuh
To stay off uh horses with wings.

—Curley Fletcher, "The Flyin' Outlaw"

Destry Forgette
(rodeo cowboy)

DESTRY FORGETTE IS ONE of the more romantic figures interviewed for this book, because of his association with the Old West. As a five-year-old, growing up in post–World War II Los Angeles, I loved cowboys. In the movies, on radio and television, and in comic books,· cowboys ruled. Roy Rogers, Gene Autry, Tom Mix, the Cisco Kid, the Lone Ranger, Lash La Rue, and the greatest of them all, Hopalong Cassidy.

I can still remember that little outfit my parents bought me—a very cool red felt cowboy hat, a matching gray suedelike vest and chaps combo, a neat pair of fancy stitched cowboy boots, and a pair of six-guns holstered on each hip. I think I wore that outfit every day. I even pretended my two-wheeled bicycle was my horse, and I rode around and around my block in pursuit of the bad guys. (I was not yet old enough to cross the street.)

One day I was out playing on the sidewalk in front of our apartment when my mother yelled out the window for me to come in. I had a phone call. Reluctantly, I left my fellow cowpokes and headed inside to see what was going on. Five-year-olds didn't receive many phone calls in those days.

I could see my mom was quite excited as she offered me the receiver and urged me to hurry up and take the call. I uttered my hello, and to my complete shock and amazement, an unmistakable voice was greeting me on the other end. "Hi, Gary, you know who this is?" I nearly died right then and there. Of course I knew who it was . . . Hoppy . . . Hopalong Cassidy . . . the greatest cowboy of them all was talking to *me*! I have no idea what words we exchanged, and the entire conversation lasted but a few seconds, I suspect. I later found out that Hoppy, William Boyd, had come to the office of my Uncle Paul, a Hollywood attorney, on some legal business. My uncle, knowing how much I loved America's number-one cowboy, asked if he would take a minute or two and speak with me. Hoppy said, "Sure," and that's how it happened.

Anyway, as soon as we hung up, my mother said I should go back outside and tell my friends about the phone call. I raced out the door in an explosion of energy, screaming, "I just talked to Hoppy! I just talked to Hoppy!" What happened next was devastating. No one believed me. "Sure, you just talked to Hoppy, and my dad is Babe Ruth." They all began to taunt and tease me, thinking this was a story I just made up. Insisting that they ask my mom did no good. It only increased the level of teasing.

To this day, I remember the excitement of that event. I never really lost my love of cowboys or tales of the Wild West, so when the occasion to interview a real-life rodeo cowboy for this book arose, I jumped at the chance.

I met Destry Forgette at a small horse ranch in Wickenburg, Arizona. He looks like a cross between Kris Kristofferson and the Marlboro Man. Destry was going to take a few of us "dudes" on a guided sunrise ride through some incredibly beautiful and rough desert terrain. Unfortunately, he had just injured his wrist in a rodeo fall and thought better about riding that morning, but we met up later in the day. He spoke of his years of rodeos and alcohol abuse. To him, the romance of the Old West was not always what it's cracked up to be.

I started drinking at a very young age, I guess about age four. I knew there was something different about me. I snuck drinks on the weekend. My dad would hide his whiskey because he was an alcoholic. We'd go to dances the fourth Saturday of each month, and all the ranchers would get together from the whole community. There was booze everywhere. This was in the 1970s, in Elizabeth, Colorado, about forty-five miles outside of Denver.

I always wanted to be outstanding. I wanted people to notice me. I strived for that because I was picked on. There was something different about me. I was kind of introverted, yet I wanted to be popular. So I fell into drinking right away. It was very easy to do on weekends. There was no school, and I had plenty of free time. Like I said before, my father was an alcoholic. And I used to drink his whiskey and then replace it with tea. I became a weekend drunk.

We had a recruiter come to my high school during my freshman year. The town I was living in had maybe 150 people. I was working at the school about eight hours a night as a janitor to help support my family. I guess I was around twelve or thirteen years of age. I was making $3.13 an hour, more than the minimum wage back then. I was doing a man's job and I was a kid. My mom wouldn't let me spend my money the way I wanted to, but I bought a car before I was old enough to drive it. We weren't wealthy, but I was very well taken care of materially by my father and emotionally by my mother. I always had what I needed, but I wanted more. So this Navy recruiter came to the school and he told me that I could rodeo, and I could be somebody, and I would learn a trade and be paid. My mom wanted me to go to college, but my dad promised to send me to Annapolis if I was successful in the Navy. It was just another of his grandiose ideas. The recruiter told me that if I joined, I could travel and see the world. And I went, "Yes!" So at the age of sixteen, I was enlisted in the Navy.

So a couple of years went by, and I was still only drinking on weekends. Partying. I had a perfect record in the military until I re-enlisted. My dad had to have open-heart surgery, and my grandfather had just passed away, so I went AWOL. My alcoholism was pretty prevalent by then. I guess I was nineteen or twenty. Around then I requested to go into alcohol treatment, which I thought would make me look good. The Navy would back off of me if I said I needed treatment before they did. So I went through treatment and stayed sober for a year, and then I got married to my first wife, Lori. After serving three years, I re-enlisted for another four. The Navy gave me a whole bunch of money to re-enlist. While I was in the Navy, I was allowed to participate in rodeo riding. I continued to get into trouble and finally received a court-martial. Afterwards I got a letter from the Bureau of Naval Personnel stating that if I was ever in any more trouble relating to alcohol, I would be released from military service. I took that personally, even though the notice was a formality. So I wrote a letter back to them stating that I had no desire to let anybody tell me when or where I can take a drink, and I have no desire to finish my military service. So a week later, I had my discharge and I was on my own.

I was married by then, and I was so insecure I couldn't leave her. I had to know where she was all the time. She was getting real tired of my drinking and abuse. Anyway, I took off and I rodeoed for a little while, and my drinking became more rampant. I drank because it made me feel like something I wasn't. It made me feel bigger than life. I was noticed by people. I didn't think I was a very good rodeo cowboy because it took courage. It took a man to do something like this. My insanity was so prevalent that I couldn't even see how sick I was. The drinking got bad enough to where I knew I needed help. I was only about twenty-four or twenty-five, and my daddy, who was an alcoholic, told me I needed to stop drinking. But I couldn't listen to that coming from him. So anyway, I went to a treatment center, which was becoming a way of life for me. I'd get well and stay sober a year or so, and I'd get a good job on a ranch, making good money. I was trying to be a man, a cowboy—"I can do this on my own. I don't need any help!" But I'd always end up crawling back to the Veterans Administration to straighten me out. I tried recovery programs several times. I would make friends and use people to get me a job or a place to live. Then I'd go back out and start drinking again.

It got to where Lori didn't want anything to do with me. I had put her through a living hell. I was moving, traveling, and expecting her to sit still and be my wife, while I was riding and running around and having all the fun. I was doing what I wanted, when I wanted, and not paying any attention to what she needed. We ended up getting divorced. About a year later, we got remarried. I met Brenda, who was young and enticing during that time, trying to make Lori jealous.

My life was turning into a nightmare, a vicious circle. I'd go out and get a good job. I'd be doing really well for six months to a year, and then I'd sabotage it because it was too good. I didn't feel I deserved this. I would end up getting fired, or I would cause some kind of crisis. I'd get injured, some kind of horse accident, or I'd get a DWI and get thrown in jail. There was always some kind of crisis that would bring me down, where I thought I should be. Then I'd get drunk in the gutter. Then I'd move on and start the process all over again. I did that for probably twenty-seven years. I've had thirteen DWIs, been in jail many times for being drunk in public, drunk and disorderly, criminal mischief, and criminal trespassing.

Brenda, the wife I have now, and whom I love very much, got pregnant right after I got divorced from Lori for the second time. We got married 'cause I was living with her, and I was afraid I would lose her. I loved her, but my drinking was becoming more important, so we got married—my third marriage between two women. It lasted a year and a half. She seen how I drank, so she left. I was binge drinking, going on these four- or five-day benders. By then I didn't have anything of material value at all. I'd lost everything. I can remember selling a belt buckle I'd won at a rodeo to get a bus ticket and a bottle of whiskey. I sold the boots off my feet to get a bus ticket and a bottle of whiskey. I sold my truck and my saddle.

Everywhere I'd go I'd have the intent of starting fresh. I'd get every-thing rebuilt. I'd establish some credit with a saddle maker, and I'd get me another saddle, get my tack built back up where I could do a job. Or I'd borrow some money from a rancher. I was such a good con artist. I would con them into loaning me a month's paycheck, so I could go buy a new pair of spurs, saddle, chaps, stuff like that I'd sold to get drunk. And that became my way of living. In the process of the twenty years that went by, I did learn how to be a cowboy and a rodeo rider. I loved being outdoors. I could relate better to the animals than I did to people, because I was so afraid of what people thought of me as a person.

Anyway, the wife that I have now, Brenda, she came back to me. She always loved me, and I told her I quit drinking. I got a really good job. I called her and said, "Hey, we can work this out. Let's get back together." She come, and she stayed for four months. She told me she was pregnant. I didn't believe her, so I denied the daughter that I have now. I was afraid. Hell, I couldn't take care of myself, let alone anyone else. I could not accept my responsibility, and I told Brenda that the baby was not mine. She'd been gone for several months, so it must be somebody else's. So she left again. Because of my selfishness. It was just another excuse to get drunk. And this time she stayed gone for seven years.

I was starting to have seizures. I had my first one when I was thirty-eight. I had gone on a bender and stayed drunk for a couple of weeks. I had just walked out of a 7-Eleven store, and I keeled over with a grand mal seizure. My heart had stopped, and I was in the hospital in a coma. When I came out of it, the doctors told me there was nothing physically wrong with me. That it was alcohol that had caused this problem. I had four or five more seizures after that, but it wasn't enough to get me to quit drinking.

Next I got thrown in jail by a judge I knew well from my career of getting in misdemeanor trouble. He was a district court judge in Wyoming. One of the first judges to start the drug court program in that state. And I was one of his first appointees to this program. I had been given a six-month sentence for domestic violence. I told the judge that I couldn't quit drinking, and he said, "It sounds like you need some help." He said, "I don't want to throw you in jail. I'd rather help you if I can." I never forgot those words, but I was so resistant to authority that I told him, "I need to be in jail." You see, I'd been on probation and violated it, so I'd get thrown back in jail for ten to fifteen days. That happened many times. I was in jail three or four times for being drunk in public. I was just a nuisance. After six months in jail, I was sent to another treatment center. There I met a girl, started a relationship, and within a couple of months, I was drunk again.

The pattern of my life was so . . . I knew I could read the future and tell you what would happen. The girls that I met and was with were alcoholics, except for my wives. They didn't really drink. Most of the women I was meeting were codependent, looking for a man to take care of. I couldn't be with anybody unless they were drinking and using. I always wanted that serene picture of having a normal person in my life, some kid, and being okay. But I knew I wasn't okay, and I couldn't ask for help. I truly needed help getting sober. I had never been by myself. I always had some-one to drag through the mud with me, because I had such a great fear of being alone. Anyway, I found a job that paid five hundred dollars a month. I got a nice house outside of Cheyenne, and I stayed sober. I bought me a pickup. I hadn't had a vehicle for five or six years. I stayed sober and got offered a bunch of jobs for more money. I wasn't making enough money. But I was told by a friend that "You need to keep that job. You're living by yourself, and you're learning something." And I learned that it is okay to be by myself. About two years went by, and then I got a phone call saying that Dad was dying. That was another thing that set me off. My dad was always dying because of his heart problem.

About that time, Brenda decided to visit me and introduce my four-year-old daughter to me. I panicked. I said, "God, here's this responsibility again, and I can't handle it." Then I couldn't deny it anymore. She was def-initely my daughter. She looked exactly like me. Once again I got scared. I quit my job, left, and went to Nevada. There I gambled and got drunk all over again. But I couldn't get Brenda out of my mind, and how much she cared. The fact that I had this responsibility and that I was ignoring child support—that was another fear factor for me and a good excuse to run and start drinking. If I stayed at my job, they would have garnisheed my wages. They'd already taken everything from me. I don't have no money. I knew if I went on like this, I'd probably spend the rest of my life in prison. So I came down here to Wickenburg, and I quit for a year. I got a job on a ranch. Brenda and I got married, for the second time. I've been married four times. Twice to two women. I started working at this ranch, and right away I got hurt. I got bucked off a horse and hurt my back. I couldn't work, couldn't straighten up. I had to have another back surgery. Anyway, we moved into town because the ranch needed the place we were living in. They needed someone who could work. They kept me on as long as they could, but I just wasn't getting any better. I also wasn't attending any alco-hol recovery meetings. I knew in the back of my head that I was aiming for trouble. Workers' comp told me they weren't gonna pay me because my back was a pre-existing condition.

I had no job, I owed rents, I had a wife and daughter to take care of, and I panicked. I went and bought a bottle, and that was my last drink. That was over three years ago. I started back in the recovery program for real this time. In reviewing my life and looking at the choices I'd made, I knew down deep in my heart it was me. Nobody else had done this to me. I knew I had run out of options. I was going to die a drunk if I didn't stop. I also thought that there was a convening power in my life that was pushing me to where I'm at now. Wanting me to be sober.

My dad passed away in these last three years. That was a big loss to me. I loved my daddy even though he was a drunk. So, I finally surrender and start going to these recovery meetings every weekend. I was working twelve hours a day at a welding shop. The thought of rodeoing hadn't entered my mind. I didn't think I could do that again because I had been so busted up from horse wrecks and previous rodeos. I also knew I would be able to get drunk again. You know, my grandfather was a cowboy. So was my dad. Cowboys and drunkenness was all I knew. I never saw a cowboy that didn't drink. It was part of the West. So being in a rodeo just wasn't an option no more.

Horses. I love horses and love ranch work, so that's what I was going to pursue. A couple months went by and I met some people here at Gatehouse [a treatment center in Wickenburg, Arizona]. I started to hear what they had to say and where they came from. I actually started to listen to people.

You know, in the Navy, I'd been around the world three times. Every once in a while, I'd go to a meeting just to keep the officers off my back. To look good and show 'em I was doing something about my drinking problem. I never went with the intent to stop drinking.

After about eight months of sobriety, I got offered this job at Gatehouse Academy for a lot more money than I ever made in my life, but still thought, "I don't have anything to offer anybody. I haven't been sober that long." But I went ahead and made a decision to give it a try. A year went by, and I was really getting into the program. Dealing with my character defects and asking God for help. Trying to help other people. I was moving forward and staying sober. It's better than getting on any bucking horse in the world!

I never experienced anything like this. You know, I've helped my mother and I've helped my sister and my brother, but to help some of these kids in recovery . . . Whoa! . . . You know, I'm forty-five years old and some of them are seventeen and eighteen and they're getting a wake-up call. I'm like Rip Van Winkle, asleep for twenty years.

I thought I was destined to be a ranch hand, a cowboy, in a go-nowhere job, until I went to work at Gatehouse. After about a year here, I started to find some happiness. I started to find some serenity. I'm meeting all kinds of wonderful people. I got friends that come here to visit me. People call and say, "Hey, Destry, we hear you're sober. Is that right?"

I even started thinking about rodeoing again. I got all fired up about it. I got a brother-in-law who's fifty-four years old, and he started riding bulls again. He's been sober twenty-three years. So now I have the courage, without anything to alter my mind to lend me the artificial courage. I still have the passion for horses and rodeo. I also think that it's sort of a test to see if I was ready, ready to stay sober while being around the rodeo crowd. And I'd do it again tomorrow if the opportunity presented itself.

My first rodeo in Prescott, I entered the bareback riding. I hadn't been on a bareback horse in about sixteen years. I joined the PRCA [Professional Rodeo Cowboys Association] and went to the rodeo. I was standing behind the chutes, talking to a couple of cowboys. They gave me some guidance about the different things they are doing. I climbed up the chute and sat down on my horse, and pretty soon it was over. I got bucked off. I got up and walked out of the arena and discovered that my wrist was broken. There was some big pain, but I told my wife that if I'd had a rodeo the next day, I would have rode because of the elation I was feeling. That I did it and I didn't have to drink!

You know, I drank to get the courage to ride, the courage to do a lot of things. If I had to talk to somebody that I was afraid of, I'd have a couple of drinks. I needed a couple of shots to get on a bucking horse, to push me to the edge. There were times where I'd have no memory of getting on a horse. I'd always have a couple of shots. I went to a lot of rodeos in the military where I'd enter as a local contestant (not as a member of the cowboy association at that time). And every time I rode, I'd go behind the chutes to take a shot or two of whiskey . . . liquid courage! The courage I didn't have to follow through. Otherwise I couldn't have done it because of the fear. The fear of getting hurt, looking bad, not being able to cover your horse (ride him in the required time). This last time I felt better. Whether I got bucked off or not, it didn't matter. It was just something I had to prove to myself. I had to experience it clearheaded.

Before I was always there for the drink and chasing the girls. I wasn't there to get on the horse. The party. That's what rodeo was to me. This was the first time I went to the rodeo to get on the horse, and I plan on doing it until I can't.

I met a girl whom I got pregnant when I was seventeen. She was twenty-four. I was going to do the honorable thing. Since I was in the military, we were going to get married in a military chapel. Three days before the wedding, she comes to me and says, "You're not ready for this, Destry. You've got too much living to do. You can't handle this right now." She said, "I'll tell him about you when the time is right."

I was twenty-one when I'd entered a rodeo and got hurt, and in the hospital, I wrote a poem about how things go with being a cowboy on the rodeo circuit. It goes like this:

I was sitting at the bar back home.
I was staring at my beer, and stoned.
This big fella walked in and come up and sat down,
And me and him got to talkin',
And he asked me what was wrong.
I looked at him and decided to tell him my unhappy song.
I said, "I was just thinkin' about a girl that left a long time ago, with a
    boy I didn't know.
I was thinkin' what my boy'd grow up to be,
And I was praying to God that he was nothing like me.
But you see, Stranger, she moved away from where she used to stay.
All she left me was a letter that said I had a son whose eyes were brown.
So I traveled through the years from town to town.
I finally said I'd quit lookin' and came back here.

But through those years became nothing but a drunken ole rodeo
  clown with a lot of cares."
You know that big fella looked at me with a tear in his eye,
And for a moment I thought he was going to cry.
This is what he said . . .
He said, "You can quit lookin' now,
'Cause you came to the right town.
That lady you was lookin' for, well,
I'm sorry, sir, she passed on about nine years before.
Well, me, I've grown and became a world champion in professional
  rodeo.
So put down your drink. Get rid of those tears.
You ought to be happy.
I know I've never met you before—
I'm your son, Dad. It's been almost forty years."

I wrote that poem when I was twenty-one and thinking about the girls
that I'd left, and how I had a boy I was never going to see, and about drinking and the despair and loneliness that go with it, and how life has a twist
and a turn.

So the lady took off and went back to San Diego, and my mom got a
letter saying she had a baby boy. He'd be twenty-seven. He called me not
too long ago. I was in the hospital with a broken back. I'd entered a rodeo
and got hurt, just like when I wrote that poem, only today I am sober with
a beautiful loving wife and daughter. I am thankful for what God has given
me in my sobriety. Of course, there were many people and events affected
negatively by my alcoholism and behaviors. Today, by being sober and of
service, my life and behaviors have changed.

A man is never so on trial as in the moment of excessive good fortune.

—Lew Wallace, *Ben-Hur*

Nile Rodgers
(musician)

ONE OF MY FAVORITE MOVIE bits from the inimitable Three Stooges features the lovable buffoon, Curly, on the receiving end of a piano being moved down two flights of stairs. Moe and Larry are above, guiding the piano down the stairs, inquiring every few steps as to how Curly is holding up. "I got it, I got it, I got it, I got it . . . I ain't got it" he understates, as the piano starts to roll over him.

This was exactly how I felt while chasing down Nile Rodgers, one of the preeminent R & B music makers, in pursuit of an interview for our book. "I got him, I got him, I got him, I got him . . . I ain't got him."

Nile and I both live in Westport, Connecticut, a fashionable community for around 27,000 seemingly prosperous inhabitants. As small as our town is, you couldn't help but run into Nile every once in a while. In these parts, it's hard to miss a dreadlock-sporting African American driving in a new yellow Range Rover.

I knew of Nile from recovery circles as well as from the music business, though our paths had never truly crossed. I had this sense, though, that his story would make an important contribution to this book, so I made a few inquiries and finally was given his home number by a helpful friend. Calling cold, I caught him home one winter afternoon about a year ago. When I explained the nature of my call and my desire to interview him, Nile tentatively agreed but asked that

I set it up through his New York office. I quickly called the number he gave me and was greeted by his most accommodating English assistant, Sooze. "Why of course we'll set this up," she assured me. And set it up she did. Several times.

"Nile is delayed in the recording studio." "Nile had to leave for Milan." "Nile's on a conference call he just can't get out of." I ain't got it. After doing the Nile shuffle for several months, and with the deadline to deliver the book fast approaching, I made one last try. "Sooze, this is it. If we don't do the interview today, I'm sunk." "Don't worry, dear," I was assured. "Nile has an appointment that will end at 10:30 a.m., and he has instructed me to set it up right after that." At 11:30 I got an e-mail from Sooze: "He had to take a call but should be done around 1:00 p.m. Why don't you call me then." Dancing with Sooze throughout the day led to a combination of anxiety mixed with no small amount of despair. I was losing my last chance to get this interview. Exchanges of e-mails during the afternoon were getting nowhere, and finally, at around 7:00 p.m., I admitted defeat to myself, packed up a few things from my office, and headed home.

After catching up with my kids and eating a brief dinner, I went upstairs to check my computer one last time in hopes of some sort of miracle. And there it was: a note from Sooze: "Nile is home expecting your call." I dashed down the stairs, scared the dog into one of his yapping fits, kicked my unsuspecting daughter off of the phone, plugged in my handy-dandy recording device, and sat down to listen to what turned out to be a riveting recounting of a truly amazing story from a man who speaks with rare insight and candor.

⟶

I was a very shy kid, born to a mother who was very young. She got pregnant at thirteen, so, needless to say, she was ill equipped for motherhood. Consequently I had a very nomadic childhood. All my family are substance abusers. My natural father died of cirrhosis of the liver before he was forty, which is incredible. In his mid-thirties, he had no liver. My stepfather, the guy my mom married, was a heroin addict all of his life, and both of his siblings died of drug abuse when I was quite young. Drug abuse and alcoholism is very, very prevalent in my family. It was everywhere.

Let me put it to you like this—one picture is worth a thousand words. For many, many years, I believed that only children slept lying down, and adults slept standing up, because when I would come home from school, the number of junkies nodding in our living room was amazing. All the adults would be standing up with cigarette ashes dangling, never falling and hitting the ground. They looked like they were asleep standing up. I didn't know they were heroin addicts. They were just adults—family and friends—just standing up sleeping. Sort of the opposite of vampires!

When you're a child and you see images like that, it's just normal to you. So me being a typical rebellious kid, the last thing I wanted to be was like them. So alcohol, heroin, and drugs like that were the furthest thing from my mind. You know, most kids don't want to be anything like their parents, and I was no different.

I came up in the hippie era of the sixties, when psychedelic drugs were very popular. I started out sniffing glue. That was sort of the rage in my community. We went from sniffing glue to amyl nitrate. In the junior high school I went to, they had amyl nitrate in the athletic department. It was used to revive people who passed out. We'd go in there and raid the medical chest. It wasn't under lock-and-key in those days. We used to steal the amyl nitrate from the gym. We had a poor man's teenage speedball. We'd sniff glue and do amyl nitrate. Boy, how deadly was that?

When I was about thirteen or fourteen, I met Timothy Leary in Los Angeles. We went to this event called The Teenage Fair, and somehow we ended up in the Hollywood Hills with Tim Leary and a bunch of hippies . . .

I'm sorry . . . my family was sort of bicoastal. Most of the time when I'm talking about my family, I'm talking about our life in New York, mainly in Greenwich Village, the Lower East Side, and the Bronx. My mom was always sort of pawning me off to my grandparents, either my paternal or maternal grandparents, who all lived in Los Angeles by that time. So I was bicoastal. At thirteen, I was doing a stint with my paternal grandmother, who was a great influence in my life. She named me after my dad. I'm Nile Rodgers Jr. She tried to instill in me stuff that my dad just didn't get. When I was born, my dad was eighteen or nineteen, but it was already clear that he was not going to make it. He was a musician and hot guy around town, but he just couldn't overcome his problems. Even though I was thirteen and my dad wasn't much older than me, I guess she felt like she had a second chance.

I was in L.A. with my grandmother at the time, and I was just doing the glue sniffing and amyl nitrate, and I went to this thing called The Teenage Fair, and somehow wound up meeting Timothy Leary. I didn't know that he was anything special. He may have been in the news in those days, but it was just starting to happen. He just looked cool and interesting. Leary asked us if we wanted to take a trip, and we thought he meant to go away someplace, so we said yes. I was with my friend who also did the same kind of recreational drug-taking that I did. We used to go to a place in Hollywood to roller-skate. It was in close proximity to the Hollywood Palladium, which is where The Teenage Fair was. So we happened to see those very odd-looking people . . . In Los Angeles I hung out with only black people. In New York it was a very mixed crowd, because my step-father is white. My stepfather is Jewish. So they were the sort of heroin addict beatnik hip crew in New York.

My parents were very, very cool. My family, now that I understand addiction, were always doing geographics. We never lived in the same place more than a few weeks at a time. So consequently, I never completed a semester in a school, ever, until I was about fourteen years old, and I was somewhat in control of my own destiny. I was at the mercy of whomever I was staying with. I never checked into a school the day that every other kid checked in, like the first day of school. And I never made it to the last day of school. Ever! I never completed one semester in any school in my life until I was fourteen, which I find extraordinary.

In those days, the American public school system basically had a standardized curriculum. For a kid that had a nomadic existence like I did, it sort of helped, because no matter what city I was in, what school, or what district, I could pretty much walk into a class and they were reading the same books. I would go to L.A. and be in the hard-core ghetto, and it was still "See Spot run. See Dick go. See Jane run." Same thing. I'd go back to New York and it was "See Spot run." That helped me to be somewhat grounded. Intellectually I sort of excelled. I could enter a classroom and, even though the other kids made fun of me 'cause they do that to a new kid, and usually I was the only black kid in an all-white class or something, I just sort of took to reading. That helped me adjust. Even though I would check into a class late, I knew all the lessons or could fake my way through it at least. I felt like an outcast, but I would grab on to any little thing that would masquerade as consistency. Even though I was the new kid and everyone made fun of me, I could pick up the reader and say, "Yes, on page 37 Dick said . . . whatever." That would sort of impress the teachers on some level. I was really a people pleaser, who did everything to belong and try to fit, because I never fit. Kids are trendy, and I'd move to a new neighbor-hood, a new school system, and the kids would have their own little fads that they were into, and of course I wouldn't know what they were into. I never fit in.

At the time I grew up, roller-skating was a very black kind of thing. There were some white kids there, but it was a real R & B thing. The rinks played R & B music predominately, although every now and then you'd hear The Archies or some pop song. But mainly it was Motown. I lived in south central L.A., and when we got to the skating rink this one day, we saw all of these people who looked very different from the people we hung out with. They were the precursors to hippies. They didn't call themselves hippies; they called themselves freaks. My family were beatniks, and the freaks followed them. Then they became hippies. At least that's how I remembered it. So when we went to The Teenage Fair and I saw all these freaks hanging out, we said, "Man, this is great." We couldn't understand how they saw through all that hair. I'll never forget, we saw a bunch of them who said, "Oh wow, spade cats!" I didn't know what that meant. So when Timothy Leary asked us if we wanted to take a trip, we said, "Yeah, where are we goin'?" We didn't know that meant LSD. We went up to this house in the Hollywood Hills, and there was this guy that they were all calling a guru. That was the first time I heard that word. Just think about this . . . we were kids, maybe thirteen years old. I'll never forget it.

We took LSD. I think it was on a sugar cube. I don't recall the amount of time it took us to get high. We had already been smoking pot, so we thought we *were* high. We had no idea what was about to happen. They were playing this record I had never heard before, by The Doors. Over and over again. The song was "The End":

This is the end, beautiful friend
This is the end, my only friend
The end of our elaborate plans
The end of everything that stands
The end

No safety or surprise
The end
I'll never look into your eyes again

We had never heard anything like that before. We were used to "Don't Mess with Bill" and "Going to a Go-Go." After a while, after we achieved LSD highness, we found ourselves watching this television set that had no picture tube inside it. They had Christmas lights with angel hair, flashing off and on, off and on, off and off! There was a bunch of really gorgeous girls and guys hanging out in front of this TV set looking at these light flashes for hours and hours, while The Doors blasted in the background.

So that was my initial experience in that type of drug taking. Before that we had really only sniffed glue and taken amyl nitrate. We'd go to the model shop and buy a bunch of glue. We were connoisseurs. You can only snort Testers, in the orange-and-white tube. I should've known I was in trouble 'cause I was a glue connoisseur at ten!

See, I tried to be different from my parents who drank, smoked pot, and did heroin. So after I dropped acid, it was like, "Whoa!" I knew my parents never did this. I felt superior to them on some level: "I'm doing stuff that they couldn't even fathom." My mom wouldn't take acid in a million years 'cause she's a control freak. So after we took acid, psychedelics became my drug of choice. I only wanted to do acid, smoke pot, and do magic mush-rooms. You won't believe this, but for a very long time, my drug of choice was rat poison. Rat poison had belladonna in it. We were smart kids. Smart enough to know that belladonna was a psychedelic. We would separate the little granules of belladonna from the rat poison. We didn't know if we could really tell which were the belladonna granules. Imagine, we were taking something that could kill you, and we were taking it to get high.

We knew all the hippie stuff—the *Alice B. Toklas Cookbook*. Remember the thing about if you scraped the inside of a banana peel that would get you high? Going to the plant nursery for morning glory seeds? All that hip-pie stuff about how to get high.

I remember reading a book by William Burroughs called *The Yage Letters*. It was about the most powerful hallucinogenic. It grew on a vine in South America. Burroughs went down there and did it with the Indians. It was more powerful than LSD or STP. It was unbelievable. And all we wanted to do was go to the jungles of Brazil and do yage with the Indians. That shows you how completely sold I was on this life-style. It came as a complete surprise to me, but at the end of the day, I ended up becoming just your garden-variety alcoholic, because I had such a flair for getting high when I was younger. It should have been very exotic, but what brought me to my knees was just vodka and cocaine.

I could have started just like my parents right away. Cut to the chase. Stopped all the bullshit. "Hey, Mom, give me some vodka. Pass me some of that coke you guys are selling, and I can be there with you right now." I had no idea that's how I would wind up.

So after living like that as a teenager, I started to develop my musical skills. My mom, dad, and stepfather loved great music, and it was always playing in our house.

One thing I forgot to mention: Part of the normal school curriculum in those days had art class, gym, and music class; all these interesting things you could learn. Every school had those. For some reason I gravitated towards music. Every school I went to had bands and orchestras, or some reasonable facsimile. So because I always checked in late, I was assigned whatever instrument was left or lacking in the orchestra. A by-product of that existence was that, by the time I was eleven years old, I could sort of play or get something discernable out of every instrument in the symphony orchestra. I knew how the instrument worked, so to speak. Its function in an orchestra. By the time I became sixteen or seventeen years old—and I've now chosen my instrument, which is guitar, which was not part of the symphony orchestra—I had all of this inadvertent training in the elementary and junior high school. I knew how all that stuff worked. So when I became a professional musician, I magically knew what to do.

"No, no, no, French horns don't play that part! You don't want to give an excessive amount of fourths to these instruments because they can't play them quickly enough." I just sort of had it down.

When I was in my sophomore year of high school, I really started studying guitar, and I sort of perfected it by my senior year. At that time the world was very political, and my life was incredibly political. I was really hard-core into the anti-war movement and every kind of liberation struggle. Women's lib, gay rights, bring home the troops. I joined every organization from the Hari-Krishnas to the Black Panthers. Every trendy little thing. By the time I was sixteen, I could hang with anybody from any religion, all that stuff. My knowledge of music and drugs, which went along with this alternative culture, was very extensive. And in my political background, I started out getting beaten up all the time and wound up a Black Panther. So I ran the gamut of every religion, every movement, every alternative cool thing.

When I turned eighteen, I decided that I was not going to drink or use drugs. Live a completely drug-free life, because I wanted to concentrate on the things that were important, which was saving the world and becoming a great musician. So for a long time, I would not drink or smoke pot or do any drugs. It was of no interest to me. I led this cool quest-for-knowledge life-style from the time I was eighteen until about twenty-three, which doesn't sound like a long time now, but then it was an eternity. It was a fifth of my whole life. By twenty-three I was a pretty good musician, and things were happening to me. One thing I noticed though. When I became drug and alcohol free, I reverted back to my real personality, which was very shy and introverted and afraid of people. I wasn't comfortable with people because I didn't like the way I looked. Everything about my existence reinforced my belief that I wasn't good enough. The fact that my mother never kept me more than a few months at a time, I felt that no one wanted me. But when I was high, everyone loved me. Everyone wanted me. I lived in communes. It was great.

So when I went on this quest to become a better musician and a better person, and I was drug and alcohol free, I reverted back to being afraid of people and very, very introverted.

Sometime during that period, I met my great music writing partner, Bernard Edwards, and we formed a band called Chic that changed my life and, if you read *Rolling Stone*, changed the life of many people: "One of the fifty moments that changed rock 'n' roll." In the mid-seventies we had our first hit. *Dance, Dance, Dance*, the first record we ever recorded under our name, was also a big hit. And from that moment on, we never looked back. The second record we recorded was also a big hit. And the third and the fourth and the fifth. We just had this huge run of success. The interesting thing was that after our first hit, before there was video, you had to go on the road to support it. You actually had to go on the road and play live concerts. And I was fundamentally very shy, even though I had done all sorts of gigs before then. I was always in the band, off to the side. I wasn't the star. But now I've got a hit record, and I'm the boss. I got to go carry a show.

The first show we did was in Atlantic City. A big disco called Casanova's, and there were thousands of people. The very next day, we played for 75,000 people at Oakland Baseball Stadium, and I walked out and saw that sea of people and I was petrified. I panicked. I couldn't go out on stage. And my roadie came over to me and said, "Hey, boss man, try a swig of this." He had a Styrofoam cup with Heineken's in it, and I just sort of swigged it down almost like cough medicine. Heineken is definitely an acquired taste, if you haven't had a beer in years, and I swigged it down. In one instant this warm glow sort of came down my body, tracing the path of the liquid. I turned around to 75,000 people, put my hands over my head, and screamed "OAKLAND!" And the crowd yelled, "CHIC!" And I went, "This is fantastic," and I played the show. Afterwards I said to my roadie, "Before we do every show, can you always have one of those cups of Heineken ready?" And to show you how quickly the disease of alcoholism progresses, by the end of that tour, I went from starting out each show with one Heineken to having the entire drum riser covered in white Styrofoam cups. Thirty or forty cups worth of beer all the way around the riser, and because the alcohol dehydrates you—it's liquid and water, you think you're quenching your thirst. Drinkin' and drinkin', and the lights are hot. Liquid evaporating. You're just getting drunk. At least for the day. But it's also giving me confidence that I'm putting on a good show. I'm a natural. Playing big baseball stadiums like I belong out there. It was great.

I carried on like that for many years quite successfully. My shrink used to call it "falling forward through life." That even though you're falling, you're spiraling down, you're going forward. You're functioning. You're doing great. I was really doing great. Writing songs like "We Are Family," "Freak Out," and "Good Times." Producing David Bowie, Madonna, Duran Duran, Steve Winwood, and Eric Clapton. Fantastic! I couldn't do anything wrong. I can't even mention all the people I've done. Hit after hit after hit. And it went great for a long time, but now I can clearly see where I crossed the line. I crossed the line on that first tour. I was young and could take it, but . . . ten years of this. I'm still glamorous. I can hang with it. But there's a big difference. Now records are costing a million, two million a record. I'm doing more coke than you can imagine. Drinking more booze than a human being should be able to drink.

I suffered many, many attacks of acute alcohol poisoning, especially on long flights. I remember once I flew from Honolulu to Los Angeles, which isn't really that long. At the end of the trip, the flight attendant came over to me and said, "Wow, you just set some kind of record!" I didn't know what she was talking about. She said, "Well, whenever we get on the plane"—this was a 747—"we carry forty of each type of drink, and you drank every whiskey sour we had on this flight." She said, "Well, you actually only drank thirty-seven, 'cause one other guy drank three. Thirty-seven whiskey sours in six hours!" I remember her words perfectly. "That's got to be some kind of record." And of course, when I got in the limo and went to my hotel, I felt very sick. I went to the hospital and was told I had acute alcohol poisoning. First time that had happened.

After that, I subsequently had two bouts of pancreatitis. The first time I had it, the doctor said, "You can never drink again." I said, "Why?" He said, "Because right now you should be dead. Pancreatitis is quite often fatal. You don't usually survive this. You die. You don't leave the hospital." So I was like, "Wow, I don't feel *that* bad."

And I recuperated after a few days, and went back to drinking. He had told me, "Never drink again. Alcohol always attacks some organ. Usually the liver, but in your case, it went after your pancreas." He explained to me that pancreatitis is just like cirrhosis of the liver. I didn't get it. I kept drinking.

I had a second bout of pancreatitis maybe a couple of years later. The doctors were like, "Wow, you're killing yourself. You're killing your pancreatic tissue." And I didn't quite get it 'cause it didn't sound that dangerous. Or I just wanted to keep going. Who knows? The second bout of pancreatitis didn't make me stop drinking either. Then one night I came home from an after-hours club. It was probably ten or eleven the next morning. Maybe earlier than that. The handyman was putting out the garbage, so it was probably eight in the morning. This was in New York. I lived on the twentieth floor at the time, and I got in the elevator, and somehow I pushed thirteen. When the door opened, I passed out and fell into the thirteenth-floor hallway, and a janitor happened to be there. He called 911, and the ambulance came and revived me.

It was a typical alcoholic incident. You pass out, you throw up, you choke on your own vomit, your heart stops, and there you go. I had done coke and whatever else, and that's what happened. Nothing glamorous, just a typical alcoholic death. They were able to revive me. Because of the amount of coke in my system, though, my heart kept stopping. Finally, after they tried to revive me the seventh or eighth time, they gave up. The doctor was filling out the death certificate, and my heart just started beating again. As quickly as it stopped, it started going again. And I only know this because the doctor told me. I certainly wasn't conscious of it; I was really lit. Anyway, the doctor was on staff, and he stayed around the next day until I came to, and explained to me how hard they worked to save my life, and maybe I was the kind of person who cared about other people. If I knew how hard they worked, I might have enough respect for their effort to go on living, because they saved my life. If I can't do it for me, I could do it for them.

And I went, "Man, is this guy laying a guilt trip on me." But you know, I thought it was really incredible for him to say that. Of course, I didn't listen to him. In fact, I don't think I waited even five days before I went back to drinking. I couldn't drink right away because I felt so bad. My chest was killing me because of everything they had to do to get my heart going. They had brought me back from the dead, and I didn't care.

I kept going for some time until ten years ago. I was down in Miami Beach at Madonna's birthday party, and I was living the life. I had a gorgeous Hollywood movie star as my date. I picked her up in some stupid grandiose car I rented. She was down there doing a movie, and I had just finished doing the music for a big film that she was in, and somehow our paths crossed. Wow, I get to date these gorgeous girls! All my life I thought I was ugly, and now I'm dating movie stars. This is fantastic. And she likes me. She said, "Nile, you're the greatest guy!"

Funny, but that was the last time I ever saw this woman. She couldn't even make it through the date. I just went nuts. I was there with a bunch of very famous people who were all my buddies. We were all in the bathroom doing as much coke as we could. I was the last person to leave Madonna's house the next day. I had to be carried home by friends. They deposited me in my hotel room in Miami. It was the first and last time I ever suffered from cocaine psychosis.

I got to my hotel room, the phone rang, and I answered it. It was a Mafia hit man telling me I only had a little while to live. He hoped that the last time I was up in New York partying with his girlfriend that I had a good time because I was going to pay for that good time with my life. I called some heavyweight detectives in New York to come down and protect me. Another grandiose gesture! A private jet. The whole bit. These detectives had to take this threat as real. They didn't know that I was just imagining this shit. So they're trying to find out who this "killer" is. In the meantime, I hid in the closet of my hotel room with a gun and a samurai sword waiting for this hit man to come and get me.

I had this wise-guy friend who took this threat very seriously. He started calling around town to try and figure out who put this contract out on me. Probably about an hour or two later, he called me on the phone—and I'll never forget this—he said to me, "Hey Nile, I got to ask you a question. Are you doing coke?" I said, "Yeah, but what's that got to do with anything?" He said to me, "You fucking moron, the coke is talking to you!"

I never heard the phrase before. I mean, I've been doing drugs all my life, and no one said that to me: "The coke is talking to you." Sounded like Greek or hieroglyphics. What is this guy saying? And then I reached out to a number of my friends who loved and cared about me, and they all said the same thing: "Hey Nile, don't worry. That's just the coke talking to you."

What did they mean? Finally, one of these tough guys said to me, "Nile, there's no fucking contract out on you. But I'm going to tell you something. If you don't stop doing that coke, I'm going to come down there and kill you." I knew he wasn't playing, and I took his shit seriously.

For some reason I couldn't hear all of my friends that were trying to help me, but this guy I could hear. For some reason, his words resonated. I still didn't understand cocaine psychosis, but I did understand "Motherfucker, I'll come down there and kill you if you don't stop doing coke." So I somehow, reluctantly, threw two half-ounces of coke down the toilet, and I sat there trying to sober up.

In those days, I believed the thing that made a person an alcoholic was brown liquor. You couldn't be an alcoholic if you drank vodka or champagne or gin—although gin was pretty hard-core for me, I didn't like gin. Even though I drank like a fish and almost died and all that stuff, I still didn't think of myself as an alcoholic. And then two things happened to me in that hotel room, by myself. One, my friend said he was going to come out and kill me, so I threw the coke away. And two, I realized I had finished all the white liquor, all the clear liquor, and had to now drink something brown. I opened the liquor cabinet and saw that the only thing left was Scotch. I'll never forget it 'cause it was the only time I did it in my life. I said, "This tastes fantastic! What have I been missing all these years?" And for some reason, that rang as if I had crossed the line. Now I'm an alcoholic. I can drink brown liquor straight and it tastes great to me. It tasted wonderful. I said to myself, "Damn, all these years I could have been doing *this*?"

For some reason, that dose of reality resonated and sent me a big message, like, "Hey pal, you're an alcoholic. And you're a drug addict. And your life is changing." I felt my music deteriorating. This whole trip to Miami was very revealing. I was down there commissioned to do a record, and went and played live at this club one night. I thought I was doing a great job. The crowd was cheering and going nuts. The artist I was working with, who happens to be the most anal artist I've ever known, recorded every single note of music that night. The next day I went to his house and he said, "You want to hear what you played last night? You thought it was great, right? Well, check this out." He played it, and it was the worst thing I ever heard. I was so embarrassed. So what brought me to my knees was realization and embarrassment. Not me being destitute, not me being poor and losing all my money, or any of that stuff. It was pride. I had worked so hard to develop a sense of belonging and accomplishment and achievement, and it was all going to be taken away from me because I couldn't even play guitar anymore. And here's the proof. This is what I play like. But meanwhile, I thought it was great. I realized all at once that I could think one thing, but it not be true. That people were after me, and it not be true. I could think I'm a great musician, and it's not true.

I realized that I was deluded, and that dose of reality started me on a quest to find what was real and what wasn't. I called my shrink, whom I'd been seeing for many years, and he convinced me to check into a hospital called Silver Hill. And I did. And for some reason, maybe because I believed I was going to lose what I worked so hard to achieve, my problem became real to me. I got a new focus and sense of purpose when I realized that drinking and drugging was as natural to me as breathing. So to not do it required a huge amount of discipline. My music teacher used to always say to me, "What do you consider the working definition of discipline?" I would think about it, and he'd say, "Discipline is the ability to delay gratification." He says, "You practice now to be on the stage later. One day you're going to be gratified."

And when I crossed over, that's what I kept thinking. A lot of alcoholics have a tough time dealing with time. "Hey, you made it to thirty days, now you got to get to ninety." For me I thought, "All I have to do is be disciplined." So now I had to take that discipline and not drink for one day, one day, and the next thing you know, I'll have ten years. Then twenty, or whatever. That's my take on sobriety.

I remember once I worked on that big charity project Live Aid. You know, "We Are the World." Lionel Richie told me and Clapton and all these people, "When we go on stage, no one can grab the microphone, because the sound-mixing guy is so far back he won't be able to tell which microphone you're on, and he might turn up the wrong one and get feedback."

And we all looked at Lionel and said, "Lionel, come on man, we're all professionals, we know that." The next thing you know, we play the intro to the song, and Lionel starts the song off 'cause he wrote it. And as soon as he goes to sing, he grabs his mike and starts stomping up and down just like what he told us not to do. What I realized is that people do what they're comfortable with. They go back to the things that they know. I knew what it felt like to do the same thing over and over again until it became second nature. To me, getting through one day sober was the same as practicing the scales.

The words still resonate to this very day: "The working definition of discipline for me is the ability to delay gratification." I don't need the gold record today. I can work towards that gold record, and the day I get it, well that's cool. My music teacher used to say, "Doing the work teaches you how to do the job." And when I got into a program of recovery, the work was getting through a day. I was so glad to get through it without taking a drink. That was work. It wasn't natural. Natural was "Forget this, let's get some vodka." So not to drink was almost an oxymoron, because not to do an action was an action. That's how the practicing of the scales was the same as "don't drink." So I sat there and didn't drink today. And it was incredible. Once I was able to come up with a philosophical approach to my recovery, it all felt natural.

To this very day it still feels natural. I'm in the rock-and-roll business. I'm around people who get drunk and do stuff all the time. I'm not a hypocrite—I loved it. I'd probably love it now if I could do it safely. But I'm an alcoholic, I'm a drug addict, and I can't do it safely. If I take a glass of champagne, I'm not stoppin'. I want all the glasses of champagne. It's pretty clear to me. A sip is not interesting. I'm a very grandiose personality. Working at being humble is discipline. That's my job. I have to work hard at keeping grounded. It's very natural for me to say, "All right, let's go to Paris for lunch." Now that the Concorde isn't flying, it's hard to be so grandiose, but I would do that just on a whim. Twenty thousand dollars to go have lunch. It was grandiose, and alcoholics are grandiose. Like they say, an alcoholic is the only person who could be lying in the gutter and think he is better than you. Do you know what an alcoholic uniform is? A crown, a scepter, and a diaper! And that's how it is. There I am, I'm lying on the floor saying, "I'm the guy who wrote 'We Are Family.' I'm a genius."

I'm so thankful that I found recovery, so thankful that I can be an honest person and not be a hypocrite. I love alcohol. I love drugs. I have all my life. And I know, if I could use them safely, I probably wouldn't be the person I am today. Now that I know that I do have a life without it, the person that I am would not choose to get high, because I like the way I feel sober. It took a long time before I could feel comfortable in a room full of strangers and face embarrassment. Now embarrassment doesn't kill me. I go talk to strangers, and if they don't like me, I'm not going to commit suicide. In the old days, I could walk past strangers and hear them laughing, and think they were laughing at me. Now I realize, whether they were or not, it's none of my business. I can actually live by that now. I can be in situations that used to devastate me, and I handle them with relative peace.

> Hey you all look out let a man come in
> I got to have fun I'm gonna do my thing
> Way over yonder can you dig that mess
> The sister standing out there dressed up
> In a brand new mini dress
> Look hey over there
> do you see that boy playing that horn
> And dig that soul brother look at him doing the popcorn
>
> Hey everybody I got a brand new start
> Hey, hey everybody I got a brand new start

I ain't gonna hurt nobody
I just, I just, I just wanna help my heart
Gonna have a ball sure as you're born
Gonna have a ball sure as you're born
I'm gonna dance, dance, dance do the popcorn
—"Let a Man Come In and Do the Popcorn"

About the Celebrities

Dick Beardsley (b. March 21, 1956)
Dick Beardsley is the fourth-fastest American marathon runner of all time. His race with Alberto Salazar at the 1982 Boston Marathon was touted as "an epic duel," and it was one of the closest in the marathon's history. Beardsley, twenty-six, and Salazar, twenty-three, ran together the entire 26.2 miles, with no other competitors in sight for the last nine miles. Beardsley finished the race in 2:08:54, losing to Salazar by two seconds. Beardsley retired from his professional running career shortly thereafter. Born in Rush City, Minnesota, Beardsley lives in Detroit Lakes, Minnesota, runs a fishing-guide business, and is a motivational speaker for youth groups.

Gerry Cooney (b. August 4, 1956)
Nicknamed "The Gentleman" and "The Great White Hope," former professional boxer Gerry Cooney was the number-one heavyweight contender in the 1980s, with a professional record of twenty-eight wins and three losses, with twenty-five knockouts. In 1982, in one of the biggest boxing showdowns in history, Cooney lost to Larry Holmes for the World Heavyweight Championship. Cooney helps run FIST (Fighters' Initiative for Support and Training), an organization devoted to helping former boxers find new careers. He was born in Manhattan.

Alice Cooper (b. February 4, 1948)
The original "shock rocker," Alice Cooper was born Vincent Damon Furnier in Detroit and grew up in Phoenix, where he and a few of his high school friends formed a band called Earwigs, which later became the Alice Cooper Group. The band is credited with bringing theatrics to rock and roll. Cooper's signature eye makeup, his boa constrictor and guillotine props, and fake blood shocked audiences and helped the band to earn twenty-five gold albums and sell 50 million records. The band's albums include *Killer* and *Welcome to My Nightmare*.

Pat Day (b. October 13, 1953)

Racing Hall of Famer Pat Day won his first professional horse race in 1973 at Prescott Downs in Arizona. Since then, Day has won the Eclipse Award—presented to North America's most outstanding jockey—four times. In 1997, he became the fourth rider in history to be able to claim seven thousand career victories. Born in Brush, Colorado, Day has won the Breeders' Cup Classic, the Canadian Triple Crown, and the Preakness. He is a spokesman for the Race Track Chaplaincy of America and is involved with the Disabled Jockeys Fund.

Steve Earle (b. January 17, 1955)

Steve Earle, a country rocker, has contributed much to the merging of progressive country music and rock audiences with works such as "Guitar Town," "Ellis Unit One," and "I Feel Alright." Born in Schertz, Texas, just outside of San Antonio, Earle quit school in the eighth grade and hit the road at age fourteen. A guitar and bass player, Earle hooked up with Guy Clark and Townes Van Zandt, two of the most legendary songwriters in Texas at the time. Earle is not shy about using his music as social commentary and has been called "the real thing" in a town "overflowing with songwriters." Earle has also written *Doghouse Roses*, a collection of short stories.

Dock Ellis (b. March 11, 1945)

A highly regarded major-league pitcher from Los Angeles, Dock Ellis spent most of his professional baseball career (1968 to 1979) with the Pittsburgh Pirates. In 1970 Ellis pitched a no-hitter against the San Diego Padres. He started in two World Series games: for the Pirates in 1971 and for the New York Yankees in 1976. Ellis was known as one of the more controversial players in baseball, for antics such as wearing hair curlers on the field, and for speaking out against racism on and off the field. He's also credited for his many charitable acts and currently works helping inmates overcome addiction to alcohol and other drugs.

Destry Forgette (b. December 13, 1959)

Destry Forgette grew up in the small ranching community of Elizabeth, Colorado. He participated in rodeo riding while in the Navy. Later he traveled throughout the western United States living the life of a cowboy. Forgette is a member of the Professional Rodeo Cowboys Association.

Pete Hamill (b. June 24, 1935)

Novelist, columnist, and journalist Pete Hamill, sometimes referred to as "the quintessential New Yorker," began his writing career in 1960 as a reporter for the *New York Post* and has since been editor and columnist for both the *New York Post* and the *New York Daily News*. His most recent books include the novels *Forever* and *Snow in August*, and a memoir, *A Drinking Life*. Hamill was born in Brooklyn.

Mariette Hartley (b. June 21, 1940)

Actor Mariette Hartley studied with John Houseman at the repertory at Stratford and with Eva LeGallienne at Lucille Lortel's White Barn Theatre before appearing in her first movie, *Ride the High Country*, with Joel McCrea. Over the years, she has appeared in dozens of television shows, including *Peyton Place*, *Dr. Kildare*, *The Twilight Zone*, *The Love Boat*, *Diagnosis Murder*, *To Have and to Hold*, *Caroline in the City*, *WIOU*, and *Law and Order*. In 1987, Hartley held the position of news anchor on the *CBS Morning Program*. Hartley was born in Weston, Connecticut.

Anne Lamott (b. April 10, 1954)

Best-selling author Anne Lamott writes with wit and rigorous honesty on the subjects of alcoholism, motherhood, and faith. Her novels include *Blue Shoe*, *Hard Laughter*, and *All New People*. Nonfiction works include *Bird by Bird*, *Traveling Mercies*, and *Plan B*. Lamott wrote a biweekly column, voted "The Best of the Web" by *Time* magazine, for Salon, and has taught at the University of California, Davis. Lamott is from San Francisco.

Richard Lewis (b. June 29, 1947)

Richard Lewis is best known as the neurotic comedian who originated "the date from hell." A Brooklyn native, Lewis began his career as a stand-up comic and went on to star or appear in TV series, including *Anything but Love*, *Curb Your Enthusiasm*, and *Hiller and Diller*. His movie credits include *Drunks*, *Hugo Pool*, and *Gameday*. *The Other Great Depression*, his autobiography, was published in 2002.

Malachy McCourt (b. September 20, 1931)

Born in Brooklyn and raised in Limerick, Ireland, Malachy McCourt returned to his home state as a young man and opened Malachy's, New York's first singles bar. He became a local celebrity and developed an acting, broadcasting, and writing career. His theater work includes *Playboy of the Western World*, *Da*, *The Hostage*, and *A Couple of Blaguards*. He has appeared in several films, including *Reversal of Fortune* and *Bonfire of the Vanities*. He has been a regular on *Ryan's Hope*, *Search for Tomorrow*, and *One Life to Live*. His memoir is entitled *A Monk Swimming*.

Malcolm McDowell (b. June 13, 1943)

Actor Malcolm McDowell is probably best known for his role as gang leader Alex in Stanley Kubrick's *A Clockwork Orange*. He played leading roles in *O Lucky Man!*, *Caligula*, and *Time After Time*. His more recent films include *Hidalgo*, *I'll Sleep When I'm Dead*, and Robert Altman's *The Company*. Born in Leeds, England, McDowell worked at his parents' pub and as a coffee salesman before joining the Royal Shakespeare Company as an extra.

Chuck Negron (b. June 8, 1942)

From his humble beginnings in the Bronx, Chuck Negron became a household name in the late sixties and early seventies as a lead singer in Three Dog Night, one of the most successful rock bands ever. His career started with his first music recording at the age of fifteen, with The Rondells. From 1969 to 1974, Three Dog Night sold nearly 50 million records, including the hit singles "Joy to the World," "Old Fashioned Love

Song," "One," and "Mama Told Me (Not to Come)." Negron now performs solo for audiences around the country.

Richard Pryor (b. December 1, 1940)

Born Richard Franklin Lennox Thomas Pryor III in Peoria, Illinois, Richard Pryor grew up in poverty, raised in his grandmother's brothel. Comedy became his outlet, and Pryor began his career in the 1960s as a clean-cut imitation of Bill Cosby. In the early 1970s, he transformed his image to become the first black comedian to humorously depict African Americans as an underclass, and to do it before an integrated audience. No longer clean-cut, Pryor portrayed characters from the streets with honesty and insight. In 1977, he starred in NBC's *The Richard Pryor Show*. His film credits include *Stir Crazy*, *Wild in the Streets*, and *Superman III*. Pryor is best known for his live performances and record albums.

Jim Ramstad (b. May 6, 1946)

Minnesota congressman Jim Ramstad was first elected to congress in 1990. He serves on the House Ways and Means Committee, the Health Subcommittee, and the Trade Subcommittee. He co-chairs the Law Enforcement Caucus and the Medical Technology Caucus. Ramstad, known for his efforts to ensure that people with a substance abuse problem or a mental health issue have access to treatment, was named "Legislator of the Year" by the National Association of Alcoholism and Drug Addiction Counselors in 1998 and the National Mental Health Association in 1999. He was born in Jamestown, North Dakota.

Mac "Dr. John" Rebennack (b. November 20, 1941)

Dr. John, one of the most distinctive voices in jazz and popular music, embodies the rich musical heritage of his hometown of New Orleans. His hit songs include "Right Place, Wrong Time" and "Such a Night." Born Malcolm John Rebennack Jr., the musician in 1968 created Dr. John, the "Night Tripper," a psychedelic medicine-man persona suited to the times and linked to the cult and voodoo culture of the Crescent City.

Nile Rodgers (b. September 19, 1952)

Voted in 1996 by *Billboard* magazine as "Top Producer in the World," Nile Rodgers began his prolific music career at *Sesame Street* and then by playing guitar in the house band at the Apollo Theater in Harlem. In 1977, he and musical partner Bernard Edwards formed the "supergroup" Chic, and "Dance, Dance, Dance," the first single off their debut album, became an instant hit. "Everybody Dance," "Le Freak," and "Good Times" quickly followed suit. Rodgers has produced music from the leading artists of the seventies and eighties, including Sister Sledge, Madonna, David Bowie, Duran Duran, Grace Jones, Mick Jagger, and Eric Clapton. In July 2002, Rodgers founded the We Are Family Foundation to promote tolerance and multiculturalism and to support victims of intolerance.

Grace Slick (b. October 30, 1939)

In the 1960s, Grace Slick became an icon as the lead singer of Jefferson Airplane and later Jefferson Starship. Her strong vocals ("White Rabbit" and "Somebody to Love"), her striking looks, and her bold irreverence garnered much attention. Slick began her music career with The Jefferson Airplane in 1966 and retired from rock and roll in 1989. She is now a successful painter. Born in Evanston, Illinois, Slick grew up in San Francisco.

Paul Williams (b. September 19, 1940)

A gifted and prolific lyricist and composer, Paul Williams wrote some of the most famous songs of the seventies. His hits include "We've Only Just Begun," "Rainy Days and Mondays," "Evergreen," "An Old Fashioned Love Song," "Rainbow Connection," and the theme song for *The Love Boat*. Born in Bennington, Nebraska, the Oscar-, Grammy-, and Golden Globe–winning songwriter is also an actor, most known for his role as Little Enos in the *Smokey and the Bandit* movies. He's also provided voice-overs for several animated series, including the role of Penguin in *Batman: The Animated Series*. A devoted father, Williams considers his children, Cole and Sarah, to be his best work.

Franz Wright (b. March 18, 1953)

Franz Wright is winner of the 2004 Pulitzer Prize for poetry for *Walking to Martha's Vineyard*. His searing yet luminous poems have been noted for their ability to "heal through expression." Wright's books of poetry include *The Beforelife*, *Ill Lit*, and *Rorschach Test*. He has received the PEN/Voelcker Award for Poetry, as well as grants and fellowships from the Guggenheim Foundation, the Whiting Foundation, and the National Endowment for the Arts. Born in Vienna, Austria, Wright is the son of poet James Wright, and grew up in the Northwest, the Midwest, and northern California. He and his wife, Elizabeth, a translator, live in Waltham, Massachusetts.

About the Authors

Gary Stromberg co-founded Gibson & Stromberg, a large and influential public relations firm of the seventies. He represented such luminaries as the Rolling Stones, Pink Floyd, Muhammad Ali, Barbra Streisand, Boyz II Men, Neil Diamond, Ray Charles, The Doors, Earth, Wind & Fire, Elton John, Three Dog Night, and Crosby, Stills & Nash. Stromberg co-produced the motion pictures *Car Wash* and *The Fish That Saved Pittsburgh*. He currently runs The Blackbird Group, a small public relations firm in Westport, Connecticut, where he serves on the board of directors of Positive Directions, a center for prevention and recovery. His son and daughter are in high school.

Jane Merrill has written on popular history, art, style, and relationships for dozens of popular magazines, including *Cosmopolitan, New York, The New Republic, Penthouse, Town & Country, American Health, Redbook, Connoisseur, Gallery, The Christian Science Monitor,* and *Vogue.* She has written several books on diverse topics, including bilingual education, beauty, child rearing, jewelry, and China (for young people). In the nineties, she switched to ghostwriting and research for several of the most noted writers in America. She has three master's degrees from Harvard and Columbia, has worked and lived in Iran and France, and has raised four children bilingual.